Zukunft und Forschung

Band 6

Reihe herausgegeben von
Martin Lu Kolbinger und Elmar Schüll, Puch/Salzburg, Österreich

Wissenschaftliche Schriftenreihe "Zukunft und Forschung" der Forschungsgruppe Innovation und Gesellschaft am Fachhochschul-Masterstudiengang Soziale Innovation

Weitere Bände in der Reihe http://www.springer.com/series/8154

Roman Peperhove · Karlheinz Steinmüller ·
Hans-Liudger Dienel
(Eds.)

Envisioning Uncertain Futures

Scenarios as a Tool in Security, Privacy and Mobility Research

Springer VS

Editors
Roman Peperhove
Berlin, Germany

Karlheinz Steinmüller
Berlin, Germany

Hans-Liudger Dienel
Berlin, Germany

Zukunft und Forschung
ISBN 978-3-658-25073-7 ISBN 978-3-658-25074-4 (eBook)
https://doi.org/10.1007/978-3-658-25074-4

Library of Congress Control Number: 2018966708

Springer VS

This Springer VS imprint is published by the registered company Springer Fachmedien Wiesbaden GmbH part of Springer Nature
The registered company address is: Abraham-Lincoln-Str. 46, 65189 Wiesbaden, Germany

Content

II. Scenarios in Practice

III. Synopsis

Foreword

Yair Sharan

The term *scenario* appears regularly in different contexts and with different intentions. Sometimes a scenario describes an opportunity and sometimes an image of the future. Sometimes it demonstrates risks, sometimes an economic situation and sometimes a smart speculation. Most people know the term itself even though there are different interpretations. In research, a structured development of scenarios became popular after World War II in order to be prepared for coming challenges in the emerging bipolar world. The formerly exclusive military usages have been replaced by a broad variety of contexts in which scenarios play a prominent role today. However, in our increasingly complex world it seems to be more necessary than ever to think about potential future developments beforehand – to be aware of threats and opportunities. This is true for economy and politics but especially for research.

In research projects it is possible to shed light on aspects which are not yet widely recognized. Using different qualitative and quantitative methods, researchers seek to build a complete information bank to be able to answer the most important questions: What might the world of tomorrow look like? What kind of challenges will we have to face in the future?

It is not possible to answer such questions easily to the satisfaction of everybody. It is not possible to *predict* the future for complex and volatile environments. It is not even possible to predict future events in closed contexts with absolute certainty (it is, however, possible to have a surprisingly high hit ratio…). Experts in foresight methods do not deny this fact. They might reply that it does not diminish the need to figure out potential future events or developments. That is: to be aware of potential future events. The questions remains, how might it be possible to build a structured picture of a future?

One answer to this question is: by developing scenarios. Scenario research affords a long history and is accepted in the military, the economy and social science. Most scenario methods offer the option to develop not just one scenario but a number of varying scenarios – for instance all shades from worst to best-case scenarios. It is possible to depict the futures of different shapes and characteristics including stable factors and even very unlikely events. Unlikely events, so called wild cards, might be useful to test scenario construction or to focus on uncertainties or neglected aspects of futures. Developing scenarios is thus a combination of several steps, some of them formal and some of them innovative. This is a kind of an out of the box thinking process – creative but convincing.

Scenarios enable researchers to deal with complex information: Either by structuring single factors and assessing their influence on each other or by using creative methods to gather relevant information for other possible scenarios. Either way, scenarios are and can be seen as an analytical tool- a very powerful one. They serve also as a communication tool between the analyzer, the researcher and the user, the decision maker. They are not a method for data collection but data processing and depend, therefore, heavily on the input. The quality of the input and the skills of involved researchers influence the value of scenarios.

It is not easy, however, to combine creativity with scientific input in order to develop scenarios. A scenario, which is not coherent, plausible, consistent, perceivable, useable and developed transparently, will not be convincing. Such criteria can be used for (self-) evaluation and assessment. A criterion which is not always useful – but often quoted – to assess the quality of a scenario is *likeliness (how high is the prospect of its realization. It should be clarified here that likelihood is actually the probability of the scenario happening. Likelihood is perceived as a "softer" word to present this parameter rather than probability, which is perceived as a "precise" number however small or large. A decision maker who considers things in a more relative and qualitative context might therefore prefer likelihoods or probabilities)*. However, even if a scenario is deemed to be unlikely it might still be useful as it opens decision makers' eyes to unsuspected events which may be important for early preparation purposes. The decision maker is confronted with an alternative scenario and he is free to consider and prioritize taking into account aspects like likeliness, desirability and impact. (In this context, for example, a wild card, which is a scenario with a low probability and high impact, will receive higher priority than a scenario which results in low effects.)

People tend to take likely scenarios into consideration much more than unlikely ones, even if the unlikely scenario may have a much bigger impact. From a security perspective it is a difference that matters: Due to media coverage, movies and books people in general overestimate the realization prospects of some threats. Others are not present at all. New technologies and an increasing interconnectivity between systems can lead to threats which are still under the radar. A simple computer bug installed by a skillful terrorist or criminal can set off a cascade of failures and breakdowns, which will result in horrific effects. Either way, potential threats, which come along with new technologies might not be likely (yet) but can have a huge impact on societies. Summarized, it is not always the likely scenario which should catch our attention but the unlikely ones, especially those which will result in great consequences – the so called Wild Cards.

This aspect is important in order to understand the scope of the FESTOS project[1], which inspired the idea for this very book. The goal of FESTOS was twofold- first to assess the potential misuse of future technologies, which will be in use in our society in the coming decades. Second goal was to focus on future threats which seem to be rather unlikely but have a high potential to have harmful impacts on society. Most of the technologies considered are not yet available for use today. Some of them are only in their basic research phase. However, all of them are going to be available – perhaps sooner than people might expect. The pace of technology development increases significantly with time. Awareness and advanced thinking might help us avoid unwanted surprises in the future.

Several experts admitted they became aware of the potential for misuse of evolving technologies for the first time in the context of FESTOS. This was one of the project's objectives: raising the awareness of a wide range of experts and policy makers to the possibilities of intentional misuse of pending technologies. The FESTOS scenarios along with the thoroughly detailed evaluation completed in the project intended to present various future situations to the reader. What might be the impact of a misuse of a technology in the future? Which aspects of the daily life would be affected? Would it have an individual dimension only or a wide societal one? Would it be regional, national or even global?

The FESTOS project team received very positive feedback – from researchers, decision makers and end-users in the field of security and beyond. A number of people – although involved in the field – became aware of these kinds of future challenges for the first time. The project team realized two important points: First, the scenarios served the project quite well and contributed much to the threat assessment completed and to counter policies considered. Second, scenarios do not get the attention they deserve once a project is finished.

It was against this background that the idea for the present book emerged. The fundamental aim of this book is to present scenarios from different projects embedded in a practical context – scenarios should not be displayed as such but be combined with a description of how they were developed and used. It might be

[1] EU funded project: FESTOS (Foresight of Evolving Security Threats pOsed by emerging technologieS)

difficult to understand a scenario without its context. Therefore, the scenarios are contextualized accordingly. It has been an additional intention to enable readers to take advantage of the study of the development of scenarios in two ways: First, to be able to comprehend their development but second, to learn from shortcomings or weaknesses.

Although projects and scenarios are connected to security topics, neither the scenario method nor practical insights are limited to security research. The contrary is the case. Scenarios are useful in all contexts where they are needed to activate much information and to present it in a coherent picture. However, the emphasis on security research projects shows vividly, that scenarios might be useful not only to identify the (positive) chances of the future (normative scenarios) but also for identifying potential future threats.

Scenarios, which describe a dangerous situation or a threat, need to be developed carefully. It might be necessary to emphasize repeatedly the fact that scenarios have a generic character. They need to take into consideration a balanced selection of potential threats and dangers. The power of mental pictures should not be underestimated. The reader may be hooked by one scenario and pay no attention to other options any more. Scenarios are *not* designed to measure likelihoods. All recipients should be aware that threats may differ regarding their potential for materialization – and even that they might never happen.

A critical question is however, how threat scenarios affect the perception of threats, and how scenarios affect the assessment of a potentially threatening situation by depicting them in a vivid way. Scenarios that describe a threat are meant to shed light on a (potentially) underestimated factor. It is important to address threats and insecurities where they may arise in the future and to initiate thoughtful discussion about them. That is what a scenario is made for – offering a basis for communication. It is important to avoid demonization but to show what could happen.

The examples given demonstrate that scenarios are neither developed in the same way nor used in the same way. They can show wishful or dreadful futures, or show a future with less security measures than we have today. Is that unlikely or even unrealistic? All scenarios described bring up an important issue: the security and stability of our future. They make us think about options and threats, political agendas and social circumstances. What kind of future that finally materializes is based on our decisions, visions and values.

A lot of research projects address this aspect by looking for options and frameworks to increase the security of society in various situations and protect it from various emergencies, but often do not get the attention they deserve. They are recognized by the core community and a number of outsiders – but not noticed by the public. When it comes to security and the very crucial question of how we are going to live one day, it seems necessary to open the debate, for example by publishing these scenarios and the projects within which they were developed. Such a step will make it possible to expose a wide range of experts and public opinion leaders to results of research activity, which may be otherwise neglected. It also presents issues of interest to the wider public in a very transparent and understandable way. The selected projects represent a broad range of topics and contexts. They serve thus to demonstrate the use of complexity scenarios and clarify the advantages in the decision making process.

A specific feature of this volume is its focus on narrative scenarios. Narrative scenarios are not yet common. Narrative scenarios often possess the format of short pieces of fiction, which include a great number of aspects explicitly and implicitly. Most of their content is gathered from experts or other people involved. The scenarios are therefore not developed at random but represent the input of all participants in the process.

Narrative is considered to be a powerful tool for describing the future of technology (Elina Hiltunen, Kari Hiltunen: Technolife 2035: How Will Technology Change Our Future? Cambridge Scholars Publishing (Mai 2015). A successful narrative depends mainly on two important aspects: Firstly, it needs the courage to step back from numbers and statistics. Clients have to be aware of what narrative scenarios are and how they can be used. It might depend on their role in a project or process if they are useful.

Secondly, a skillful writer is indispensable - to be able to develop and – more importantly – to write a convincing and coherent narrative. Narratives thrive on atmosphere and persuasion. It is only such an atmosphere that can enable readers to immerse themselves into the story. Writing a persuasive story is more difficult than most people think. Not everybody has this ability. Having an experienced writer who is able to translate the input into a story is therefore a precondition to be able to adapt the method after all. Names mentioned, contexts and situations send a message to the reader, which may influence their perception. The selection of names and special contexts has to be completed very carefully. Even if the intention is not to write an "objective" story the invention of characters and names – not to speak of the plot or fable - is a crucial aspect.

Finally, the articles in this book do not only present research projects and their corresponding scenarios, but also offer an insight into the implementation of scenarios in relevant policies and counteractions. To support further scenario work it seems to be necessary to enable such a process. Not all aspects of scenario development can be addressed in a single volume however.

It is a frequently stated argument that the future is still unknown. Nobody wants to argue that. However, by thinking about potential future developments and events we might be aware of the challenges of tomorrow. Our reactions to developments and changes will thus be quicker and more efficient. Furthermore, by planning and preparing now, there may be a chance to avoid threats or reduce the likelihood of their realization or impact. More importantly - we won't be caught by surprise when things are happening. We will be prepared with preplanned counteractions, with trained forces and necessary measures. Scenarios thus do not predict future events but enable an advanced change of behavior and readiness as well as the preparation of timely means and counter policies.

To grasp the complex issues of tomorrow, it is necessary to dispute potential futures. The articles in the present book are examples of scenarios in a security context. That is a start but should not be the end. Scenarios – and other foresight methods – help to initiate discussions and make the future tactile. They make the future more realistic and visualize the challenges we have to face – if we want to or not. Scenarios can help us to be aware of future threats and to initiate preparations – we should use this chance.

Introduction

Roman Peperhove

For several decades, foresight studies have been receiving more attention in science, economy and politics. Originating from war games and military strategy planning, foresight studies offer a great number of methods to identify potential futures. Rather diverse methods and their combinations have been applied in the last decades in relation to numerous studies and in a great variety of contexts. A solid number of theoretical descriptions, manuals and study results exist, which are written by experienced practitioners. This present volume approaches scenarios from two distinctive perspectives: Firstly, from a special thematic angle and secondly from a methodological angle.

The thematic focus that is present in all given articles is: Security and privacy issues of different kinds. People might think that *Security* is a national issue and doesn't really affect them– but that is a misunderstanding. Security issues are present in everyday life as well as in complex regional or global contexts.

Security issues are omnipresent, if people are aware of them or not. The majority may think about security whilst withdrawing money from an cash machine (ATM) and wondering if anyone is able to spy on their pincode. Only few consider security implications when using new gadgets or think about food supply. In statistical terms, people in Western Countries are more secure than ever before but, rather ironically, feel less safe. That may be caused by an increasing complexity of (inter)national politics or technical systems and devices. It is this increasing complexity at which security research is aiming when future potential security issues are at stake.

The improvement of security measures in aspects of everyday life as well as on national or international levels therefore became one of the leading issues in research and politics. Nowadays, interrelations between people and technical systems are increasingly intertwined *inter alia* by globalization in all fields. The so-called information revolution is a strong symbol for this development. New technologies, international cooperation, climate change or the global markets and traffic can lead to emerging challenges and threats but also new chances – depending on the perception of threats, their assessment and according countermeasures.

R. Peperhove et al. (Eds.), *Envisioning Uncertain Futures*, Zukunft und Forschung 6, https://doi.org/10.1007/978-3-658-25074-4_1

Security challenges differ strongly depending on region or the field of interest. Where high-tech systems and devices are common, the Internet of Things (IoT) may cause security implications. In rural areas, water distribution in a disruptive state may be the main challenge. On an international level, the future of forthcoming UN Peace operations may change with significant ramifications. Such examples do have the potential to have serious impacts on day-to-day life – be it on the micro level or the macro level – and are worth shedding light on. To be able to think about future challenges and possible measures to deal with them, it is necessary to look ahead and try to display potential developments – based on existing knowledge and estimates for the future.

What is a serious and useful way to address such challenges? How is it possible to catch the attention of decision makers as well as the general public to a matter? How can identified challenges be discussed properly in order to initiate countermeasures or solutions? This is the point where the methodological focus of this volume comes into play. The challenge is not only to think about the future but to establish a method or procedure for a structured approach, which is accepted by relevant stakeholders.

A number of foresight methods are available and used regularly but one of the most favored is a scenario method. Scenarios differ in style and development process but are meant to enable easy access to complex situations or relationships. Foresight offers reasonable arguments as to why something might happen and something else not. This way, foresight research provides methods to describe (different) potential futures. Such potential futures do not appear out of nowhere but are the product of systematic research and analysis. It depends, however, on the relevant actors if and which one of these materializes actually.

This volume centres upon a special form of scenario that receives increasing attention in research but is not represented accordingly in literature: narrative scenarios. Narrative scenarios combine a number of specifications, which enable implementation in a broad range of contexts. Using different security issues in this volume, the method will be presented through its characteristics, its preconditions and advantages as well as limitations.

Narrative scenarios can be roughly described as short stories, which aim to include relevant aspects of a topic and transform it into a vivid narration with characters in an everyday context. This way, recipients are immersed in the story and the respective characters and are able to perceive a context as much intuitively as deliberately. They focus on a specific problem - and take into account (in a coarse, sketchy way) the wider context.

For security issues, this method appeared to be very useful since future threats or challenges are difficult to communicate through blank statistics or descriptions. Narrative scenarios depict a potential future situation and trigger pictures and images in the mind's eye. They display scenes, which the reader finds easy to perceive and provoke a reaction – ranging from approval to rejection in all its facets. Whatever it may be, the reader thinks about a scenario and wonders if he likes it or not, how he would react or if there is a way to circumvent or counter the threat.

Such mental pictures are important for a comprehensive analysis. Pictures, drawings and stories have a long history in terms of warnings and oracles. They have always been used to warn people about the future – for return and change or as a promise. Dürers' famous *Four Horsemen of the Apocalypse* shows, in warning, the divine apocalypse and the Last Judgment and reminds people of the inevitability of death. The same applies to pictures of the Ten Plagues or other images that are intended to maintain people's belief in a monolith god, a sinless life or other concepts. The mythological Delphic Sibyl became more famous than the practice of interpreting omens from the observed flight of birds (Augury), as in Roman religions. What they have in common is people's desire to be ahead of the future: To be prepared when catastrophe hits or to avoid it completely, to guarantee an afterlife in heaven and not in hell, or to be successful in life. The reasons differed but the intention is similar: To influence the future by "knowing" what is going to happen.

In opposition to historical creations, scenarios do not predict the future or claim to "know" what happens in the future. The only similarity is the approach of being interested in the future and to think about possible developments and according measures to influence it. In contrast to oracles, scenarios develop different images of a potential tomorrow based on different qualitative or qualitative methods in order to facilitate a necessary discussion on future challenges. The scenarios and research projects in this book use pictures and images not to predict, but to transform potential threats into perceivable mental pictures.

Dark scenarios in projects like FESTOS use narratives to depict potential threats in a future society with reason. Like historical dystopias they are intended to shed light on critical aspects, be it intended technological misuse by a terrorist or a looming conflict on water distribution. Today's actions – or non-actions – might have severe consequences in the future, for future generations. By describing different plots, decision makers and people concerned are able to attain a comprehensive understanding, which is a precondition for reasonable decisions.

A timely adjustment of strategies may save resources of all types in the medium or the long run. One of the aims of foresight is to reduce surprises or to be prepared for sudden events and enable a solid course of action instead of ad hoc solutions, which are seldom the best.

Narrative scenarios push their recipients to think about the implications of future events and situations. Scenarios convey sociopolitical questions through narration in a broader context: How do we want to live in the future? Are we aware of the explicit and implicit threats we might face in the future? How can we set the course for a secure and desirable future?

The articles in this book have been gathered to answer the question on how scenarios can be developed based on research experiences and to give a number of examples to show how such a scenario could look and be implemented further.

Often scenario development is described as a theoretical task. In this volume researchers show how they adjusted the theory to fit implementation. Implementation is marked by limited resources (e.g. time, money, manpower) or specific topics (e.g. security, local government). Such limitations lead to specific adaptions of methods and therefore influence the output. All present articles are experience-based descriptions of scenario development written in a way that addresses the formation of scenarios and give samples of the final scenarios or suggest how to utilize them. Most articles are written so that they can be used as an experienced-based manual for scenario development.

It was the intention of the publishers to bring researchers and experts for foresight and scenarios together in one volume with the goal to improve foresight and scenarios through a more frank exchange of experiences, perspectives and visible results with the motive to learn from each other. Mostly, the results of research projects or studies end up being cast aside, into a drawer or elsewhere. What a waste! In order to deliver results to a broader audience and initiate more exchange between researcher, recipients and clients it seems to be necessary to initiate an open discussion on the chances but also the limits of scenarios. In the *lessons learned* chapter we tried to address critical aspects of scenarios and their development and contribute in this way to a more realistic understanding of the power of scenarios.

This book is designed to give an insight into studies executed, which applied foresight methods to gain insights into a potential tomorrow. It describes the objectives of the studies, explains the methods used and procedures which were implemented to achieve results and ends with lessons learned. In this way, this volume is designed to work as a manual showing examples and including suggestions on how to improve such studies in the future.

All articles reflect a special angle on foresight in the context of security and privacy. They illustrate how scenarios work as a vehicle to raise awareness for security and privacy issues in very different contexts.

In his article *Narrative Scenarios as an Analytical Instrument*, Karlheinz Steinmüller constructs a red line from early scenario works until today. He describes the typology of scenarios and reflects the use of story lines as an artistic form of scenarios. To be a writer on one hand and bound to a specific scenario on the other enables the introduction of contextual backgrounds, everyday behavior as well as action and interaction, which can lead to new insights. In this way, narrative scenarios become an analytical instrument and a "collective learning process".

Scenarios that tell a Story. Based on this statement, Robert Gaßner and Karlheinz Steinmüller explain the several steps in the development process of narrative scenarios. They present several examples of its implementation and their comprehensive experiences with this technique. The core claim of their experiences is the impact of the process itself, in which the client is involved. By being part of the development, participants are affected by it and the scenarios reach a higher level of impact. However, Gaßner and Steinmüller emphasize that scenarios are meant to work "in the minds of their readers".

Lars Gerhold and Karlheinz Steinmüller discuss the impact scenarios are able to evolve in their article *Security 2025: Scenarios as an Instrument for Dialogue*. The scenarios themselves are only a part of a wider concept. In the context of future security concepts, threat scenarios were utilized to trigger fundamental questions, how risks are perceived and communicated, assess uncertainty and how politics is embedded in dealing with security concepts. It is stated that "scenarios do not give answers – they ask questions and point out problems". These questions are a precondition to gain new perspectives and a deeper understanding of the complexity of problems.

The authors Massimo Moraglio, Hans-Liudger Dienel and Robin Kellermann address the important aspect of the utilization of scenarios by looking at a real life market. In *The Didactical Functions of Dark and Bright Scenarios: Examples from the European Transport Industry*, the authors highlight the impact of several dark scenarios on the transport industry market and highlight the adjustment of the industry as a reaction to them. The dark scenarios successfully displayed a decreasing market for European companies if nothing changes. As a communication instrument scenarios triggered adjustments which enabled a (re)strengthening of the European transport industry in the global market.

One of the core questions regarding the content of scenarios is, how many different futures are they able to display and remain reliable? In *Surprising Scenarios,* Hauptmann and Steinmüller focus on Science Fiction literature as a fruitful source to enrich scenarios. Although science fiction writers are usually more interested in a good story than in scientific accuracy, SF literature places the stories in a regular future social environment and is much more tangible than usual scenarios. By pointing to Wild Cards and Weak Signals, the authors emphasize the usefulness of implementing more un-consensual views in scenarios to challenge usual scenarios and prepare for unlikely but high impact events.

In *The Future of Water Use: Scenarios for Water Management in Telangana,* Jain and Dannenberg show how scenarios can also be used- as a trigger for future visions. These visions were developed through the implementation of an innovative follow-up method: the salon method. Confronted with the increasing problematic context of water distribution in rural India, narrative scenarios were constructed in close collaboration with local experts not only to highlight potential future developments but also to utilize them as starting point for the development of common visions and strategies on how to deal with the problem in the future – in practical but also political ways.

Björn Theis and Stefan Köppe deal with a global security problem in their article: International peacekeeping missions. In *Peace Operations 2025* their scenario process for identifying potential future action in this sensitive field is elaborated. Based on iterative workshops and continuous reflections, key factors, which may influence the development of international missions, could be identified and are presented here,. The detailed explanation of thoughts and decisions during the whole process enables the reader to follow the whole process and gives insights for future works.

Roman Peperhove describes in his article on *The Development of FESTOS Scenarios* the preparation and generation of narrative scenarios in a security research project. The challenge in general and more specifically in security projects is to show not only the first impact of an event which comes to mind, but also side-effects or cascade effects. Besides, the FESTOS scenarios take place in future societies, which had to be reflected. In the article, the whole process from research design to the finalization of scenarios is explained to enable transparent access to the process and results.

The FESTOS Scenarios contain the four detailed narrative scenarios that were developed in context of the EU-funded security research project FESTOS (Foresight of Evolving Security Threats Posed by Emerging Technologies). Designed as short stories including characters and future daily life contexts, they show vividly the easily accessible complexity of potential misuse of future technologies. This is shown with varying story lines from the vulnerability of future society to emerging technologies and several levels of impact in case of intended misuse.

Liisa Luoto and her colleague Annika Lonkila give a detailed example on how to exploit the explicit or implicit information included in scenarios. *The Use of SWOT Analysis for Future Scenarios* is not only a theoretical explanation but also a critical reflection on the advantages and limits of SWOT for scenarios based on experiences in an international foresight study. Their aim is to evolve the method in order to enable "a more detailed, transparent and systematic analysis of scenarios". Their concept allows a value-based interpretation of scenarios for better decision making.

Finally, in *Reflections on how to Improve Future Scenarios,* Roman Peperhove discusses a number of critical aspects in the development of scenarios, which go by the board too often. He claims for a more transparent and frank handling of information on the development process in order to increase not only the reliability of the output but also the reputation for foresight as a serious profession.

I. Scenarios – A Methodological Tool

Narrative Scenarios as an Analytical Instrument

Karlheinz Steinmüller

Abstract

This paper analyses the advantages of narrative scenarios. It begins with an exposition of scenario typology: synchronic (snapshot) vs. diachronic (future history) scenarios, exploratory vs. normative scenarios, abstract presentations vs. narrative descriptions.

Writing narrative scenarios, i.e. scenarios told as stories, can be regarded as an analytical procedure since it allows in depth assessments of the scenario's topic – its prerequisites, its implications and side effects, its risks and opportunities. Fictionalised scenarios are thought experiments with a high degree of imagination and realism; they explore in particular the human and social dimensions in the setting of everyday life.

The main challenge of writing narrative scenarios lies in the necessity to integrate all ideas into a consistent, convincing and compelling plot. There is always a tension between two structures: the "idea line", defined as the sequence of scenario elements that have to be conveyed, and the "plot line", defined as the sequence of events that belong to the plot and that trace the unfolding of interactions of the characters.

Narrative scenarios help to understand how people and whole societies may react to technological trends, to innovations, or to future security threats.

Introduction

Scenarios are one of the basic tools of future studies and foresight respectively. They allow advance thinking, performing mental experiments with alternative futures, with desirable ones, possible ones, and even with rather improbable ones. It is therefore no wonder that during the last decades, the number of scenario studies has grown steadily, and the term itself is applied to a broad range of topics: There are scenarios studies about climate change and about urban development, companies use technological scenarios and business case scenarios, governments

R. Peperhove et al. (Eds.), *Envisioning Uncertain Futures*, Zukunft und Forschung 6, https://doi.org/10.1007/978-3-658-25074-4_2

commission scenarios of future energy systems and demographic change … The media frequently employ the term, they speak about the "scenario for the end of the euro" or call the disturbance of air traffic due to volcanic ash a "Hollywood scenario", thus bringing the term back to where it originated, the movie world. Short and sketchy descriptions and lengthy elaborations are titled scenario, sometimes a scenario consists only of a chart with some notes, and sometimes scenarios are communicated in cartoon-like drawings or even put into the format of a short animation movie. There is a large diversity, and given the tendency to call any fragmented idea about the future a scenario, futurists may warn, that "scenario" is the most abused term in futures studies (Glenn 2009, 2).

Historically, the term "scenario" originated within the American school of military-strategic thinking in the late 1940s. The "scenario" for a "theatre of war" consisted of a description of a possible situation on the battlefield. What means and options were available to the adversaries? How would they act, how would they react? Most probably the word was introduced into foresight through the RAND Corporation, the first post-war think tank. Herman Kahn, who at first worked at RAND and later founded the Hudson Institute, made scenarios popular (Wilson 1978, 225). In his famous study "The Year 2000. A Framework for Speculation on the Next Thirty-Three Years", he defined a scenario as "a hypothetical sequence of events constructed for the purpose of focusing attention on causal processes and decision points" (Kahn 1967, 6). Scenarios should answer two questions: How does the hypothetical future situation arrive? And what are the options of each actor either to impede the unfolding situation or to divert its evolution in another direction?

Companies like General Electric and Shell soon adapted the scenario concept to their aims, mainly in strategic planning. They focused on branching points, potential discontinuities and contingencies (Wilson 1978: 228ff), "rapids" in the terminology of Pierre Wack (1985). These companies mainly used scenarios to test out the robustness of their strategies. Morphological analysis, introduced by Fritz Zwicky, provided a powerful tool to take account of possible future alternatives (projections) with a multitude of factors (Jantsch 1967, 174): Which projection of key factor A is mutually compatible (or antagonistic, or synergistic) with which projection of all the other key factors B, C …? First software packages for scenario construction were developed in the late 1970s, e.g. BASICS by Battelle. It included cross impact analysis and a calculation of Bayesian probabilities (Millet: 2009). Today, scenarios of many different types have spread into multiple fields – from regional planning and corporate foresight to long-term environmental studies and policy-making. Scenario methods, the ways to generate and to utilize scenarios, have diversified in parallel, and studies about scenarios proliferated (Schwartz 1991; van der Heijden 1996; van Notten et al. 2003; Wilms 2006; Kosow & Gaßer 2008; Steinmüller 2012).

Types of Scenarios

In contrast to Kahn, most futurists define scenarios primarily as a future state of affairs that can, optionally, be complemented by the development leading to this state. "A scenario can present future conditions in two different ways. It can describe a snapshot in time, that is, conditions at some particular instant in the future. Alternatively, a scenario can describe the evolution of events from now to some point of time in the future. In other words, it can present a 'future history'" (Becker 1982, 96).

Synchronic, future state of affairs scenarios, on the one hand, put the emphasis on consistency: The picture of the future must not contain any contradictions, it has to be at least in a very abstract sense possible, all its elements have to fit into the overall picture, and usually one tries to make the scenario plausible, i.e. after some reflection easily acceptable by others. Internal consistency analysis is therefore a cornerstone of generating snapshot scenarios. It is mostly based on tools like morphological boxes or consistency matrices. Synchronic scenarios are frequently employed. Companies rely on snapshot scenarios on the future business environment to streamline their strategies – or to design new strategies (Schulz-Montag & Müller-Stoffels 2006; Godet & Durance 2013). A case in point is the scenarios of logistics in the year 2050, developed by Deutsche Post DHL with the support of Z_punkt GmbH (Deutsche Post 2012).

Diachronic, future history scenarios, on the other hand, put the emphasis on causalities, on the interplay of factors that give rise to the scenario's future. As a rule, they are not constructed by combining future projections in a consistent way, but by assumptions about the interaction of trends, about actors and their strategies, about obstacles and barriers, "show stoppers", "drivers" and "inertial forces", about "game changers", including secondary and tertiary impacts etc. Typical examples are policy driven scenarios in which the effects and consequences of policies implemented and measures taken are explored. These two types differ deeply by the modes of narration: Whereas snapshot scenarios provide a *description* of a future state, future history scenarios provide an *explanation* of how this state could originate. A case in point is the scenario study on the future of German forests until the year 2100 (Steinmüller et al. 2009).

Depending on the aim of the scenario exercise one has to also distinguish exploratory and normative scenarios. As the name infers, exploratory scenarios are used to explore or "map" possible futures, or, more precisely, expectations about what may happen under certain conditions. They need a systematic analysis of options or alternatives for framework conditions, trends – and sometimes wild cards. As a rule, a whole set of exploratory scenarios is constructed, which in most cases is intended to cover the major relevant possibilities. A specific problem lies in the term "possible" itself. Some studies try to extend the realm of the possible to the limits; more abstract options, possibilities in a purely logical sense are demanded. Such an approach has the advantage of tearing down mental barriers. Other studies are designed to capture what realistically can be expected, maybe at the cost of narrowing down vision.

Normative scenarios depict desirable futures, or, in rare exception, future states of affairs that should be avoided. Their aim is to identify goals and objectives and to paint a rather optimal, desirable end state, a vision. Normative scenarios have the advantage of making the values, attitudes and the mindset of their authors explicit (Glenn et al. 2009, 7; Steinmüller 1999). Usually, either individual preferences or normative orientations of a society (like sustainability) serve as starting point. But the preferences of two people never perfectly coincide – there may be even some tacit conflict between the values one person adheres to – so that most normative scenarios exercise aim at finding common ground, shared values, consensus on objectives. Very rarely more than one normative scenario is generated. As with exploratory scenarios, there are the extremes of unbound, effusive visioning and too narrow realism: On one hand, there is the risk of losing any link to realistic expectations, to boundary conditions that can already be predicted. Such scenarios become utopian. However, sometimes even utopian scenarios have their merits, since they allow very clear and distinct value statements. On the other hand, there is the danger of becoming trapped by excessive realism and level-headedness, too close adherence to present-day concepts, patterns, models that may hamper vision and prevent more radical innovative thinking. In general, one may require that a normative scenario should stay within the realm of the "in principle" as possible (Gaßner & Steinmüller 2006, 133), a term that can be stretched if necessary. As projections of a desirable, ideal future state of affairs, normative scenarios at least in the beginning are pure snapshot scenarios. Almost regularly, they are supplemented by backcasting: Identifying steps and measures required for a realization of the scenario, adding to the desirable snapshot scenario a history of successful measures and helpful circumstances which lead to it.

However, one has to be aware that the scenario concept as used in security studies differs in some respects from the concept of foresight scenarios. As a rule, security scenarios depict possible situations, mostly situations of crisis, catastrophes, and situations with specific security challenges that could arrive today or rather soon. As far as scenarios in security studies describe an abnormal, irregular, anomalous (present or future) situation, they are exploratory (snapshot) scenarios. As far as they focus on catastrophic incidents, they can be regarded as scenarios of the undesirable, frequently close to a postulated worst case.

Table 1: Generic Types of Scenarios[1]

Types of Scenarios		
Time	Synchronic (Snapshot)	Diachronic (Future history, evolution)
Modality	Exploratory (Mapping possibilities)	Normative (Desirable, undesirable)
Description	Abstract (List of scenario elements)	Narrative (With storyline)

Narrative Scenarios

Generally speaking, scenarios tell stories about the future for the purpose of directing today's action. However, from a literary point of view, most scenarios are rather abstract presentations of a certain state of affairs or path of development,

[1] A more comprehensive scenario typology is given by Van Notten et al. (2003).

at best in an essayistic manner, without (or even avoiding) colorful detail, without acting persons (characters). They don't have much in common with fictional stories. From a storytelling point of view they lack – last but not least – a plot. This is not necessarily a disadvantage: An excess of colorful detail may distract the recipient, an intriguing plot with much suspense may even obscure the main message of the scenario; and there is perhaps no need at all to communicate a scenario about, e.g. the returning age of fossil fuels as an invented story about future workers in a carbon sequestration and storage plant. In many cases, it makes sense to narrate the scenario not as a typical story with an unfolding plot, but in other literary forms: as an interview, a newspaper report or a speech.

Unfortunately, the term "narrative" itself is rather ambiguous. Narration encompasses any type of textual description or exposition of the scenario, not only storytelling: all synchronic or diachronic descriptions, with or without acting characters. The main point is that there exists a red line throughout the narration, something that binds the elements of the scenario in a logical, consistent, convincing way together, some general idea, some main pathway of development, the "storyline". For diachronic scenarios this is very often the unfolding of events, where one event gives rise to the next, where boundary conditions restrict the impact etc. Such scenarios follow the model of history textbooks that do not simply describe a sequence of more or less connected events, but expose the driving forces behind history.

In a certain way, storytelling is easy for diachronic scenarios: They are based on assumptions about cause and impact, action and reaction – and they can be used to construct the storyline. In synchronic scenarios, there exists only a set of mutually consistent projections or items of the (possible or desirable) future state of affairs. Therefore one has to invent a storyline for the scenario, a line that combines in a convincing manner all the diverse elements. This can be done by taking refuge in the means of fiction.

There are ample cases of narrative scenarios, written like short science fiction stories. This kind of narration is not only well suited to communication, it forces the scenario writer(s) to write in a very realistic, down-to-earth style. If you want to present a desirable future in the most convincing way and as close to everyday (future) reality as possible, and if you want to give it a human angle, to show the perceptions of ordinary people, a narrative scenario is first choice. Normative narrative scenarios have been used repeatedly within the framework of the German High-Tech Strategy for depicting future applications of emerging technologies – with a focus on their benefits, but also including risks to be avoided (see Gaßner & Steinmüller in this volume). Putting technological visions into an everyday setting implies looking for their probable – and sometimes unexpected – social, political, economical, environmental, and cultural consequences and their relations to other technologies. Primarily a means of communicating and inciting debate about normative requirements to emerging technologies, these scenarios allow, during their generation, some in depth analysis and add important elements to the picture of the future. Seen from this perspective, writing a narrative technology scenario comes close to "technology assessment in a nutshell" (Gaßner & Steinmüller 2004).

Sometimes narrative scenarios have also been employed to explore the social and human dimensions not of desirable, but of possible futures. As a case in point, the narrative exploratory scenarios about impacts of demographic change (Bieber 2011) serve mainly illustrative purposes, but they also expose human sentiments and modes of reaction that would never become equally prominent in a more abstract description.

The same holds true for the rare examples of narrative scenarios in security studies. Besides the FESTOS scenarios, the public security scenarios of the Forschungsforum Öffentliche Sicherheit should be mentioned (Steinmüller et al. 2012). The four scenarios based on a major failure of banking software, reactions to a disaster, and urban and airport security put specific challenges into a societal context and allowed the identification of weak spots in security communication and management. Fictionalized scenarios used in this way are thought experiments with a high degree of imagination and realism.

Idea Line vs. Plot Line

Writing narrative scenarios is an art in itself. It requires a certain literary craftsmanship and a certain discipline, even restriction in storytelling. In principle generating a narrative scenario can be broken down into several distinctive steps, including scenario content generation (in most cases during a workshop), elaboration of a scenario exposé, construction of the storyboard, writing and enriching the scenario. Since these steps are exposed in detail in the contribution of Gaßner and Steinmüller to this volume, they need not to be recapitulated here. Specific features of the FESTOS scenario process are also explained in Peperhove's paper in this volume.

We will focus here on one challenge of scenario writing: the tension between scenario content and scenario presentation. As a rule, there is no lack of good ideas. Large workshops or small team brainstorming sessions regularly produce rich content for the scenario, and all methods of scenario generation put much emphasis on avoiding manifest inconsistencies in the scenario. In some cases the items generated do not fit perfectly into an overarching image of the future, but at least they do not contradict each other. These items, ideas, aspects – "seed visions" in the terminology of the *Futur* scenario process – make up the content core of the scenario. The challenge is, to tell them as parts of one story.

Imagination and a clear understanding of the content are required – and all the craft of a fiction writer. In a way, writing the scenario gives "flesh and skin" to the "skeleton" of core content. The writer has to be able to integrate everything into one single piece: the contextual background (future world/setting), the whole portfolio of ideas – and everything he or she invents to form not a textual collage but a real story. As in fiction, a plot is needed, and the plot requires protagonists (characters, "heroes") with their motives, perhaps conflicts. One has to decide, for example, on their name, age, profession, their relationships etc. Even trivial things such as names have to be chosen carefully since they share a lot about society and culture. But this is still the more simple part. Inventing a suitable plot is the big challenge. Of course, one can take refuge in stereotypical plot patterns: the detective story, the quest – but these are rarely adequate. Some narrative scenarios are based on the simplest plot: Somebody (e.g. a journalist) visits an expert (scientist, engineer…), who explains everything. Schwartz (1991; 1992) stresses, that a plot for a scenario should at least generate a certain measure of excitement or suspense. Explanations never achieve that.[2] Further on, the plot should allow an integration of all ideas, all content into one line of action without overloading protagonists – and the readers! – with too many tasks, too many places to visit, too many explanations to listen to.

There is always a tension between two structures:

- The "idea line", defined as the sequence of scenario elements or portfolio of scenario ideas that have to be conveyed,

[2] This problem is well known from utopian literature: The description of the utopian state of affairs in classical utopias as a rule lacked a convincing plot.

- The "plot line", defined as the sequence of events that belong to the plot, as the unfolding of interactions of the characters.[3]

A good narrative combines both; it may even be regarded as a criterion of quality whether the "entanglement" of idea line and plot line produces convincing results. Goeminne and Mutombo (2008) argue that there "seems to be a trade-off at work between both: Either, scenario's focus on the rational and logical aspects (e.g. explicated in a conceptual framework) which seems to work as a straitjacket curtailing the imagination and creativity needed to come up with compelling plotlines or, vice versa, the focus is on creating original, memorable, provocative and compelling with the risk of loosing hold of the underlying core messages." (Goeminne and Mutombo 2008, 20)

However, the tension between idea line and plot line can be utilized in a productive way. From this perspective, scenario writing is not just translating ideas into a narrative. Storytelling enriches the image of the future; it goes beyond the input of core ideas. Putting these ideas into a contextual background forces the author to think about the implications of the setting, about relationships, links, interactions, about causes and reactions not thought of before. The human side of protagonists comes vehemently into play: emotions and sentiments, the everyday behavior of human beings. The plot generates its own dynamics and its actions and interactions not only "decorate" the scenario but also produce new insights. Sometimes, logically following the sequence of events leads to counter-intuitive results – these are of particular value. Story telling implies enriching the scenario, adding depth to the analysis and putting assessments into concrete terms (Steinmüller 1999, 675).

As mentioned above, there is a down side. Writing the scenario story is a creative activity on its own right. As an artist, the writer is inclined to decorate and embellish the narrative with details, to elaborate on the characters, to give them psychological depth, perhaps even to use low puns or a slightly satirical touch or to smuggle in very personal opinions. However, everything that distracts attention has to be avoided – as do common stereotypes. In difference to fiction writing, a focus on the core ideas is needed, not individualistic style, no all-encompassing inventiveness. Metaphorical or rhetorical beauty is only valuable as far as it supports the core ideas.

---

[3] Rasmussen (2005) uses the terms "storyline" and "plotline", which could easily be confused.

Decoding and Using Narrative Scenarios

Scenario generation is an analytical as well as a creative process. Using a scenario comprises of both aspects too, with a clear emphasis on analysis. In a way, ideas about the future are coded in the scenario, and using the scenario means decoding it. At best, utilization of the scenario is completed on a hermeneutical basis (Steinmüller 2012) that allows an identification of latent meanings, e.g. elements of hidden agendas, tacit assumptions, cultural bias etc.

In principle, fully-fledged causal layer analysis (CLA) can be applied (Inayatullah 2004; 2009). CLA intends to expose not only the current conditions, key trends or key factors ("the litany" in CLA terminology) and the interrelations, interactions, and consistencies ("the causal layer") on which the scenario is based. It aims at exploring the underlying values and cultural icons ("the worldview") and at unveiling psychological archetypes, subconscious predispositions with a long pre-history ("the myth / metaphor layer"). In practice, an analysis beyond the "causal layer" is rarely completed, and one may even argue that it has for most uses, especially for strategy building or supporting innovation processes, only limited relevance.

In security studies, CLA would allow looking for the manifest and deeper meanings of "security", for hopes and fears of specific (or unspecific) dangers and threats embedded in the concept, for shared values and views, for images of safety and hierarchies of risks, for perceptions and prejudices.

In these cases, a workshop with the "implementation team", the people within the company or other organization who are supposed to work with the scenario, could be the first choice. In such a transfer workshop the content of the scenario is systematically made accessible and analyzed with respect to conclusions for the addressees. In particular, the workshop participants discuss the question "So what?" What are possible implications of the scenario? Which measures could and should be taken to realize opportunities and to avoid the threats of the scenario? Sometimes, comprehensive strategies can be derived; sometimes specific measures are integrated into a road map for action. (Gaßer & Steinmüller 2004)

To some extent, the discussions on public security scenarios (Steinmüller et al. 2012) provided an informal CLA.

Conclusion

Scenario writing can be understood as a collective learning process. It is an analytical instrument in as far as it allows in-depth assessments of the scenario's topic – its prerequisites, its implications and side-effects, its risks and opportunities – in a more informal way.

Narrative scenarios have the great advantage of including the background of a possible future world, the setting of everyday life in an imagined future – if necessary with the whole scope of social, cultural and psychological factors. In that way, narrative scenarios add to the human dimension.

One may argue that in general scenarios do not provide answers about what the future will really be like. Nevertheless, they sharpen our perception about what is relevant, what is uncertain, and what is desirable. Narrative scenarios in particular help us to understand how people and whole societies may react to technological trends, to innovations, or to future security threats. Scenarios do not provide answers on what we shall do. But they help us to pose the right questions.

References

Bieber, D. (Ed.) (2011). *Sorgenkind demographischer Wandel? Warum die Demografie nicht an allem schuld ist.* München: Oekom Verlag.

Denison, E. S. (2012). When Designers Ask "What If?". *World Future Review, 4* (2), 38-43.

Deutsche Post (2012). *Delivering Tomorrow. Logistics 2050. A Scenario Study.* Bonn: Deutsche Post AG.

Gaßner, R. & Steinmüller, K. (2004). Scenarios that tell a story; Normative Narrative Scenarios – An efficient tool for participative innovation-oriented foresight. In *Proceedings of the EU-US Scientific Seminar: New Technology Foresight, Forecasting & Assessment Methods.* Seville, Spain, 3-14 May 2004.

Gaßner, R. & Steinmüller, K. (2005). Freizeit mit Agenten, Avataren und virtuellen Butlern. In R. Popp (Ed.) *Zukunft : Freizeit : Wissenschaft. Festschrift zum 65. Geburtstag von Univ. Prof. Dr. Horst W. Opaschowski* (99 – 112). Wien: LIT Verlag.

Gaßner, R. & Steinmüller, K. (2006). Narrative normative Szenarien in der Praxis. In F. Wilms (Ed.). *Szenariotechnik. Vom Umgang mit der Zukunft* (133-144). Bern: Haupt Verlag.

Gaßner, R. & Steinmüller, K. (2009) *Welche Zukunft wollen wir haben? Visionen, wie Forschung und Technik unser Leben verändern sollen*. Berlin: IZT-WerkstattBericht Nr. 104.

Glenn, J. & The Futures Group International (2009). Scenarios. In J. C. Glenn (Ed.). *Futures research methodology. Version 3.0.* Washington, D.C.: The Millennium Project.

Godet, M. & Durance, P (2013). *Strategische Vorausschau für Unternehmen und Regionen*. Paris: Dunod.

Goeminne, G. & Mutombo, E. (2008). *The Field of Scenarios: fuzziness as a chance for building appealing future visions.* Working paper for the CONSENTSUS project 2008. Available at: http://consentsus-project.pbworks.com/f/Scenarios-Fuzziness.doc [15.03.2013].

Inayatullah, S. (2009). Causal Layered Analysis. An Integrative and Transformative Theory and Method. In J. C. Glenn (Ed.). *Futures research methodology. Version 3.0.* Washington, D.C.: The Millennium Project.

Inayatullah, S (Ed.) (2004). *The Causal Layered Analysis (CLA) Reader: Theory and Case Studies of an Integrative and Transformative Methodology*. Taipei/Taiwan: Tamkang University Press.

Jantsch, E. (1967). *Technological Forecasting in Perspective. A Framework for Technological Forecasting, Its Techniques and Organisation; a Description of Activities*. London: HMSO.

Kahn, H. & Wiener, A. (1967). *The Year 2000. A Framework for Speculation on the Next Thirty-Three Years*. New York: Macmillan.

Kosow, H. & Gaßner, R (2008) *Methoden der Zukunfts- und Szenarioanalyse. Überblick, Bewertung und Auswahlkriterien*. Berlin: IZT-WerkstattBericht Nr. 103.

Millett, S. M. (2009). Should Probabilities Be Used with Scenarios? *Journal of Futures Studies, 13* (4), 61-68.

Rasmussen, L. B. (2005). The narrative aspect of scenario building – How story telling may give people a memory of the future. *AI & Society, 19* (3), 229-249.

Schulz-Montag, B. & Müller-Stoffels, M. (2006). *Szenarien. Instrumente für Innovations- und Strategieprozesse*. In F. Wilms (Ed.). *Szenariotechnik. Vom Umgang mit der Zukunft* (381-397). Bern: Haupt Verlag.

Schwartz, P. (1991). *The Art of the Long View: Planning for the Future in an Uncertain World.* New York: Doubleday.

Schwartz, P. (1992). Composing a Plot for Your Scenario. *Planning Review, 20* (3), 4-9.

Steinmüller, K. (2012). Szenarien – Ein Methodenkomplex zwischen wissenschaftlichem Anspruch und zeitgeistiger Bricolage. In: R. Popp (Ed.). *Zukunft und Wissenschaft. Wege und Irrwege der Zukunftsforschung* (101-137). Berlin/Heidelberg: Springer Verlag.

Steinmüller, K., Gerhold, L. & Beck, M.-L. (Ed.). *Sicherheit 2025.* Schriftenreihe des Forschungsforums Öffentliche Sicherheit Nr. 10, Berlin 2012.

Steinmüller, K., Schulz-Montag, B. & Veenhoff, S. (2009). *Waldzukünfte 2100. Szenarioreport.* Köln: Z_punkt GmbH. Available at: http://www.z-punkt.de/fileadmin/be_user/D_CorporateForesight/Wald2100_Szenreport_090603_kons.pdf [28.3.2011].

Steinmüller, K. (1999). Szenarien in der Technikfolgenabschätzung. In S. Bröchler, G. Simonis & K. Sundermann (Eds.). *Handbuch Technikfolgenabschätzung* (669-677), Vol. 2, Berlin: Sigma.

Van der Heijden, K. (1996). *Scenarios. The Art of Strategic Conversation.* Chichester: Wiley.

Van Notten, P. W.F., Rotmans, J., Van Asselt, M. B.A. & Rothman, D. (2003). An updated scenario typology. *Futures, 35* (5), 423-443.

Wack, P. (1985). Scenarios: Shooting the Rapids. *Harvard Business Review, November/ December,* 139-150.

Wilms, F. E. P. (2006a). Szenarien sind Systeme. In F. Wilms (Ed.). *Szenariotechnik. Vom Umgang mit der Zukunft* (39 – 60). Bern: Haupt Verlag.

Wilms, F. E.P. (Ed.) (2006b). *Szenariotechnik. Vom Umgang mit der Zukunft.* Bern: Haupt Verlag.

Wilson, I. H. (1978). Scenarios. In J. Fowles (Ed.). *Handbook of Futures Research (*225-247). Westport/ London: Greenwood Press.

Scenarios that tell a Story. Normative Narrative Scenarios – An Efficient Tool for Participative Innovation-Oriented Foresight[1]

Robert Gaßner, Karlheinz Steinmüller

Abstract

Normative scenarios are scenarios that depict preferable future visions without transgressing the realm of the possible. Ideally, they make the values, attitudes and the mindset of their authors explicit, and they can therefore be used as a starting point for discussions about visions and values. They are narrative since they are told like a short story.

This paper describes how normative narrative scenarios are constructed and used, taking the scenarios for the German HighTech Strategy as the most prominent example. According to the experience of the authors, normative narrative scenarios are optimally generated in a collective, participatory process with seven or eight separate stages, definition and bounding (focus of the scenario), vision workshop (developing the central visionary ideas), elaboration of the scenario exposé (background, content, general plot idea), construction of the story board (detailed plot with protagonists), writing the scenario, enriching the scenario through feedback with workshop participants, interpreting the scenario (e. g. within a special workshop), and, if intended, publication. Main difficulties and challenges in each step are discussed, as well as ways to communicate and use the scenarios.

Introduction

In the last decades, scenarios embarked upon a tremendous career. They are used by companies as a tool for strategic decision making (Van der Heijden 1996), and they provide orientations for governmental planning activities. Quite often they serve as a means of communication, e.g. to incite discourse or to make the public or the employees of a company sensitive towards future developments.

[1] This contribution is an updated and extended version of a paper presented to the EU-US Seminar "New Technology Foresight, Forecasting and Assessment Methods", Seville 13-14 May 2004, available at http://foresight.jrc.ec.europa.eu/fta/papers/Papers%20from%20posters/Scenarios%20that%20tell%20a%20story.pdf [09.03.2013].

R. Peperhove et al. (Eds.), *Envisioning Uncertain Futures*, Zukunft und Forschung 6, https://doi.org/10.1007/978-3-658-25074-4_3

Depending on their use, scenarios focus on different issues and possess different formats (Kosow & Gaßner, 2008; Steinmüller 2012). Scenarios, which serve as an exploration tool within a research project, are subject to other criteria than scenarios that are used as a starting point for a future creation workshop or for municipal future discourse (*Leitbildprozess*). Depending on their function and on their addressees, scenarios are formulated abstractly and in technical terminology or written in a popular way.

Within the framework of the German HighTech Strategy – and before that within the German Research Dialogue *Futur* – normative narrative scenarios have been developed from a participatory process with the aim to outline future technological and social innovations and their everyday implications (Gaßner & Steinmüller, 2005, 2006, 2009).

These scenarios are called *"normative"*, since they make the values, attitudes and the mindset of their authors explicit (Glenn et al. 2009, 7; Steinmüller 1999). They depict preferable future visions (in the case of the German Research Dialogue *Futur* so called lead visions), but without transgressing the realm of the possible. Contrary to explorative scenarios, which are as a rule based on assumptions about trends, trend interactions and possible disruptions or wild cards, normative scenarios are developed on the basis of desirable future images. Frequently backcasting techniques are used. After having set a desirable future state of affairs, one identifies steps, decisions or prerequisites that are necessary to reach this state.[2] Whereas usually a whole set of different explorative scenarios is developed (e. g. by means of consistency analysis), in many cases just one normative scenario, constructed from a consensus of wishes, suffices. But sometimes there are discrepancies or outright contradictions between different values. In such a case, different normative scenarios have to be generated (e.g. one scenario which highlights gender mainstreaming, another which puts an emphasis on ecological sustainability and a third one which minimises unemployment).

"Narrative" means that the scenarios are formulated in a literary way, as very short stories about some person or an organisation. A fictional formulation is not only suited to communication, it forces the scenario authors to write in a very realistic, down-to-earth style. They have to think about the characters they introduce, about their everyday life, how they use technology etc. Putting visions into an everyday context implies looking for their probable – and sometimes unexpected – social, political, economical, and cultural consequences and their

[2] Backcasting for scenario construction is also called "retropolation" (Eberl 2001).

relations to other technologies. Ideally, writing a scenario comes close to "technology assessment in a nutshell".

Normative, narrative scenarios are frequently, but not always, constructed in a *participatory* process. Within the framework of the Research Dialogue *Futur* so called focus groups of experts (one for each subject) took this role. As a kind of expanded scenario team the focus group developed the main visions that were to be incorporated into the scenario, and they supported the process of writing the scenario through comments and additional ideas. Of course, writing itself cannot be done through a committee. Nevertheless, close, elaborated feedback at certain stages of the writing process was crucial. The main point however, is that the group finally took ownership of the written scenario as a kind of legitimation and as a prerequisite for successful implementation.

In a similar way, normative narrative scenarios were developed for the German national Automobile Association ADAC. In this case the expert group consisted of colleagues from the ADAC headquarters and interested stakeholders (Gaßner & Steinmüller, 2011).

Normative narrative scenarios can be generated for almost any topic. As a case in point, the scenarios for the German HighTech Strategy cover a broad scope from ambient assisted life, novel approaches to education, bionic buildings, and nutrition to health technologies, global water issues, individualised manufacturing, and – last, but not least – public security: Scenario "Silvestre at Brandenburg Gate" (Gaßner & Steinmüller, 2009, 131).

The Process

Creating a normative narrative scenario is a process with seven or eight separate stages:

1. Definition and bounding
2. Vision workshops
3. Elaboration of the scenario exposé
4. Construction of the story board

5. Writing the scenario
6. Enriching the scenario
7. Interpreting the scenario
8. Publication (if intended or useful)

From our experience, an appropriate format for a normative narrative scenario consists of the following elements:

- A short introduction, if necessary a listing of the premises (assumption about trends in the scenario environment etc.) and/ or "recommendation for reading" the scenario with notes about its aim, the process in which it has originated, intended uses etc.
- As the main part the "story": a narrative account of the future state by way of a course of events (or plot) with fictional characters and/ or fictional organisations.
- Marginal notes to highlight specific elements, to provide additional explanations and to facilitate understanding of crucial contents.

It should be stressed that any scenario is open to discussion. Scenarios can neither be complete, i.e. describe all aspects of a topic, nor satisfy all the different individual mindsets and perspectives of their creators or addressees. On the contrary, giving rise to much discussion should be appreciated as a criterion of success. A scenario, which provokes solely a general nodding of heads, is most probably too smooth and superficial, it will neither contribute to the analysis of the problem nor have any stimulating effect on its recipients. Ideally, the presentation of a "good" scenario leads to spontaneous, often emotional reactions and to an exchange of opinions about its subject and to a reflection of its underlying premises and of the convictions of its recipients – regardless whether they had much knowledge of the subject before, whether they belong to a younger or an older part of the population or a specific social class.

Definition and bounding

During the first step, the aim of the scenario, its function, addressees and last but not least its organisational framework have to be defined. If this has not been done earlier, the project team is convoked, questions of the scenario process (time frame, workshops, feedbacks) have to be agreed upon, and the format of the scenario (size and style …) have to be fixed. The time horizon of the scenario and its subject are specified. Sometimes the most problematic part is bounding: to agree upon the aspects that do *not* belong to the scenario. For all these points the core team (consisting of the people who will actually write the scenario or who organise the project) may put forward a proposal; otherwise these points may be discussed and decided upon during a workshop (for pragmatic reasons the first part of the vision workshop may be used for that).

In the first step, other preparation measures may take place too, e.g. – if necessary – a primary gathering of data and analysis (aka "horizon scanning") or inquiries for experts who should participate.

Vision workshop(s)

The main task of the second step consists in pinpointing the central content of the scenario (so-called scenario premises):

- Which topics, situations, aspects of life should be addressed within the principal subject of the scenario?
- What general assumptions about the background of the scenario (the stage/ setting) have to be made?
- Which key factors or key drivers of change respectively (e.g. from demography, technology, political life...) are important for the background of the scenario? Because they distinctly describe the background, because they are influenced by the scenario subject or influence it themselves?
- Which future visions for the subject should be featured?

The main instrument of this step is team brainstorming. Within the framework of the German HighTech Strategy – and also within the ADAC scenario study – this was done in a specific one-day workshop without any former preparation of participants. Within *Futur* the third session (the final one) of the focus groups served as a kind of vision workshop. For certain subjects it makes sense to start the workshop with a presentation by an (external) expert, e.g. about the main trends in the field. Such input can provide a basis for reflection, further elaboration and the prioritising of key factors to be identified. From our experience we prefer another way; the workshop participants themselves develop trend assumptions.

Identifying and analysing key factors is also a good way in which to get into the right mindset for later brainstorming.

During brainstorming, different creativity techniques and tools can be used to obtain a comprehensive set of "seeds" or "fractals" of visions (*Visionskeime*), ideas that have the potential to be evolved into holistic visions. We use mainly techniques like an imaginary "travel into the future".[3] Within *Futur* we worked with fictional "future headlines"; short descriptions or "announcements of success" respectively, modelled on newspaper headlines. Brainstorming should produce a sufficient number of concrete seed visions, which are agreed upon as positive future options by all participants. In the first part of the brainstorming session we aim at sheer quantity and originality of visions; in the second part we ask for concrete underpinnings, examples, and prerequisites.

- How can we get to the visionary future state of affairs, make the vision come true?
- What are the links, interconnections, relations between the visions?
- Do they really depict preferable futures?
- How plausible are these visions?

In all the projects mentioned, we put a distinct emphasis on everyday life. This emphasis has proved to be very helpful for connecting social and technological imagination. From the point of view of group dynamics, the whole process is designed to result in maximum commitment of all participants for "their" scenario.

Scenario Exposé

Scenario premises and seed visions are the first steps towards the scenario. The next is an exposé which comprises of:

- The scenario background: premises, especially the supposed evolution of key factors (or trend assumptions) within the given time frame and normative assumptions (value statements)

[3] This tool is widely applied in the "utopia stage" of future creation workshops, see e.g. Jungk & Müllert, 1989.

- The seed visions which are to be incorporated, usually highlighting their normative content
- First ideas for the plot of the scenario, for the protagonists, for the style (story, interview, report, speech…)

The exposé has to show how seed visions can be integrated into a whole. As a rule, not all seed visions are compatible with each other, and usually not all of them can be brought into one consistent picture of the future. Therefore a selection may be necessary. This of course has to be agreed upon – just like the exposé on the whole – with the participants of the scenario process.

Story Board

As with movies, the storyboard comes first, the actual shooting after. Scenario writing needs not only a clear guideline for style and content, it is very much facilitated by a fairly detailed outline of the plot. Naturally, the necessary items include the "personae dramatis" with their names, some remarks on their biographies, the relationships amongst them. The plot has to be both consistent and plausible; to achieve both can be quite difficult. Very often it is a tricky task to integrate all seed visions into one plot, without overloading the acting "heros" with too much content, too many and too varied partial plots and without moving them around on a lengthy trip from vision to vision, from explanation to explanation. One solution of this problem consists in giving protagonists professions or occupations which are related to the scenario subject. If no other solution is available, journalists or other media personnel can be introduced, who gain insights into the subject by means of their job. Furthermore, characters should be of different age and sex, and therefore contribute different views on the visions to be described. Last but not least: an attractive story needs a captivating and meaningful beginning and a pointed ending.

We do not recommend inviting the larger team to comment on the storyboard. If necessary, this can be done, but from our experience, usually the additional ideas, hints, and comments of the team can only partially be integrated into the plot. Since they come from different people, they are not usually compatible. But not taking them into account leads often to disappointments and may diminish the commitment of the participants in the scenario.

Writing the scenario

The main step on the path to narrative scenarios is of course scenario writing itself. Here, the craft of a writer is called for, much imagination and a clear understanding of the content. Being an apt writer alone is not sufficient. All the different elements – the visions, the protagonists, the background – have to be integrated into a plot with at least a certain measure of excitement or suspense (Schwartz 1991, 1992). The following questions can be helpful in this demanding task:

- What are the relevant aspects of the future social, economic, political etc. environment?
- What prerequisites and framework conditions are necessary for the realisation of the visions?
- How can the visions fit together into a consistent overall picture?
- What are the motives (wishes and dreams, aims and objectives) of the protagonists?
- How can explanations be integrated – without interrupting the plot? Which aspects of technology and future social life really have to be explained – and to what extent?
- Which ambivalences (differing attitudes of people or groups, assumed risks and negative effects) have to be described?

Much emphasis has to be put on appropriate and intuitively understandable labelling for social or technological innovations. Stereotyped images of the future have to be avoided; the same holds true for low puns and (unintended) satire on the present state of affairs.[4]

Protagonists have to be plausible and lively people, but delving too deep into their personal life is as a rule not very helpful. Embellishing and decorating the "story" with too many trimmings distracts the reader. Concentration on the subject is the principle, any deadwood should be avoided. Technical details of future gadgets could be such ballast.

[4] According to Horace, it is difficult not to write satire.

Generally, all descriptions should be tangible and specific, in a way naturalistic. But often it makes sense to leave some points open, to avoid a too detailed description. The reader is invited to fill in these gaps unconsciously with his or her own imagination. Scenario writing is like a tightrope walk, and not only in this respect. Furthermore, the scenario should make for easy reading; it should be short, easily comprehensible and contain at least a pinch of humour.

It goes without saying that narrative scenarios cannot depict the "real" world of, say, the year 2030. Until that time, not only technology but also society, culture and even language itself will evolve. We may foresee some of the cultural and linguistic changes within the time frame of the scenario, but we do not speak the language of the future, and scenarios are addressed to readers who live in the present. Too much inventiveness in cultural and linguistic matters could erect an additional barrier to understanding.

According to our experience, seed visions sometimes bear a more or less metaphorical character. Such visions cannot be taken at face value into the scenario; the realistic core of the idea has to be carved out. E.g. "hospital on wheels" could mean comprehensive ambulant medical services or chirurgical services near to one's home.

The draft of the scenario is given to the client and to the larger scenario team for discussion, comment, and any amendments.

Enriching the scenario

The feedback from the client and from the larger scenario group helps not only to amend possible discrepancies or obscurities in the scenario, it helps further to enrich the scenario with new ideas and visions that fit into the general setting, with more hints to possible applications of a technology, to social and political implications, juridical aspects, other related technologies etc. Of course one has to beware of overloading the scenario with too many different elements. Each item has to contribute to the main subject and be consistent with the aim of the scenario.

In principle, the draft scenario can be presented and discussed in a specific workshop. Generally, we do not advise to do so, not only because of the additional expense of time, but because a premature discussion can lead to tearing the scenario to pieces: Every participant could be inclined to put his or her favourite ideas into the scenario or to reformulate this or that paragraph (problem of "too many cooks…"). Writing is certainly not a committee task.

Nevertheless, in the final editing procedure all hints, comments, and critical remarks should be taken into consideration as far as possible, i.e. as far as they fit well into the general picture. Usually, not all suggestions can be implemented. A well-rounded, conclusive, self-contained scenario rarely permits the integration of many additional ideas. In this case, the suggestions – which are in themselves all valuable – have to be treated with diplomatic care. Any move that could reduce the commitment of the participants to their scenario has to be avoided.

Final editing includes clearing up all ambiguities, ironing out cumbersome phrasings and uncommon terminology, correcting misleading associations and other obstacles for the reader. As a result, the scenario has found its final enriched and well-edited shape.

Interpreting the scenario

Depending on the framing research or communication process, normative narrative scenarios are used in different ways. In most cases they are primarily a means of communication, as for example the scenarios of *Pictures of the Future*, a company journal of Siemens AG. In the case of *Futur t*hey primarily serve as a visualisation and evaluation tool that focuses on results from a discursive process and provides a starting point for implementation (being part of the so-called lead visions, specified descriptions of a new research topic).[5]

But how can implementation best benefit from the scenario? It is crucial that the visionary content of the scenario is made accessible and utilized systematically. As we experienced, a workshop with the "implementation team" (whoever that may be) could be the best choice. During such a "scenario interpretation" workshop the participants give their individual comments on the scenario and then collectively evaluate it. Guiding questions could be:

- What about the desirability of the visions within the scenario – socially, politically, economically, ecologically?
- Are there "blind spots", aspects that escaped notice?
- What are the implications for action of the scenario?

[5] For an example of the *Futur* scenarios see: http://www.aal-deutschland.de/aal-1/tina-and-her-butler.pdf [09.03. 2013].

- Which measures should be taken to realise the opportunities and to avoid the threats of the scenario?

Sometimes, measures can be elaborated upon or integrated into a road map for action.

Communication and Impact

Obviously the form and the formats of scenario communication depend on its target group. Generally, specific "taking benefit from the scenario" workshops are the first choice. But usually some form of publication makes sense, in particular if the scenario is to be communicated to a larger audience. Expert circles are to be addressed in another, more technical language than the broader public. For an expert, explanations and description should be more specific, for the man from the street more general, etc. Therefore a scenario from a priority setting project (like the German HighTechStrategy) may have to be "tuned" to its new recipients and their reading practice before publication. At least a kind of preamble and some "reading instructions" can be of much help.

Scenarios are designed to produce certain results – in the heads of their readers and in the organisations of their recipients. Obviously, such an impact cannot be measured by quantitative means, and sometimes impacts manifest themselves only with some delay. In general, the feedback from the recipients of the three normative narrative scenario processes mentioned above has been rather positive. In the case of the German HighTech Strategy an accompanying evaluation (Kosow & Gaßner, 2010) indicates that almost all participants appreciated the scenario work. They gained benefits from the thematic penetration of the scenario's topic and profited also with view to their work and their professional networks.

References

Eberl, U. (2001). Pictures of the Future – ein Verfahren, die Zukunft zu erfinden. *Pictures of the Future – Die Zeitschrift für Forschung und Entwicklung – Siemens AG, 10/2001*, 4-5.

Gaßner, R. & Steinmüller, K. (2009) *Welche Zukunft wollen wir haben? Visionen, wie Forschung und Technik unser Leben verändern sollen.* Berlin: IZT-WerkstattBericht Nr. 104.

Gaßner, R. & Kosow, H. (2010). *Szenario-Methodik zur Begleitung strategischer F+E-Prozesse am Beispiel der Hightech-Strategie der Bundesregierung.* Berlin: IZT WerkstattBericht Nr. 111.

Gaßner, R. & Steinmüller, K. (2005). Freizeit mit Agenten, Avataren und virtuellen Butlern. In R. Popp (Ed.) *Zukunft : Freizeit : Wissenschaft. Festschrift zum 65. Geburtstag von Univ. Prof. Dr. Horst W. Opaschowski* (99 – 112). Wien: LIT Verlag.

Gaßner, R. & Steinmüller, K. (2006). Narrative normative Szenarien in der Praxis. In F. Wilms (Ed.). *Szenariotechnik. Vom Umgang mit der Zukunft* (133-144). Bern: Haupt Verlag.

Gaßner, R. & Steinmüller, K. (2011). *Verkehr von morgen. Szenarien & Visionen.* München: Broschüre des ADAC.

Glenn, J. & The Futures Group International (2009). Scenarios. In J. C. Glenn (Ed.). *Futures research methodology. Version 3.0.* Washington, D.C.: The Millennium Project (CD-Rom).

Jungk, R. & Müllert, N. R. (1995). *Zukunftswerkstätten. Mit Phantasie gegen Routine und Resignation.* Munich: Heyne.

Kosow, H. & Gaßner, R. (2008). *Methoden der Zukunfts- und Szenarioanalyse. Überblick, Bewertung und Auswahlkriterien.* Berlin: IZT-WerkstattBericht Nr. 103.

Schwartz, P. (1991). *The Art of the Long View: Planning for the Future in an Uncertain World.* New York: Doubleday.

Schwartz, P. (1992). Composing a Plot for Your Scenario. *Planning Review, 20* (3), 4-9.

Steinmüller, K. (1999). Szenarien in der Technikfolgenabschätzung. In S. Bröchler, G. Simonis & K. Sundermann (Eds.). *Handbuch Technikfolgenabschätzung* (669-677), Vol. 2. Berlin: Sigma.

Steinmüller, K. (2012). Szenarien – Ein Methodenkomplex zwischen wissenschaftlichem Anspruch und zeitgeistiger Bricolage. In R. Popp (Ed.). *Zukunft und Wissenschaft. Wege und Irrwege der Zukunftsforschung* (101 – 137). Berlin/Heidelberg: Springer Verlag.

Van der Heijden, K. (1996). *Scenarios. The Art of Strategic Conversation.* Chichester: John Wiley.

Surprising Scenarios. Imagination as a Dimension of Foresight

Aharon Hauptman, Karlheinz Steinmüller

Imagination is more important than knowledge.

Albert Einstein

Abstract

This paper explores two ways to integrate more imagination into foresight studies: through the use of wild cards and through the utilization of science fiction. Both follow the principle of "What if…" and both are aimed at imagining surprising events or developments. In both cases, thought experiment starts with an assumption – the invented wild card or the novum of science fiction (element of difference to our real world) and searches for possible implications. Foresight needs neither pure daydreaming, nor incoherent fantasies, but – paradoxically – stringent, methodologically controlled kinds of imagination. With this background, differences and commonalities of science fiction and foresight are discussed. Whilst the science fiction writer often indulges himself in an excess of imagination, futures studies often lack it.

Two EU projects – IKNOW and FESTOS – are taken as examples for the methodological integration of collective and individual imagination within foresight processes. Putting wild cards or science fiction ideas into context implies to fathom plausible social, political, economical, and cultural consequences, counter-intuitive findings and surprises included.

Introduction

The future is a time fundamentally different to our age. Most efforts of futurists are aimed at identifying and describing at least the main differences. Trends are of some help, but as they follow the principle of "more of the same", they are a kind of prolongation of the present and do not enable us to grasp the real great tectonic shifts that transform the present into the future. Some of these shifts can be predicted in one way or another, but history tells us that there are always surprises.

R. Peperhove et al. (Eds.), *Envisioning Uncertain Futures*, Zukunft und Forschung 6, https://doi.org/10.1007/978-3-658-25074-4_4

One may even say like Herman Kahn that a surprise-free future would be the biggest surprise of all.

This however poses a fundamental problem. How can we include surprises into futures studies? It is obvious by definition that we cannot analyse the real unknown unknowns, the things we do not know that we do not know. As soon as we identify them and make them available for analysis they are no longer totally unknown. The best we can do is to work with "proxies", with invented, simulated near-unknowns. They are within our reach. They can provide us with some idea of what the future could be like, the weird "flavour" of things to come.

In an age of deep transformative shifts and high volatility in all spheres of life, futurists have tried to tackle the problem of surprises and disruptive change in different ways. Two of them are outlined in the following; the use of wild cards and the utilization of science fiction. These two approaches have much in common. They build on a voluntary detachment from the present and from mainstream thinking: It could happen otherwise. They are both rooted in the "What if…" principle. And both require a lot of imagination. At best, wild cards and science fiction provide a good test bed for thought experiments.

It is commonly acknowledged that foresight needs imagination. But imagination is a broad field, including all forms of wishful or fearful daydreaming and of incoherent fantasies. It is obvious that not all forms of imagination are suited to foresight processes. But what kind of imagination can contribute to foresight? There is no easy approach to delimit the realms of "useful fantasy". One can pose only some requirements: Imagination in the service of foresight should not be too narrow, and not without any focus, any borders. Counter-intuitive ideas are highly welcome, but they should be sufficiently consistent, logically coherent. On one hand, the resulting visions should be understandable by others, but on the other hand one should not fall into the trap of watering the "freakish" visions down for ease of communication.

Paradoxically, we need stringent fantasies, methodologically controlled visions, reasoned irrationalities, counter-intuitive intuition.

Imagination in science fiction: "What if..."

Science fiction (SF) is one of the most successful and influential contemporary genres. Quite generally, it shapes our images of science, technology and – last, but not least – the future. As an integral part of post-modern culture, science fiction has penetrated all fields of the media landscape: fiction, comic books, computer games, movies, even plays and musicals. Science fiction themes and images surface sometimes quite unexpectedly in everyday life, in TV commercials, video clips, and technical shoptalk. For the public, technology is science fiction come true. And for many scientists and engineers science fiction provides the imagery of (or the inspiration for) their visions.

Despite a multitude of studies, science fiction still defies a simple, commonly accepted definition. Ever since the term SF came into use during the 1930s there have been attempts to bring all its different currents and subgenres into one formula.[1] For our present aim it may suffice to follow Moskowitz, who defined science fiction as a "... branch of fantasy identifiable by the fact that it eases the 'willing suspension of disbelief' on the part of its readers by utilizing an atmosphere of scientific credibility for its imaginative speculations in physical science, space, time, social science, and philosophy." (Moskowitz 1974, 11)

As long as the future is highly determined by the progress of science and technology, science fiction is future fiction. Of course, it is never literature about the future as it will be, but "futuristic" fiction in the sense that it gives its imagery an exciting character combined with a touch of amazement. Science fiction in its most original works (not the repetitive mainstream sci-fi trash) can prompt what Darko Suvin (1979) calls "cognitive estrangement"; fantastic imagination in the service of intellectual discovery, not as vehicle for escapism. However, one should not mix up cognitive value with prediction. "What if..." does not aim at forecasts, but at implications of a presupposed novum (element of difference to our real world). SF, from this perspective, comes close to a kind of fictional technology assessment. Or, as the SF writer Fred Pohl put it: "A good science fiction story should be able to predict not the automobile but the traffic jam." (Lambourne et al. 1990, 27)

---

[1] Compare e.g. the entry on "Definitions of SF" in Clute & Nicholls (1993).

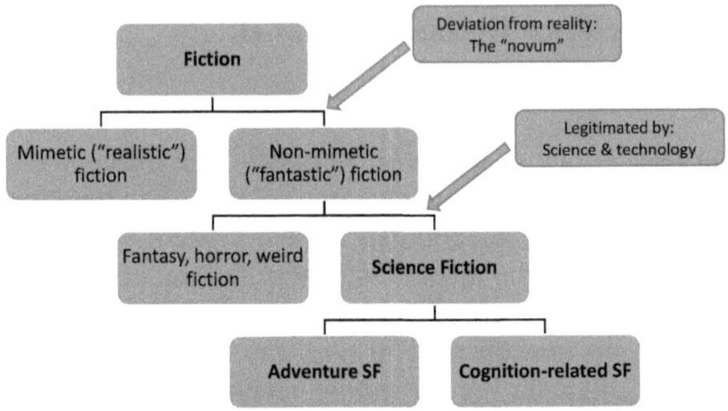

Figure 1: The Place of Science Fiction (Steinmüller 2010, 20)

The general principle of imaginative speculation in SF has often been described as the "What if..." approach (comp. Steinmüller 2003). What if interstellar travel or time travel were feasible? What if machines could be made more intelligent – or more ethical – than human beings? What if a self-replicating nano-assembler escapes from a laboratory? What if the internal combustion engine had never been invented? In some rare cases, writers do not ask for implications but for prerequisites, for reasons or causes: "How could this happen?" How could a sustainable economy based mainly on renewable resources work? How could we inform our distant descendants, perhaps living in a new medieval age, of the hazards of nuclear waste deposits? Or, seen from a distant future: How was the collapse of our civilization brought about? In any case, a lot of imagination is needed to invent starting points full of potential, rich, fascinating settings, plots with unexpected turns and, primarily, convincing characters.

Following these questions, SF can be understood as a kind of thought experiment similar to thought experiments in science (Steinmüller 2003). The experimenter – the writer – begins with a hypothesis and sets up initial conditions. Following the inherent logics of these conditions (i.e. the plot) they derive some results, perhaps surprising ones, as in pointed short stories with twisted or double twisted endings. Use of imagination is as central to the fictional thought experiment as to the scientific one, with the difference that the imagination of a writer is not controlled by scientific, methodological constraints, but by aesthetic, narrative principles. Characteristically, the writer does not look for the most plausible outcome of the experiment but for the most striking, most dramatic, most surprising. Perhaps the most profound reason why so many scientists feel attracted to science fiction, is that – without the methodological restrictions of science – SF opens up vast opportunities for a playful manipulation of scientific concepts, for speculations on alternative laws of space and time, on more than two genders or on changed sexual roles, on machine self-reproduction and last but not least on cunningly devised political and sociological models.

Science fiction and foresight

Science fiction and futures studies anticipate the future in specific ways however – and they are in some respects even complementary. As literature, science fiction narrates stories in a pseudo-realistic setting, a detailed, complex world of the future, with people acting in it, heroes and villains. Everyday human needs and behaviour patterns along with emotional aspects play a fundamental role, and the writer uses explicit or tacit value statements. Foresight, on the other hand, stays mostly at a certain level of abstraction, details have only an illustrative function; to be too specific makes a forecast less probable (except special cases of quantitative trend extrapolations or forecasts focused on specific technical developments), or burdens it with unnecessary additional hypotheses. Value statements, if given at all, have to be transparent and explicit and not hidden in attributes or perspectives.

Finally, science fiction writers are not bound by questions of technical (or social) practicality and thus can be particularly vivid when depicting desires, goals and concerns in their scenarios. One could even argue that science fiction writers – because they take into account everyday human behaviour patterns and by way of example include at least speculatively the options for abusing any given technology – have a more correct (more complex!) perspective on people and technology than some futurists. Naturally the great majority of science fiction does not satisfy this ideal model.

Table 1: Comparing Science Fiction and Foresight

	Science Fiction	Foresight
Aim	• Entertainment • Intellectual stimulation	• Provide orientation for action
Approach	• Intuitive, creative (with artistic methods of fiction)	• According to scientific / best practice methodology (including creativity)
Guiding questions	• What is imaginable? • What are the most striking, amazing, disastrous implications?	• What is possible? • What is likely? • What is desirable? • What are plausible implications?
Challenges	• Suspension of disbelief • Inducing a "sense of wonder"	• New convincing and useful insights about the future(s)
Criteria for quality	• Originality • Powerful, compelling visions • Style, dramatic quality • Convincing characters	• Plausibility, logical coherence • Realism • Methodological transparency (e. g. with respect to value statements)
Success criteria	• Readers' pleasure / satisfaction • Sales	• Client's satisfaction • Usefulness in making better decisions

Both kinds of anticipation – SF as well as foresight – possess certain disadvantages. SF writers do not intend to describe a future that a futurist would regard as probable or plausible. They play with ideas. Frequently, SF writers combine futuristic technology with traditional social models. Sometimes SF becomes FS ("fictional science"), where imaginary inventions are inconsistent with physical laws (e.g. faster-than-light travel) and only the *atmosphere* of scientific credibility (prescribed in Moskovitz's definition mentioned above) prevents the story to be labelled as pure (non-scientific) fantasy. Sometimes the quest for the spectacular leads to exaggerations that are almost absurd. And which writer is not inclined to sacrifice scientific plausibility or even consistency for the sake of a good story?

Foresight, on the other hand, often remains too abstract, shrinks back from the specific item, the small detail, even in cases where details would be helpful. Perhaps more importantly, most futurists feel obliged to stay within the realm of the plausible and realistic. But narrow realism amounts to "presentism", to perpetuating present conditions, and plausibility often equals to nothing more than consistency with shared images of the future, not to mention preconceptions and prejudices. While the SF writer indulges himself in an excess of imagination, futures studies often lack it. In these cases, a slight touch of the science fiction mentality could be helpful to foresight. It could help to overcome some of the limitations of "presentism", and it could even make foresight studies more tangible – and therefore more realistic (in the sense of giving it a touch of literary realism) by adding concrete details.

Livingston (1969, 1978), Gaßner (1992), Steinmüller (1995) and others have repeatedly emphasised the value of science fiction, the "epistemological genre par excellence" (Malmgren 1991, 172), for foresight. SF can be used heuristically as a "mind opener" and source of inspiration, e.g. in the framework of specific types of workshops. Short readings from a SF story or a sequence of a SF movie transport the participants into the unknown land of the future; they can help to overcome mental barriers, and to sensitise the participants to change and to boost their imagination.

Sometimes SF is used as an indicator for social or cultural trends, expression of fears of future catastrophes, possible technological or scientific breakthroughs, or the impact of these breakthroughs on man and environment. Seen in this way, SF is not only an inroad to popular expectations about the future, but also a fragmented early warning system for the big transformations to come.

Cases of a systematic scanning of SF for foresight purposes are rare. Within the EU project iKNOW (see below), lots of SF books have been screened for interesting wild cards and weak signals (see below for definitions of these terms), and SF writers have been invited to share their ideas in workshops. The quality of items found in SF was not so different to wild cards and weak signals derived from other sources.

Another example for this kind of utilisation of SF is the study "Innovative Technologies from Science Fiction for Space Applications" (ESA 2002), commissioned by the European Space Agency. This stocktaking included many technical ideas from novel space suits and propulsion systems to space elevators, terraforming, and asteroid mining. This study induced much debate between the participating ESA experts and SF specialists. Even if one has to assume, that no idea of the study has direct influence on ESA planning, one has to acknowledge that a broad field for further research has been opened.

Perhaps the great problem, as the SF writer and futurist Arthur C. Clarke held many years ago, is finding people who combine sound scientific knowledge with "a really flexible imagination". Clarke regarded the *failure of imagination* as a major "hazard of prophecy". Based on many examples of scientists who suffered from such failure, Clarke concluded that "too great a burden of knowledge can clog the wheels of imagination". At the same time Clarke was confident that although only a very small fraction of SF readers would count as "reliable prophets", "almost a hundred percent of reliable prophets will be SF readers – or writers" (Clarke 1974, 14-15, 32). Today, one would of course replace "prophets" with "futurists" and "technological visionaries", but nevertheless Clarke hits the point.

Quite generally, it is no easy task to identify weak signals, or hints to future developments, in SF.[2] SF encompasses a cornucopia of fascinating ideas – but which ones can be seen as useful "weak signals", as early indicators of possibly approaching events? The main difficulty lies in the concept itself: Weak signals cannot be taken at face value; they have to be interpreted, since they are not factors of impact by themselves but (only) early indications, hints on an emerging trend or a possible future wild card. Therefore, an idea taken from a piece of SF becomes a weak signal only by the interpretation given to it, by making sense of it. Take e.g. the "Beggar" novels by Nancy Kress.[3] In this trilogy, a new kind (or species) of human being has developed within mankind: the "sleepless". We could interpret this idea a) as a near satirical extrapolation of the present trend of shortening of sleep, b) as the anticipation of the future evolution of man, c) as a criticism of the increasing phenomenon of cognitive overload...

These examples prove that imagination can produce many compelling and surprising items, but the value for foresight lies in their interpretation. Making sense of fantasies however, is a tricky thing. Too easily one can fall into the trap of an arbitrary attribution of meaning, driven by preconceived ideas, prejudices,

[2] For more on the concept of weak signals see below.

[3] "Beggars in Spain" (1992), "Beggars and Choosers" (1994), "Beggars Ride" (1996).

ideology. Who seeks inspiring ideas in SF, shall find. The question is: How to filter out the really relevant portents of the future?

Wild cards: Imagining surprising events

The future is unpredictable. Even many aspects of the physical world governed by the "exact" laws of physics are not practically predictable, either due to high complexity or due to inherent fundamental uncertainty – as manifested by quantum effects. Even more so when human whims and desires are involved. Foresight must cope with the many potential outcomes of the complex interaction between human decisions and the physical world, hence with *alternative* futures rather than a "deterministic" one that cannot exist. In the past, many typical foresight studies used a single method, either quantitative (e.g. trend extrapolation) or qualitative (e.g. Delphi survey). But no single method can cope with the complex situation of alternative futures with inherent uncertainties, which become ever more severe and influential with the accelerated pace of interrelated technological, societal and other changes. Therefore, in contemporary foresight studies more effort is devoted, whenever possible, to using an appropriate mix of different and complementary approaches and methods, which synergistically may better cope with the inherent uncertainties and disruptions. In particular, experience shows that the reality is very likely to surprise us, time and again, even when good foresight studies are available on the relevant subject matter. Decision makers need foresight studies that challenge their conventional thinking and force them to think "out of the box" (Steinmüller 2007). Therefore, naturally foresight itself needs systematic "out of the box" thinking, and it is very important to challenge the "conventional wisdom" and the basic assumptions on which forecasts or scenarios are based. This is where the idea of wild cards and weak signals comes in (comp. Mendonça et al. 2004; Hiltunen 2006, 2010).

Wild cards are potential future events with low likelihood of occurrence (at least as currently perceived by most people) but with high impact if they occur (Petersen & Steinmüller, 2009).[4] *Weak signals* are slight changes in the current

[4] Wild Cards should not be confused with Nassim Taleb's *Black Swans*, "unknown unknowns", unprecedented events that never have been on any mental map till they occur and that therefore surprise everybody (Taleb 2007).

state of affairs or in existing trends that – if observed and correctly interpreted – *may* hint at potential wild cards (more on weak signals later).

The concept of wild cards was first introduced in 1992 by BIPE Conseil (France), the Copenhagen Institute for Futures Studies (Denmark) and the Institute for the Future (USA), and at that time it focused mainly on the business arena (BIPE et al. 1992). Petersen (1997, 2000) later extended the concept to other areas. Today it is understood that the impact of a certain wild card can be on the society at large, on some segments of it (e.g. certain country, region or age group) or on a particular system (e.g. air transportation). Wild cards may result from different processes or incidents, broadly divided into "planned events" (often with unplanned consequences) such as technological breakthroughs resulting from R&D, and "unplanned events" (e.g. natural disasters). Because wild cards have by definition a low likelihood of occurrence, they are surprising events when they happen. And because they have high impact, the surprise is a major one. But this does not necessarily mean that every wild card is a surprise for all people. The level of surprise can be subjective. Certain events may be surprising for many people but not for experts who envisioned them (and certainly not for people who planned them, in the case of "planned events").

Wild cards are the ultimate challenge to "business as usual" scenarios (and even to "business as not so usual" scenarios). Many past foresight studies tended to focus on the most likely possible futures. This is hardly the best way to anticipate strategic surprises, although experience shows that unexpected events always happen and surprise decision makers (and all of us). Major surprises are often caused simply by denial (which in turn may be the cause of neglecting and missing relevant weak signals). Denial is a powerful psychological self-defense mechanism that usually protects us against things offending our self-image, but makes us at the same time more vulnerable by distorting our perception. Schwartz and Randall (2007) stress the importance of using imaginative "unlikely" scenarios to counter this effect:

"There is a tendency to deny strategic surprises altogether […] Denial is a powerful form of cognitive bias found in organizations of all sizes […]. Denial can stifle creativity and make companies and nations susceptible to strategic surprise [...] Because denial is such a strong influence, one of the most important steps in constructing an imaginative and systematic analysis of the future involves making the analysis believable. […] Well-crafted scenarios can help organizations that suffer from denial about future change to rehearse it in advance […] Scenarios encourage management to 'think the unthinkable', anticipate surprises and try out new possibilities…" (Schwartz & Randall, 2007, 103)

We may conclude that in order to enrich the outcomes of foresight studies and to strengthen their effectiveness, there is a pressing need not only to strive for consensus amongst experts (as is usually done in Delphi surveys where controversial opinions, far from the mainstream group response, are often intentionally disregarded) but on the contrary – to pay attention to non-consensual views. Such views may themselves be regarded as important weak signals that may hint at surprises unforeseen by the mainstream expert opinion. In other words, there is "epistemological need for integrating disruptive ideas – to come away from the prevalent mode of constructing consensual futures" (Schaper-Rinkel 2011).

Although the likelihood of occurrence of any particular wild card is low, it can be asserted that in the long run, our future will be largely shaped by wild cards. Why? Because as we look farther into the future, the number of potential wild cards rises, with each year new ones are added to the existing ones, and the probability that *some* will occur increases and becomes significant (Steinmüller & Steinmüller, 2004) despite the low probability of any single wild card. So the elicitation of potential wild cards as part of a foresight study is not just an interesting intellectual exercise in imaginative thinking, but may prove as an essential means for preparedness to critical future surprises. As an occurrence of a wild card has a very high or even critical impact on specific systems/stakeholders, organisations are usually especially vulnerable to wild cards. Paying special attention to wild cards in foresight/scenario studies undertaken by these organisations could alleviate this vulnerability.

At this point one may wonder if from a practical point of view the "imagining" of wild cards is really useful for decision makers (after all, this is the ultimate success criterion for any foresight method or study). A creative team (or an imaginative individual) can "invent" a large number of plausible wild cards, but given limited resources it will be impossible to be prepared for all of them – even if it is almost sure that one or more will occur. But by definition we cannot know which one(s)...

There is no easy definite answer, but there are two directions that may be followed. One is the appropriate assessment and prioritisation of wild cards, based on suitable criteria. Petersen suggested a method for assessment and prioritisation called the "Arlington Impact Index" (Petersen 1997). This index is composed of the following seven "impact factors", which can be given numerical values based on experts' judgment: Timing (near, medium or far future); Reach (local, regional, national, global); Vulnerability level; Certainty of outcome (higher uncertainty implies greater impact); Opposition (ranging from strong opposition to the outcomes to strong support); Rate of resulting change (days, months, years, decades…) and Power (how close to an individual's essential being does the change strike).

The composition of the impact index and the characteristics of its components, namely the particular impact factors, are not written in stone; variations of them or other methods of assessment can be adopted or developed for specific foresight studies. For example, within the EU project RACE2050 several transportation-related wild cards were assessed in an online expert survey, in terms of likelihood, impact on different industry segments, breadth of the effect, importance for decision makers, and more. Additional insights were obtained by linking the wild cards assessment to a classical SWOT analysis (Hauptman, Hoppe & Raban, 2015).

A second important direction is making use of weak signals. Weak signals are "precursor events" or "early warnings" that may hint at a growing likelihood of occurrence of a certain wild card. The weak signals may be unclear or ambiguous, but they may become clearer in time (if monitored) or stronger, perhaps in combination with other signals. Searching for weak signals, finding the relevant ones and interpreting them are challenging tasks and an important subject of research in the Foresight field in recent years (Hiltunen, 2006, 2010; Ilmola & Kuusi, 2006; Holopainen & Toivonen, 2012). Advances in this area are still needed, in order to increase the usefulness of the wild cards concept for decision makers.

Example: The Project "iKNOW"

The growing international interest in wild cards and weak signals has been reflected for example by the project "iKNOW" funded by the European Commission's Seventh Framework Programme for Research and Technology Development (FP7)[5] during 2008 to 2011. iKNOW was probably the first publicly-funded international project that entirely focused on wild cards and weak signals. The rationale behind iKNOW was that many important issues may have remained "below the radar" of policy makers and so far have received no (or too little) attention in forward-looking activities, because of perceived low likelihood (or denial?). Therefore, the research team of iKNOW (with the help of a large

[5] Full name: "Interconnecting knowledge for the early identification of issues, events and developments (e.g. wild cards and associated weak signals) shaping and shaking the future of science, technology and innovation in the European Research Area". For details see http://wiwe.iknowfutures.eu/iknow-description.

number of experts) has elicited and collected a large quantity of wild cards and weak signals (termed “WI-WE”) potentially shaping the future of science, technology and innovation (STI) policy in Europe and worldwide. Main thematic areas under consideration were health, agro-food and biotechnology, information and communication technologies, nanotechnology and materials, energy, environment, transport, social sciences and humanities, and space and security. The iKNOW team developed a conceptual framework on how to identify and classify WI-WEs and how to assess their potential impacts on STI policy. In order to implement this framework, iKNOW developed several elements that can be found on the iKNOW website, such as iScan (for monitoring and searching WI-WEs) and iDelphi (to assess and prioritize WI-WEs). From a large collection of more than a thousand WI-WEs (available on the project’s website and still growing at the time of writing of this chapter), a sample of 60 wild cards and 60 weak signals were selected in the context of EU “Grand Challenges” like Energy security and vulnerability, Work-life balance and mental health, or Globalisation and localisation. The selected WI-WEs were described in detail and were assessed by means of the iDelphi online expert survey incorporated into the iKNOW website.

It is instructive to elaborate on the assessment approach adopted in iKNOW. In the assessment phase experts were asked to indicate what priority (on a scale 1 to 5, from “none” to “critical”) should be given by policy makers to each wild card in the short term (less than 10 years) and the long term, and what importance the wild card would have for STI policy. Then, the experts assessed the potential impact level of each wild card (on a scale 1 to 5) on the following eight domains, in specific countries and in the European Union as a whole: Physical infrastructure, virtual infrastructure, social welfare, economy, security, policy & governance, environment & ecosystems, and STI systems. Furthermore, the experts also evaluated the current level of preparedness of decision makers to cope with each wild card. Finally, they selected the most relevant RTD strategies for improving preparedness (from a given list of several strategies).

We briefly present here a few examples from the iKNOW collection of wild cards. We chose examples that have some “science fiction flavour” (and were probably partially inspired by SF, although weak signals possibly pointing to them may be found in current “embryonic” research or in emerging trends).

“Invisibility spray” available in high street stores. An invisibility spray is developed and the technology refined until it becomes available in most retail outlets and is affordable to the general public. Initially, this is seen as fun, however there are strong implications for security and the military as applications for warfare are exploited.

Automatic learning through neuro-data transfer. Automatic neuro-education is technologically possible but at a price - and therefore available only to wealthy people (or those singled out by powerful institutions). Techniques are developed for neuro-implants with cognitive targeting for subliminal learning. Wealthier schools and colleges build virtual environment 'learneries' where 'in-house' pupils and students can be kept in suspended animation, wired up to intensive edutainment systems. There are benefits for educational attainment levels, but at the cost of social mobility and segregation in EU society. There are also growing concerns about the use of such facilities for "brainwashing" and correcting unwanted behaviours, and about possible negative impacts on creativity and divergent thinking.

Nano-lab inside your body. Chips and micro-robots are inserted into the human body at birth, to monitor vital functions and inner conditions, prevent diseases and heal the body if necessary throughout the person's entire life. They can communicate with a health centre and ask for medical intervention and healing. People no longer need to visit the doctor. Healthcare is individualised and cheap.

The lottery: the way to a perfect world. Reducing the population to a sustainable level becomes a major objective in many people's mind. This leads to programmes of voluntary sacrifice in the name of saving the world. In the US, the leading political party creates a lottery, the winners of which have the opportunity to experience a period in their lives without worries, in which all desires are satisfied. The price is a sweet death, by the injection of a drug, giving very pleasant feelings of happiness. This helps to decrease the population and helps other citizens to maintain greater prosperity. The benefits of the lottery diffuse and other countries start to adopt similar methods, especially in overpopulated regions.

Nano dreams – more than a reality? Brain-computer interfaces are created to manipulate dreams. Parts of society become addicted to this quest for utopia, and false states of euphoria are created. Dream manipulation becomes a priority for parts of society and reality is neglected. People spend less time socialising as they are spending more time in the "dream world". The population decreases as there is limited opportunity to date, marry or have children.

Revolutionary space propulsion. New space propulsion technology (not based on chemical rockets) enables a dramatic reduction in the cost per pound payload to send a satellite into orbit or to propel a spacecraft to its destination in space. This is achieved because the need to carry fuel with the rocket is eliminated. Instead, the energy for propulsion is supplied from the ground (e.g. laser beams) or from space (e.g. solar “wind” or “scooping” hydrogen molecules).

Algae pathogen suddenly destroys the new energy foundation of humankind. Step by step all human kind becomes dependent on algae biofuel production. Transportation relies almost entirely on algae biofuel, but heating and electricity production rely heavily on it as well. Use of oil goes down. Suddenly, a new type of airborne algae pathogen emerges and starts to spread around the world. The new energy foundation of humankind is suddenly destroyed.

An important observation stemming from the iKNOW results is the pronounced gap between the importance of wild cards and the preparedness of policy makers (according to the judgment of experts). Evidently, in general the preparedness of decision makers to wild cards is very low (in many cases non-existent), even in cases where the importance of the wild card and in particular its impact on STI policy is perceived as very high. This observation accentuates the importance of raising awareness of the WI-WE approach amongst policy makers.

Example: FESTOS scenarios as an exercise in imagination

Similar to many SF stories, wild card scenarios are constructed according to the “What if...” principle. The starting point is the wild card as the “novum” in Suvin’s terminology (Suvin 1979). Like the plot of a story the scenario evolves on the line of possible implications of the wild card, progressing from the near and immediate reactions to the wild card all along the chain(s) of causes and effects to far implications that become more and more hypothetical.

In the case of the FESTOS scenarios, it is more than some (perhaps superficial) structural similarity. The FESTOS scenarios belong to the special type of narrative scenarios, told – narrated – like a story, be it SF or not. In difference to more abstract, descriptive scenarios they are formulated in a literary way, as very short fiction about some protagonists, people or an organisation.

The starting point for the FESTOS scenarios[6] was technology horizon scanning: What technologies (with relevance for future security issues) are just now in their first “embryonic“ stage of development? Which visions about their

[6] For more about the FESTOS methodology see Peperhove pp. 189-204 in this volume. For more about writing narrative scenarios see Gaßner & Steinmüller, pp. 37-48 in this volume.

potential uses and abuses are discussed in the scientific community? What are the possible implications not yet discussed? Based on this scanning, three broad categories of potential threats were observed: *Disruption* of certain applications, *increased accessibility* to technologies that once were confined to the military sector or to unique laboratories, and were prohibitively expensive, and *surprising malicious uses* of new technologies that are being developed for benign, beneficial purposes. For the FESTOS scenarios the project team decided to concentrate on the third category, as a source of signals to wild cards on which the scenarios would centre. Selected technologies were assessed by experts in terms of their likely time of realisation, the easiness of their abuse (by terrorists or criminals), their likelihood to actually pose a threat (in different future time-frames), the severity of the threat involved, and which societal spheres would be most threatened. The results enabled ranking the technologies by their so-called "abuse potential" and "threat intensity" (Hauptman & Sharan, 2013). The combination of relatively low likelihood with high severity (i.e. high impact) may signal potential wild cards.

During a subsequent workshop, technology, security and foresight experts were invited to share their ideas about specific technology areas. Special attention was given to potential combinations of technology trends. As a case in point, the internet of things could in combination with programmable matter and molecular manufacturing give rise not only to a revolution in manufacturing but also in the use of "intelligent", "nano-enabled" everyday objects. Such sophisticated future objects could be capable of self-healing and self-reconfiguration or automated recycling; they could receive a remote upgrade etc. But what if a virus or a malicious remote signal transforms self-healing into self-destruction?

This wild card "Disassembling of nano-enabled products by remote signal" was the basic technological idea that finally led to the scenario "At the flea market" (see Steinmüller, pp. 222-228 in this volume). During the workshop, in a breakout session called "security café", one of the participants mentioned that "nano-enabled" products could be sold on the black market. In the beginning, this was not much more than a word in a discussion. But after the workshop, when the FESTOS team reviewed the results, this idea gained momentum. At this stage, the main question was: How to expose all the technological ideas and security issues in one plausible and convincing storyline, that allows an integration of all the content and also provides a plot that everybody may understand and follow? Not a black market, but a flea market with old "pre-nano" things that did not fall victim to the virus, turned out to be the right setting. Still the protagonists, their motives and their interactions within an overarching plot had to be invented...

Science fictions stories of the "idea as hero" type are constructed this way, around a central idea. According to the "What if..." principle, a broad variety of possible consequences of central ideas had to be fathomed – in much more depth than is possible in a workshop. Thus, the creativity of the workshop participants and their specific knowledge as a precondition to stay within a reasonable frame is combined with the imagination and the narrative skills of the scenario writer(s).

The fictional style in itself has many advantages. It is not only very well suited to communication, it forces the scenario writers to be the utmost realistic with all the small items needed to create an atmosphere of credibility around the setting, the protagonists – the flea market has to come to life. The writers are forced to think about the characters they introduce, about their wishes and fears, how they use (nano-enabled or "old-style") technology, about everyday life in the assumed future: What occupations should they follow? How do they earn their living (if they do)?

Putting the wild card (nano-enabled products go "to dust and ashes"[7]) into context implies fathoming plausible social, political, economical, and cultural consequences, counter-intuitive findings and surprises included. In a way, the imagination of the futurist who derived the main features of the scenario is complemented at this point by the artistic imagination of the writer who does not only fill in the details but brings in the human aspect. And last but not least, the writer always aims at making the story compelling, with tension and suspense, a forceful beginning, a dramatic middle part, a surprising, maybe twisted ending. Of course, futurists are not necessarily born fiction writers, and not all narrative scenarios are built on a dramatic conflict; some are told in the way of old utopias and only lead their readers from one station to another, at best ending with a little smile.

Imagination, however, can go astray. There is always the danger to invent much more than is needed for the narrative scenario, to embellish it with arabesques that do not contribute to the subject but distract the reader. Imagination, moreover, can betray you; it can – in a well-hidden manner – introduce implicit value statements, not to speak of prejudices. One has to be careful with metaphors,

---

7 "To Dust and Ashes" was first discussed as a title for the scenario. It seemed too pathetic. Titles should convey the main idea of the scenario, they should be easy to remember and provoke associations focused on the topic of the scenario. Finding the right title for a scenario is sometimes very challenging.

with adjectives, embellishments of any kind. In our case, one should avoid "denigrating" nano-enabled products…

Therefore, a narrative scenario that is based on a process with many participants, who contributed their ideas, should go through some review process, where a small editorial team or experts involved earlier in the process have a look at the scenario. Such feedback is also needed to create ownership. In our experience, feedback has to be handled with care. Too much feedback, in particular with contradicting opinions, can either lead to endless review iterations or even tear the scenario to pieces. If all ends well, the scenario will still bear the handwriting of its author(s).

Conclusion

Foresight generates images of the future in a methodologically controlled way, based on the best available knowledge of the realms of the possible. Creativity and imagination are needed for several reasons: to overcome the myopia of "presentism", to integrate the human aspect into the image of the future and to bring in some of the wild chances the future is fertile with. The very thinking of such "unthinkable" wild cards may counter the natural tendency to deny major disruptions/surprises. Whereas identified and forecasted trends narrow down the scope of possible futures, wild cards (and weak signals hinting to them) broaden it up and create new vistas. They are the harbingers of fundamental changes. Without them foresight is almost blind to the future.

Imagination in foresight is a collective as well as an individual affair. It springs up in team brainstorming and it is deepened in individual reflection, perhaps a kind of "thought experiment" of "focused daydreaming" fiction writers are proficient at. Imagination, seen this way, is an irreducible dimension of foresight. However: It is quite certain that the future will surprise even the most visionary futurist and the most imaginative science fiction writer.

References

BIPE Conseil, Copenhagen Institute for Futures Studies, Institute for the Future (1992). *Wild Cards: A Multinational Perspective*. Palo Alto: Institute for the Future.

Clarke, A. C. (1974). *Profiles of the Future. An inquiry into the limits of the possible*. London: Gollancz.

Clute, J. & Nicholls, P. (Eds.) (1993).*The Encyclopedia of Science Fiction.* London: Orbit.

ESA (European Space Agency) (2002). *Innovative Technologies from Science Fiction for Space Applications*. Noordwijk: ESA Publications Division.

Hauptman, A. & Sharan, Y. (2013). Foresight of Evolving Security Threats Posed by Emerging Technologies. *Foresight: the journal of future studies, strategic thinking and policy, 15* (5), 375-391.

Hauptman, A., Hoppe, M. and Raban, Y. (2015). Wild Cards in Transport. *European Journal of Futures Research, 3* (7), 1-24.

Hiltunen, E. (2010). *Weak Signal in Organizational Futures Learning* (Thesis). Aalto University School of Economics.

Hiltunen, E. (2006). Was It a Wild Card or Just Our Blindness to Gradual Change? *Journal of Futures Studies, 11* (2), 61-74.

Holopainen M. & Toivonen, M. (2012). Weak Signals – Ansoff Today. *Futures, 44* (3), 198-205.

Ilmola, L. & Kuusi, O. (2006). Filters of weak signals hinder foresight: monitoring weak signals efficiently in corporate decision-making. *Futures, 38* (8), 908-924.

Lambourne, R., Shallis, M. & Shortland, M. (1990). *Close Encounters? Science and Science Fiction*. Bristol/New York: Institute of Physics Publishing.

Livingston, D. (1969). Science Fiction as a Source of Forecast Material. *Futures, 1* (3), 232-238.

Livingston, D. (1978). The Utility of Science Fiction. In J. Fowles (Ed.). *Handbook of Futures Research (*163 – 178). Westport/Conn.: Greenwood Press.

Malmgren, C. D. (1991). *Worlds Apart. Narratology of Science Fiction*. Indianapolis: Indiana University Press.

Mendonça, S., Pina e Cunha, M., Kaivo-oja, J. & Ruff, F. (2004). Wild cards, weak signals and organisational improvisation. *Futures, 36* (2), 201-218.

Moskowitz, S. (1974). *Explorers of the Infinite. Shapers of Science Fiction.* Westport/Conn.: Hyperion Press.

Petersen, J. L. (1997). *Out of the Blue, Wild Cards and Other Big Surprises.* Washington: The Arlington Institute. (Re-edition as Petersen, J. L. (2000). *Out of the Blue, How to Anticipate Big Future Surprises.* Lanham: Madison Books.)

Petersen, J. L. & Steinmüller, K. (2009). Wild Cards. In J. C. Glenn (Ed.). *Futures research methodology. Version 3.0.* Washington, D.C.: The Millennium Project (CD-Rom).

Schaper-Rinkel, P. (2011). Foresight. Presentation in "Framing Futures Studies: Science, Technology and Global Challenges". *International Workshop, 19-21 July 2011.* Available at: www.futures-studies.rwth-aachen.de/engl_workshop.html

Schwartz, P. & Randall, D. (2007). Anticipating Strategic Surprises. In F. Fukuyama (Ed.). *Blindside - How to Anticipate Forcing Events and Wild Cards in Global Politics.* Washington, D.C.: Brookings Institution Press.

Steinmüller, A & Steinmüller, K. (2004). *Wild Cards. Wenn das Unwahrscheinliche eintritt.* Hamburg: Murmann.

Steinmüller, K. (2003). The uses and abuses of science fiction. *Interdisciplinary Science Reviews, 28* (3), 175-178.

Steinmüller, K. (2010). Science Fiction: eine Quelle von Leitbildern für Innovationsprozesse und ein Impulsgeber für Foresight. In K. Hauss, S. Ulrich & S. Hornbostel (Eds.). *Foresight – Between Science and Fiction* (19-31). iFQ-Working Paper No. 7. Bonn: Institut für Forschungsinformation und Qualitätssicherung.

Steinmüller, K. (2007). Thinking Out of the Box. Weak Signals and Wild Cards for European Regions. *Futura, 2/2007,* 22-29.

Suvin, D. (1979). *Metamorphoses of Science Fiction: On the Poetics and History of a Literary Genre.* London/New Haven: Yale.

Taleb, N. (2008). *The black swan. The impact of the highly improbable.* London: Penguin.

Security 2025: Scenarios as an Instrument for Dialogue[1]

Lars Gerhold, Karlheinz Steinmüller

Abstract

Threat scenarios as used in security research depict very specific threat situations without much focus on societal or other contexts. In particular, future social and political developments resulting from the actions of science, politics, end-users and society usually are not elements of these scenarios. In contrast to this, the scenario process "Security 2025" of the Research Forum on Public Safety and Security was aimed to relate broader visions of future security situations with selected research questions on, for example, unintended consequences, multi-systemic risks, the influence of social resilience etc. Within the project, four narrative scenarios were developed; two of them are displayed in abbreviated form in this paper.

In 2012, these four scenarios were presented to an expert audience at the conference "Civil security. Security in an open society". They were evaluated, contextualized and critically reflected upon by experts from politics and science and by security practitioners. The paper analyzes the rich discussions inspired by the scenarios, focusing on risk perception, risk communication, politicians as stakeholders, and a new security culture that embraces uncertainty. As a result, security dialogues, fueled by scenarios, have to be seen as an indispensable task of security research.

Introduction

Since the turn of the millennium, new threats and risks, in combination with technological and social change, have led to the development of security research as an independent research field with an explicit view on future developments relevant to security. Terrorist attacks and power outages, instabilities in the financial markets and organized crime indicate the broad scope of these studies. But as in any new field, methodologies are still in development and the transformation of research results into practical policies is still somewhat lagging behind. With this paper, we intend to present and discuss a specific novel approach, partly rooted in foresight, and to draw conclusions from our experiences.

---

[1] This text is partly based on: Steinmüller, K., Gerhold, L., & Beck, M.-L. (Eds.) (2012). Sicherheit 2025. Forschungsforum Öffentliche Sicherheit. Schriftenreihe Sicherheit Nr. 10. Berlin.

R. Peperhove et al. (Eds.), *Envisioning Uncertain Futures*, Zukunft und Forschung 6, https://doi.org/10.1007/978-3-658-25074-4_5

Threat scenarios

In the second period of the Research Program for Civil Security, German security research focuses on developing solutions for "concrete threat scenarios" aimed to serve the needs of end-users and operators: "Taking global and societal challenges in civil security as a starting point, the scenarios are based on concrete risk and threat analyses and take into account security economy aspects as well as the social dimension of civil security" (BMBF 2012, 30).

Generally, publications in the context of the national security research program start with a description of such threat scenarios. For example, the threat reports of the Schutzkommission (Protection Committee, cf. Federal Office for Civil Protection and Disaster Assistance (BBK), 2011), the risk reports of the Federal Office for Civil Protection and Disaster Assistance (cf. Federal Office for Civil Protection and Disaster Assistance, 2005) and even the scientific discourse in this field (cf. i. a. Gerhold & Schiller, 2012; Lange & Ohly & Reichertz, 2009; Münkler, Bohlender & Meurer, 2010; Renn et al., 2007) determine the discussion on potential threats to the state, economy and society. The topics discussed include natural disasters (storms, floods, earthquakes), biological, chemical and radiological events, social events (political-military events, terrorism, organized crime) as well as internet related threats, threats by strong electromagnetic fields and threats by the sudden release of huge amounts of mechanical and thermal energy (cf. BBK, 2005, 9-41; BBK, 2011, 30).

Threat scenarios like, for example, "a power outage in an urban area" are used for the analysis of future threats and are intended to help to successfully cope with them. In the end they aim to control the situation described in the scenario. The objective is to prepare the responsible stakeholders for the possible incidence of a threatening situation, enabling them to develop strategies and seize preliminary training measures. However, concentrating on single threat situations and their possible consequences runs the risk of focusing only on reactive coping strategies. It does not take into account the fact that the future can be influenced and shaped. Also, this perspective ignores that stakeholders (e.g. politicians, the population, disaster managers) are following different strategies that can influence the development of a situation. Because threat scenarios do not take the application of security technologies and political action strategies into account, there is no vision of the future which allows the discussion of whether a future state is desirable or not.

Scenario Process: Security 2025

As described, scenarios in security research are generally based on the description of the threat situation. Future social and political developments resulting from the actions of science, politics, end-users and society in most cases are not part of threat scenarios. To compensate for this deficit the scenario process introduced by the Research Forum on Public Safety and Security aims for a targeted and well-founded reflection of the political and scientific practice in security research and to initiate a dialogue on different perspectives of security research.

The purpose of the scenario process *Security 2025* is to think ahead in light of the work of the Research Forum on Public Safety and Security. The aim is to relate visions of the future with selected research questions on, for example, unintended consequences, multi-systemic risks and the influence of social resilience etc. In the case of the topics "urban security" and "airport security" it is less a matter of single threat areas (e.g. technical risks, natural disasters, terrorism etc.) that have been the center of attention up until now, but more the cross-section of questions which are equally virulent in different threat areas (certainly with different peculiarities).

In contrast to trends or forecasts, the scenarios developed and discussed here do not deal with an exact prediction of a disaster or threat event, but with a detailed portrayal of what could happen under certain circumstances or how society could change respectively. Thereby the scenarios indicate the actions and event results of different stakeholders that in principle are possible, consistent and plausible under the presumed framework requirements.

Crucial for the use of scenarios in the security research community, which considers possible and probable threat situations, was that the scenarios should not be misunderstood as forecasts. Scenarios cannot describe the future as it actually will be. They show logical, plausible and realistic situations based on today's knowledge, therefore giving an approximate idea of how the future may look. Whether, one day, the portrayed "possible future" does occur, is always uncertain. Scenarios tell future stories and should stimulate different ways of thinking, even if they will certainly never deliver all-embracing future descriptions.

Scenarios will be of more use following the discussion and reflection by stakeholders who are involved in the scenario generation process. They deliver approaches for the active influencing of future developments; if the situation the scenarios describe is conceivable, one needs to ask how to deal with it! What has to be done either to avoid the described developments or to induce them deliberately? Therefore the conclusions, which can be drawn from the scenarios, are crucial: *How do we want to act and how should we act?*

In 2012, the scenario process *Security 2025* was realized in the following steps:

- Identification of key questions (What are the key questions that should be covered by the scenario?)
- Identification of key factors (What are the key factors that influence the direction and development of the scenario?)
- Defining the essence of each scenario (What is the essence of each scenario?)
- Scenario writing and illustration (How can the scenario be communicated, content-wise and image-wise?)
- Inviting selected expert feedback (What aspects of the scenario should be improved or enlarged upon?)
- Presentation and discussion with stakeholders (How do other experts review the scenario?)

In 2012, the scenarios were presented to an expert audience at the Innovation Forum of the BMBF, "Civil security. Security in an open society". They were evaluated, contextualized and critically reflected upon by experts from politics, science and end-users. These contributions and the discussion were documented and evaluated (cf. Steinmüller, Gerhold & Beck, 2012).

In the following we present two scenarios in abbreviated form to give an impression of the results of the scenario process.

Urban Security 2025: The safe city or security as a social problem (short version)

What would happen if an increasing fear of crime led to omnipresent control and surveillance?

The "safe city" is a split city; to a large extent the authorities have withdrawn from the neighbourhoods where the "socially weak" live. They are considered unsafe and "no go areas". The inhabitants themselves or gangs keep a certain order. The living areas of the middle class are well protected– as are shopping centres, cultural sites and many other public areas. Even there the authorities show little presence due to financial shortages. Private service providers and modern surveillance technologies (crime mapping and surveillance drones) provide security in response to a latent feeling of threat and mutual mistrust.

On the borders of urban districts, surveillance is particularly strict. Though the areas of the wealthy are not surrounded by a real wall, one can speak of a highly engineered virtual wall consisting of surveillance cameras with integrated motion detection and tracking functions, sensor technologies protecting certain areas, private guards and patrolling robots at night. Whoever acts suspiciously is intercepted, checked as a precaution and if necessary sent away.

Strict social norms and exclusion, the reinforcement of inequality and restrictions of freedom are the price that citizens must pay for their security. In sum, these repressive measures strengthen the social causes of crime.

At what level does an excessive orientation towards security become counterproductive? How much exclusion, inequality and restrictions of freedom are imaginable to produce security? How is the responsibility for security spread between state, private service providers and the population?

Message

Politics and politicians focus the fight on (certain) manifestations of crime, but not on their causes. Social disparities, exclusion, poverty and unemployment arc closely connected to the development of crime, which is perceived neither by the population nor by politics. The repressive instruments and strategies used are counterproductive, since they aggravate the problem; preventive strategies address the symptoms, but not the causes. Besides, the fight is ineffective, and private security companies increasingly protect citizens as well as companies. Citizens should be urged to think socially inclusively instead of socially exclusively. Examples must be generated by politics and society.

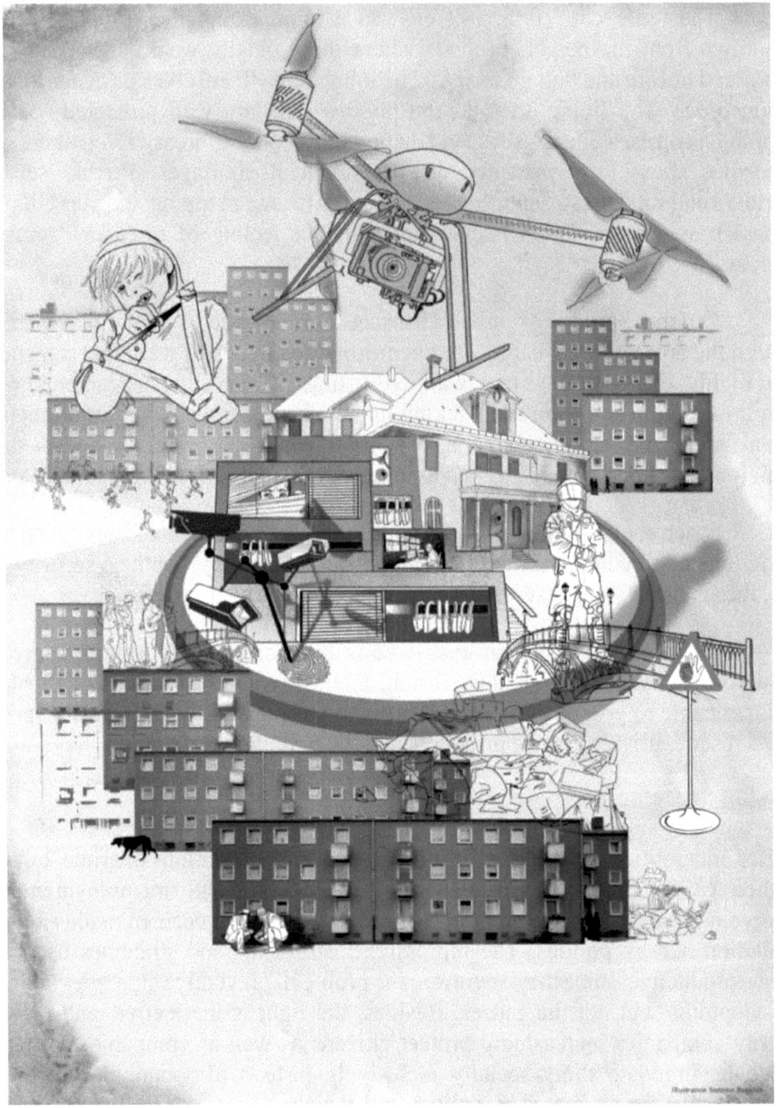

Figure 1: Illustration "Urban Security 2025: The Safe City or Security as a Social Problem" (Steinmüller, Gerhold & Beck, 2012, p. 37

Airport Security 2025: Adventure Airport or coping with uncertainty?

What would happen if citizens were so upset with the security checks at airports that politicians had to react and reduce them?

The model for airport security would be taken from shopping centres or railway stations, the airport would be an open, friendly place for shopping and entertainment and of course a gateway to the world. Visitors accept uncertainty as a part of life; there are always risks, one must only know how to handle them. Hence, the fear of terrorist attacks is less important than the fear of flying. Airport visitors have developed their individual strategies to handle uncertainties: they collect information themselves, mainly from people or institutions they trust, they rely on their own intuition and their own experience and just shrug their shoulders as if to say, “Don’t panic”.

Politics guarantees a certain “basic security”, but makes clear that 100% security is not feasible. The basic level of security at the airport is guaranteed by unobtrusive technical facilities and civil patrols, which provide a calm atmosphere and above all have an eye on everyday risks – from fire risk to pick pocketing. Besides, transparency creates trust. If an attack really happens, people refuse to go along with the scaremongering. In the media, including social media, reasonable voices come out on top. We do not allow fear to determine our life.

How could an airport look in 2025 if the protection against all possible threats was not predominant, as uncertainty was accepted as a core component of life?

Message

People accept risks and live in a “culture of uncertainty” because it adds value to life. A culture of uncertainty means fundamental commitment to uncertainty as a basis and reference point of human life and the rejection of the notion of 100% security in life. The goal of the action is not the removal of all kinds of uncertainty, but the acceptance of a sensible level of uncertainty. Coping strategies like trust, intuition and experience help to correctly distinguish and evaluate risks. Uncertainty includes risks, dangers and challenges and is never definite, but determined by time and the situation. People abstain from total protection by the state; they live an alternative to the philosophy “We must protect the citizen”.

Figure 2: Illustration "Airport Security 2025: Adventure Airport or Coping with Uncertainty?" (Steinmüller, Gerhold & Beck, 2012, 91)

Scenarios as an instrument for dialogue

Scenarios should stimulate discourse; they should raise new questions and contribute to a detailed discussion of its subject. This aim was achieved in the scenario process "Security 2025".

The starting point of heterogeneous perspectives in group discussions with stakeholders were the following questions:

- What is the exciting part of the scenario?
- Where does the scenario tie in with today's trends and developments, especially in the area of public security? Where does it strongly deviate from them?
- How plausible are the developments and actions of the stakeholders described in the scenario?
- Which aspects of the scenario are desirable, which are not?
- Which strategies could promote the desirable aspects, which help to avoid the undesirable ones?

The participants, especially the experts from the political field, but also end-users and scientists from the security sector, discussed the scenarios quite differently. They emphasized different points and behaved either critically or positively to the basic message of the respective scenarios. It can be assumed that – more than in other scenario processes – the participants interpreted the scenarios not only based on their expert knowledge, but also based on their assumptions of the security-political (not only scientific) intentions of the scenarios' authors. Hence, the discussions were not only about the aesthetic or scientific quality of the scenarios, although even these aspects were discussed sufficiently.

In general, the discussion of a scenario started with technical or organizational details and led to principal questions of security-politics and ethics, sometimes even on matters that were not indicated in the scenario. As the discussion proceeded, more and more questions were put forward: To what extent can complex technical-social systems be consciously constructed or changed? Which actors have the largest influences; stakeholders from politics, the economy, civil society or science? The evolution of technical-organizational systems (as well as their dysfunctionality) is often accepted as "naturally-grown" and therefore seen as nearly uncontrollable. Security politicians and practitioners generally stress that it is possible to shape these systems. Thinking in scenarios, in options and potentialities supports this attitude to proactively design, shape and implement systems.

Regarding the security-political aspects that ran through the discussions about the introduced scenarios, three facets should be stressed:

- Risk perception and risk communication
- The new culture of uncertainty
- Politics as stakeholder

Risk perception and risk communication

Risk perception played a key role in the scenarios; which risks are at the centre of public attention, which are consciously or unconsciously ignored? To which risks is the population accustomed and which risks are accepted as a phenomenon of everyday life? It is a well-known phenomenon that risk perception does not necessarily correspond to the probability of risks. This was illustrated by the exorbitant fear of criminal activity by the Old Town inhabitants in the scenario "The Safe City" and mirrored by the lost fear of terrorism in the "Adventure Airport" scenario.

The differences of subjective and (expert-based) objective security have often been investigated in sociology (cf. i. a. see Bonß 2011; Gusy 2010; Slovic 2010). Although the topic has already been discussed intensely in risk-sociological discourses – particularly in the 1990s – it receives new meaning in terms of threat situations, characterized by their complex, ambiguous and systemic design. This expresses itself, for example, in the discussion about the coexistence of increasing social and economic uncertainty with concurrently increasing security in terms of safety and security standards.

Not all participants followed the theory that increasing uncertainty on an individual level would cause, for example, exaggerated security expectations in the field of crime. However it was said that security expectations and security promises on no account had to apply to all social areas of life. Some risks were accepted and didn't even cause a feeling of uncertainty (e.g. traffic, the internet) others were accepted, but caused fears (e.g. security of employment) and for others zero risk was claimed (e.g. airport security). This led to the discussion of the present division in tolerated and non-tolerated risks, which again raised the question of the mandate for such a discourse.

In the end, all participants agreed that one should discuss security measures and threat situations more rationally and not without suitable contextualization; not least to provide society with a more real picture and an objective discussion about subjectively perceived and objectively available (as far as this is determinable) threats.

The new culture of uncertainty

The scenario about airport security, in particular, discussed risk acceptance as a core element of security culture; what could a new security culture look like? What risks are tolerable and acceptable for society as a whole? Thereby, the discussion adds to what in political science is understood as "security culture in the sense of the sum of convictions, values and methods of institutions and individuals which decide what is to be seen as a threat and with which measures this threat should be met" (cf. Daase 2010). Without any doubt, an aspect neglected in the scenarios, risk "education" or risk competence as a part of prevention, should be a central component of this new security culture. Some of the risks are based on the ignorance of processes in nature, technical systems and society. Hence, the question should be raised; what "ignorance tolerance" may we accept socially and in which areas? Coping with ignorance, with the unknown unknowns of security research, with the "things we do not know we do not know", in the context of systemic risks is a challenging as well as difficult security-political and risk-ethical research question.

It became clear that a "culture of uncertainty", in the sense of a fundamental commitment to uncertainty as a base and reference point of human life and the rejection of the image of complete security (cf. Bonß 2011, 65), on the one hand is hard to grasp and on the other hand even harder to communicate. There is no easy way out of the steadily increasing security demands of society and the steadily rising security promises of politics. At the same time it showed that the uncertainties, risks and threats described in the scenarios do not allow a discussion that is solely focused on the production of security anymore. In the context of the airport scenario the essential question was asked, how could one (re)turn to accept risk and threats as part of our lives so that excessive and uncontrollable mechanization cannot further be established in the future?

Politics as stakeholder

A key finding of the scenario process is the addressing of responsibility of politicians to communicate in a fair and transparent way to the public. An adequate policy can influence both the establishment of an uncertainty-culture and a better proportionality between subjectively perceived and objectively given risk as well as subjectively and objectively reasonable strategies. It is crucial that it is not exclusively the responsibility of the state to ensure security by measures such as surveillance or police protection. Rather state-organized social conditions, which allow for a high degree of social cohesion in society, must be implemented. Prevention rather than reaction is the essence of the discussion. Prevention therefore means to openly communicate to the public that it isn't possible to achieve 100-percent security and that there are always risks that belong to life.

Both the discussion of a supposed mentality of the population, that the state is responsible for everything as well as of the "risk-aware citizens" must be discussed objectively with regard to the terms of complex requirements. The difficulty for political stakeholders to make the appropriate decisions coming from this information is, however, obvious. Symbolic politics for example serve medially based perceptions in society, thus they are fulfilling an important function, because irrational and subjectively influenced perspectives on security issues also have their entitlements and need to be answered. However, careful considerations must be made with regard to the symbolic content, in order to prevent a seasonal and event-driven policy.

Conclusion: Security dialogues as a task of security research

Dialogues, such as those that took place within the framework of the workshop "Security2025" and which are documented here, aim to capture different perspectives on security, to reflect them and to think ahead. Scenarios do not give answers – they ask questions and point out problems. And they stimulate discussions about possible and sometimes seemingly impossible questions. During the workshop the scenarios have served this purpose. They thus helped to dissolve the one-sided focus on the threat perspective and the unspoken goal of complete controllability of risks.

Nevertheless, the recurring demands for a dialogue between science, politics and population still remain. The scenario process as such could be the beginning of a transdisciplinary understanding. The challenges of present discussions, however, appeared even within this small community: engaging in the inherent logic of the other (policy on science, science on population and vice versa), recognizing the special conditions of the other and not exploiting them for its own purposes. All this presupposes a culture of awareness, or at least routines of encounter, that are not yet given. At the same time it became clear that only a democratically legitimate discourse, in which all stakeholders are involved, could provide the opportunity to break the circle of increasing security promises of politics on the one hand and increasing security expectations of the population on the other.

The need for such a cross-border dialogue and the need to raise the willingness of stakeholders to be involved in it is clear. Therefore, in the future it is crucial to establish such a dialogue on a scientifically as well as politically sustainable foundation and promote financial and organizational support structures.

References

Bonß, W. (2011). (Un–)Sicherheit in der Moderne. In P. Zoche, S. Kaufmann & R. Haverkamp (Eds.). *Zivile Sicherheit: Gesellschaftliche Dimensionen gegenwärtiger Sicherheitspolitiken* (43–70.). Bielefeld: transcript Verlag.

Bundesamt für Bevölkerungsschutz und Katastrophenhilfe (BBK) (Eds.) (2005). *Problemstudie: Risiken für Deutschland. Teil 1.* Bad Neuenahr-Ahrweiler. Available at: http://www.bbk.bund.de/SharedDocs/Downloads/BBK/DE/Publikationen/Wissenschaftsforum/Bd6_Risiken-fuer-D_Teil1.pdf?__blob=publicationFile [13.02.2013].

Bundesamt für Bevölkerungsschutz und Katastrophenhilfe (BBK) (Eds.) (2011).*Vierter Gefahrenbericht* (Schriften der Schutzkommission). Bonn: BKK. Available at:

http://www.schutzkommission.de/SharedDocs/Downloads/SK/DE/Publikationen/4-Gefahrenbericht.pdf?__blob=publicationFile [13.02.2013]

Daase, C. (2010). Wandel der Sicherheitskultur. *Aus Politik und Zeitgeschichte, 50.* Available at: http://www.bpb.de/apuz/32301/wandel-der-sicherheitskultur?p=all [13.02.2013].

Federal Ministry of Research and Education (BMBF) (2012). *Research for civil security 2012–2017.* Framework programme of the Federal Government. Available at: http://www.bmbf.de/pub/BMBF_rahmenprogramm_sicherheitsforschung_2012_2017_engl.pdf [25.01.2013].

Gerhold, L. & Schiller, J. (Eds.) (2012). Perspektiven der Sicherheitsforschung. Beiträge aus dem Forschungsforum Öffentliche Sicherheit. Frankfurt am Main: Lang Verlag.

Gusy, C. (2010). Sicherheitskultur – Sicherheitspolitik – Sicherheitsrecht. *KritV, 2010,* 111–128.

Lange, H.-J., Ohly, P. H. & Reichertz, J. (Eds.) (2009). *Auf der Suche nach neuer Sicherheit – Fakten, Theorien und Folgen.* Wiesbaden: Verlag für Sozialwissenschaften.

Münkler, H., Meurer, S. & Bohlender, M (Eds.) (2010). *Sicherheit und Risiko. Über den Umgang mit Gefahr im 21. Jahrhundert.* Bielefeld: transcript Verlag.

Renn, O., Schweizer, P. J., Dreyer, M. & Klinke, A. (2007). *Risiko. Über den gesellschaftlichen Umgang mit Risiko.* München: Oekom Verlag.

Slovic, P. (2010). The Psychology of Risk. *Saúde e Sociedade, 19* (4), 731–747.

Steinmüller, K., Gerhold, L. & Beck, M.-L. (Eds.) (2012). *Sicherheit 2025.* Forschungsforum Öffentliche Sicherheit. Schriftenreihe Sicherheit Nr. 10. Berlin.

Didactical Functions of Dark and Bright Scenarios: Examples from the European Transport Industry[1]

Massimo Moraglio, Hans-Liudger Dienel and Robin Kellermann

Abstract

"Horror" or "dark" predictions, e.g. worst-case situations for the future, once well-grounded in terms of accuracy and well-related to the real world situation, could have a very high motivational effect, e.g. a didactical function, especially if they are largely debated well beyond the stakeholder milieu. We argue that in the cases here presented, dark scenarios often lead to activities to avoid their realization. The example of the European transport industry in the period from the 1960's-1980's – largely described in this essay - confirms this argument. A broad analysis of historical and present dark forecasts in the field of transport clearly shows how they indicated "no-go" paths, while the "bright" scenarios did offer "go-this-way" perspectives. This didactic impact of scenarios as a policy instrument was especially strong when dissemination targeted a wider audience, beyond the client and the stakeholders. We argue that the same principles work in the field of security scenarios, although this would need additional investigation.

Introduction

The final goal of the foresight studies has changed. More and more often, it is to scrutinize the existing forces, weight them and give clues about the interaction in the long run (Harper 2013). The target is thus to organize the best available information and knowledge, put them in a time perspective, and finally display those elements in evolving trajectories and possible (alternative) futures (declined in plural). There is also expanding literature analysing the need of better tuning forecasts and making them fit the agenda of the policy-makers (Da Costa et al. 2011; Könnöla et al. 2011), aiming to make forecasts and scenarios part of a larger debate on the future. Therefore, the foresight exercises have the need to properly address their audience, to be convincing, to raise a proper debate, and naturally, to engage policy-makers in acting accordingly. As Harper noted, offering an inspiring differentiation,

[1] Disclaimer: The research leading to these results received funding from the European Union's Seventh Framework Programme (FP7/2007-2013) under grant agreement no.314753.

R. Peperhove et al. (Eds.), *Envisioning Uncertain Futures*, Zukunft und Forschung 6, https://doi.org/10.1007/978-3-658-25074-4_6

> "one can distinguish between two main forms of foresight linked to policy. There is foresight for/in policy, relating to its advisory and strategic function, where foresight serves as a tool to inform and develop policy in any area or to "join up" policy across domains. Secondly, *foresight as a policy instrument*, relating to its instrumental role, where it serves as an instrument to implement budgetary, structural or cultural changes in the domain of research and/or innovation policy. [...] In summary, in the first category, the main benefits are strategic, whilst in the second the main benefits relate to enhancing the effectiveness of the instruments" (Harper 2013, 8).

The difficulty of being "listened to" by policy-makers is thus receiving greater attention (Da Costa et al. 2011), while there is larger discussion about the gap between forecast studies and their ability to inform action (Könnöla et al. 2011). In other words, such an ability to influence the debate on the future is considered a key factor of a successful foresight exercise. Framed in that debate, this paper aims at analyzing – retrospectively – foresight activities in the past decades concerning the European transport industry, and scrutinizing to which extent dark forecasts developed a wider debate about the future of the industry. Finally, we state how this line of investigation should be developed also about other fields, like security and environmental studies. This is not only to enable a comparative approach, but also in order to better understand the inner dynamics of dark scenarios, and their different impacts in different fields.

More precisely, this paper focuses on some historical examples of dark predictions and scenarios having some common features:

- the focus on the industrial future of Europe;
- a large debate which overlapped economic, political and societal fields;
- the role of dark forecasts in activating "bright" alternatives, the latter as a clear response to the first.

Generally speaking, the forecasts concerning the future of the European transport industry for the period from 1960-1980 had largely and obsessively focused on negative predictions, envisioning the imminent end of the European leadership in that sector, in favour of other international competitors. Those 1960's-1980's debates addressed questions already present in the political and economic agenda, but in those narratives the key factors had been turned into gloomy colors, describing a negative future, and, in many cases, taking this negative trend for granted, though picturing, at the very end, some actions to be taken.

Finally, this essay also investigates a 2012-2015 research project run by the authors, devoted to the future of the European transport industry. This contemporary research openly used the instrument of presenting a set of dark scenarios as a way to alert policy-makers, stakeholders and the larger public about the current debate concerning the European transport industry. This action has been developed in combination with a set of bright scenarios, in order to enlighten also the currently present potentialities.

In this regard, we focus on how dark scenarios can have – given some particular circumstances listed in the following pages – a positive function of alerting the public opinion about certain issues. This allows us to claim how those dark scenarios drove to a public debate and open a discussion, which finally produced i) a shifting of perceptions, and ii) clear industrial and political actions devoted to counter-fight the dark scenario statements.

Horror scenarios and their function as a policy instrument

This paper focuses on "horror" or "dark" forecasts (horror and dark will be used as synonyms in this paper). For "dark" forecasts we mean foresight exercises, which underline a decline or a collapse of a given part of the society, or of an economic activity, or the crumble of some political values. Dark "scenarios", often linked to apocalyptic outcomes (at least in the Judeo-Christian ethical tradition), have been strongly marked by religious elements (O'Leary 1994). Hebrew, paleo-Christian and Christian prophets, including Jeremiah or – for the matter – the 14th century Florentine monk Savonarola, all largely used allegory of the incoming "dark" times. The most extreme and inspiring figure is Jeremiah, who first provided a "horror" scenario for the kingdom of Israel and the destruction of Jerusalem: but, once Jerusalem was conquered by the Babylonian, he turned around to a positive vision and with his last money purchased land in Jerusalem to demonstrate that the city would recover in future.

> "This is what the Lord Almighty, the God of Israel, says: Take these documents, both the sealed and unsealed copies of the deed of purchase, and put them in a clay jar so they will last a long time. For this is what the Lord Almighty, the God of Israel, says: "Houses, fields and vineyards will again be bought in this land." (Jeremiah 32:14-15).

What usually is present in 99% of the "dark" predictions and scenarios is the combination of the inevitability of the "negative" outcomes (negative for a given audience) combined with the (slight) hope of a resurgence (again, such a resurgence is tailored for a part of the society). The dark forecasts are, in other words, like the apocalyptic tales, a "tension field" between the "bad" and the "good", e.g. a way of depicting the uncertainty of the future and its potential proneness to bad outcomes (O'Leary 1994), as well as a tiny hope of resurgence. This leads us to state how "dark" scenarios are necessarily dealing with political and ethical issues, making their development a strong responsibility.

Moving to more recent times, we can easily say that in the meantime the future is the time horizon of any foresight exercise and scenarios are often linked to the present time once they want to inform the present policy. Generally speaking, a "dark" narrative usually elaborates elements already present in the debate, it takes full advantage of the statistical data supporting its thesis, and stresses any potential trend, even if still embryonic, which confirms the main thesis. Those factors are shaped to their extreme scale, in order to persuade the audience of the inevitability (and its parallel undesirability) of the prediction. These forecasts often – but not always – embed apocalyptic or dystopian discourses, in which some forces, external to the targeted audience, benefit from this decline/collapse. As we will see below, for instance the late 1960's debate around the "American threat" stated a declining Europe, while "the Americans" would largely benefit of this weakness. According to the different targeted fields, the founding elements of the dark scenarios are a variable combination of well-grounded facts, self-explanatory statements and numerical data. However, naturally, it is not enough to assemble those factors together. What is usually necessary to gain a large audience is to step in an already existing discussion on the given topic, and to further elaborate (or better assemble) the pieces present on the stage. In order to be debated and largely discussed, dark predictions have to be rather general, but not generic; despite, at first glance this seems contradictory, they have to be well-grounded and credible, also for the experts, but nevertheless able to shock the reader and to "threat" the audience. This makes the scenario convincing *and* shocking at the same time.

The success of horror forecasts in reaching the audience is, of course, related to the cultural, political and economic debate of a given societal landscape. Usually, if not always, the timing is an essential factor. Dark predictions reach a wide audience because they were leveraging an already running discussion on the decline of their respective social environments. For instance, the French journalist Servan-Schreiber was able not only to summarise the on-going elements in his seminal dark scenario book "Le Defi Américain"; moreover he was able to address those issues in a systematic way, feeding a larger public and putting to an extreme the arguments supporting his thesis. His book was published once the discussion was already running, but not yet fully developed. And his main ability was to escalate the debate, keeping his dark scenario credible and plausible even for the experts, and, *at the same time*, his forecast was not dull or written in jargon. In other words, despite well-grounded and already debated, his book was able – as he said – "to rattle the cage" (Zimmermann 2000; De Cugis 1969).

As an additional point, the 1960's-1980's dark forecasts for the European transport industry – using an old rhetoric trick – largely objectified their statements, flooding the reader with numbers, charts, and tables. Beside the numbers, a large, carefully selected choice of arguments was added to the narrative, using, when necessary, also previous research and assessments. A sense of unavoidable trajectory was, finally, informing the texts, based on undeniable arguments, alike the economy of scale (and scope) for the American companies in the 1960's or the outstanding performance of the Japanese car manufacturers in the 1980's.

The example of "dark" scenarios for EU transport industry 1960's-1980's

Today, the European transport industry holds the leadership worldwide. The sector is one of the main voices of European export, while European brands have been able to achieve international positions and to access global markets, including emerging economies. This is not true for all the sectors: for instance, the position of the European maritime industry is relegated in sub-sector niches. But, the role of the European railway equipment sector is unquestionably globally dominant, while Airbus is holding a strong position, automobile European Original Equipment Manufacturers (OEMs) are blanketing the planet (ACEA 2012).

Against this current situation, we notice how, in the last 50 years, the European transport industry has faced several threat periods and external competitive pressures (Tilly & Triebel, 2013). The business community had been aware of some intrinsic limits of the transport industry, and above all, its national fragmentation and the lack of economy of scale and scope. In the early 1960's, once the European "Economic miracles" were at full steam, the industrial and political experts already focused on the critical points of the sector, making alarming statements about the crumbling aviation industry (MoA 1965), or assessing the business backwardness of Europe (World Economic Forum 1971). Two periods seem to be very appealing for the matter of this essay; in each of those, journalists and essayists, not-industrial experts and governmental agencies stepped in, which was both reason and consequence of a discussion reaching a broader audience than the inner circles of the "experts".

These periods were:

i) The American threat. In 1967, the French journalist Jean-Jacques Servan-Schreiber published "Le Défi Américain" (quickly translated into 15 languages), summarising the on-going debate. He argued that if the European industry was not merging and Europe did not unite, it would be defeated by American economies of scale superiority.

ii) The Japanese threat. During the 1980's, the American and European markets for automobiles were flooded with Japanese cars for the first time. At the same time, Korean ship building outperformed many American and European competitors. The American industry (and some years later, the European industry too) began to admire the Japanese organisation of car quality and lean production, fearing to disappear.

Dark scenarios about the "American threat"

In the course of the 1960's, Western Europe was experiencing a shift from predominantly transatlantic orientation to an intra-European perspective. As well known, the US had played a major role in rebuilding and influencing a war-torn Europe, being in the 1960's the latter aiming both to cope and to compete with the US. At that point, the established transatlantic system of military, monetary and economic securities was continuously put into question within Europe's political and public spheres (Zimmermann 2000). Given the contemporary unequal industrial conditions and Kennedy's less Europe-focused successors Johnson and Nixon, a growing number of European stakeholders, supported by an increasing public and political debate, stated Europe was becoming an American satellite. Those considerations were expressed in far-ranging notions like "The American challenge" or "The American threat" and led to frame many of the political and public debates of the 1960's and early 1970's. Those reports, pamphlets and books gave voice to the ambiguous feeling of fear and admiration of the US economy. According to the mainstream economic debate, the winning factor of the US industrial sector was its economies of scale. In 1967 it was the French journalist Jean-Jacques Servan-Schreiber who most outstandingly highlighted the major European weaknesses and future challenges in his milestone book "Le Défi Américan". Having sold more than 600,000 copies in France alone and being translated into 15 languages, this book was finally published passionately showing what many European economists and politicians were already discussing in the course of the 1960's. Labelling the status quo of the USA industry as the "American Colossus", he convincingly suggested, "it is the giant American firms, not the medium-sized ones, that play the major role in penetrating the European market" (Servan-Schreiber 1968, 18).

Analogue to Herman Kahn's and the Hudson Institute's future study of life in the year 2000 (Kahn & Wiener, 1967), Servan-Schreiber drew an alarming picture in which Europe, while having to fear additional threats from upcoming countries like India and China, "will belong to a different world, a world somewhere between the advanced societies and the underdeveloped ones" (Servan-Schreiber 1968, 26). Moreover, as an extrapolation of the lasting deficit of European scale economies, he stated a foresight that soon became famous and must have been the ultimate challenge to European stakeholders in all fields related to industry:

> "(…) it seems clear that we Europeans cannot hope to participate fully in that world of the future. This does not mean we will be poor; probably we will grow even richer. But we will be overtaken and dominated, for the time in our history, by a more advanced civilization" (Ibid., 32).

Although he was sometimes criticized of representing the European economy as too defensive and of not adequately reflecting the economic reality (Stoltenberg 1968; De Cugis 1969) – particularly concerning the booming car industry – "Le Défi Américain" literally described Europe soon to become subject of an American dominance.

Facing that and other alarming and negative assessments about the future of industry, and particularly about the transport industry (MoA 1965, 48), it is worthwhile to note how there was a wide discussion about such an issue, and how eventually a set of actions were concentrated in order to counter-act the trend. The first EEC Summit in The Hague in 1969, the 1971 Davos European Management Forum and the 1972 Werner Plan (European Parliament 1969; European Commission 1970; World Economic Forum 1971) can be contextualized as direct outcomes in the realm of policy and decision-making. The Concorde airspace project as well as the Airbus foundation can be also claimed as materialized industrial outcomes and reactions to the American challenge, furthermore marking distinguished approaches that very much differed in success. What for the transport industry remains a lesson to be learned is that a weak and desperate sector, like the European aviation industry in the 1960's, can in the long run become a strong and highly competitive sector. Since the car and rail industry were much less affected by the American threat, or were considered to have a stabile future, policy makers were able to concentrate their capacities on the weakest field, the aviation and aerospace sector. Consequently, instead of an announced collapse, we witnessed a winning outcome for the sector. Hence, in the long run, the American threat paradoxically appears to be a big opportunity for the European aviation sector.

Beyond that, we can learn that if a national industrial sector is threatened in its very existence, a given national state (e.g. the UK in the 1960's) can much quicker overcome exclusive domestic perspectives. Extrinsic motivations might have fuelled common decisions much stronger than intrinsic persuasions about a common Europe. Following that, as a last point we can learn that a warning "horror" scenario like "Le Défi Américain" for the 1960's might have been a more fruitful circumstance than political "Durchhalteparolen" (mere motivation slogans). In this respect, Servan-Schreiber's book was so fortunate in its timing and in its contents (although considered controversial by experts) that it provoked a very large debate. Servan-Schreiber presented nothing but the collapse, though his key concept of economy of scale could be at reach for the Europeans *once they unite*. So, it was – at the end – an impulse – among others – to strengthen the political will towards a stronger European unification process and towards competitive projects in technology, transport and infrastructure.

Dark scenarios about the Japanese threat

Japan, in the 1960's, had experienced growth rates of up to 14% through strict governmental planning in key and future industries and a highly efficient production. The Asian country was undergoing a tremendous economic rise, which eventually challenged the USA and Europe much faster than most experts would have expected. Japanese impressive export rates threatened foreign markets and their balances of trade, offering high quality, reliable capital-intensive and continuously improved products, accompanied with astonishingly low cost. In contrast to the American threat, the 'weak signals' of an upcoming Japanese threat seemed to have remained underestimated in Western Europe's perception during the 1960's.

Throughout the 1960's Japan's trade volume with the European Community was not considerable and all together it had little impact, so there was hardly any fear or even scepticism. But from the late 1960's the situation changed completely: "between 1969 and 1977 Japanese exports to Europe increased by 620%, from $1.4 to $8.7 billion" (Lehmann 1982, 41). Foresights about Japan, alike Hedberg's "The Japanese Challenge" (Hedberg 1969) or Kahn's "The Emerging Japanese Superstate" (Kahn 1970), did not gain great attention when published. But the late 1970's saw an overwhelmingly quantitative presence of Japanese exports and economic performance. European (and North-American) car companies were convinced that they had to fundamentally change production culture in order to stand and overcome the Japanese (and later the Korean) competition (Womack, Roos & Jones, 1990).

The debate around this issue ran for more than a decade. Instead of having one landmark book, as in the 1960's for the American threat, we can count three relevant documents here, namely two European Union reports (European Commission 1976; European Commission 1984) and the famous MIT volume "The Machine that changed the world" of 1990 (Womack, Roos & Jones, 1990). *Sensu stricto*, none of those texts was a scenario, not even a forecast, but the purpose was more a description of the current situation about the car industry. If that was the stated goal, nearly all of them contained very alarming (alarming, naturally, for US and European car industries) claims, depicting the strength of the Japanese car sector and the unavoidable decline of the US and Europe. The European union reports were largely a reaction to the development of a two-decade lasting industrial development, in which a mere extrapolation of the Japanese export growth was frightening (for the Europeans), but easily predictable.

A sense of panic informs the first of those texts, and as early as 1976, it was proclaimed that "the European car industry will face the greatest difficulties it has ever known" (European Commission 1976, 11). European manufacturers to that day had already lost many export markets to the Japanese, especially in the USA, where between 1970 and 1979 European share "fell from 11% to 5% while the Japanese shares rose from 4% to 17%" (Jones 1981, 11). But also the domestic markets were challenged since the Japanese had captured more than 10% of almost every national market in Western Europe.

The 1984 European Union report on the car industry shows at the same time a retrospective analysis of the past, as well as a (negative) prediction for the future: "The commercial challenge from Japan – felt in Europe and the United States alike – shows that the decline of the [European] Community car industry cannot be explained by the recession and successive oil crises alone. The demand for cars in Europe did slow down at the start of the 1980's. But the problems of the European industry flow, to a much larger extent, from the slowness of its reaction to a period of enormous change in motor manufacturing" (European Commission 1984, 2). The consequence would be that, in 2000, Europe would sink down to a mere Japanese colony, because the Japanese´s key technologies were so much more advanced to that of the Europeans. In other words, the 1984 report formulated a dark prediction, in which the European car industry would collapse. As for the American threat, the Japanese industry in the late 1970's and 1980's showed outstanding outcomes, which dwarfed the rivals´ performance. Moreover, that meant the arrival of an inexorable and unavoidable new production system that was flexible, customer oriented and much more efficient than ever before (Kenney & Florida, 1993). The only hope left was to copy the Japanese production and marketing model.

It was the 1990 MIT study that finally invented the term "lean production", which summed up a new industrial reality experienced in Japan. That volume, unpacking the key factors of the Japanese success, and blaming American and European car producers being dull and slow, depicted a gloomy forecast. The MIT investigation definitely has all the ingredients and presents a typical dark prediction: a trajectory, leading to (unavoidable and undesirable) decline or even collapse; an external agent which challenges the *status-quo*; a long set of data confirming the trend; a new formulation of concepts and ideas circulating in the debate. And, last but not least, a thin line of hope.

The experts agreed in the understanding that Japan had learned to combine foreign developments of mass production with refined domestic configurations, gaining a unique industrial organisation, based on "the achievements of economies of scale, sophisticated marketing, vigorous exploitation of technical advances, emphasis on product reliability and a substantial awareness of changing Japanese factor endowments vis-à-vis the international division of labour" (Shepherd 1981, 387). For the car manufactures, the above meant that the Japanese peers moved from "just-in-time" to "total quality" principles (Altshuler et al. 1984, 29). As in the early 1970's for the American challenge, the Japanese threat offered enough elements for reconsidering and quitting the EU status quo and to i) radically adjusting and adapting to the overarching Japanese concept of "lean production", and ii) boosting European integration towards the final goal of the 1992 Single Market.

The problem and dilemma for Europe, however, was considered that "no one quite seems to know how to meet the Japanese challenge" (Hager 1992, 23).

As a response, the political and industrial sphere was again induced to obtain a European 'critical mass' in order to overcome the stagnation of the 1980's "Euroscepticism". The dark prediction to lose Europe's car industry as the "industry of industries" pushed the sector's top-management and policy makers to learn from its main competitor and to catalyse global integration, which turned out to be a precondition for its further success in emerging markets in present times. In other words, the dark predictions in context of the Japanese threat were meant to gradually diversify Europe's industrial foundations and to shift away from the former economies of scale towards economies of learning and (international) cooperation.

The replies to this new challenge were diversified. There were, first, defensive and (neo-) protectionist policies, though, as Sachwald points out accurately, "the term itself is typical of neo-protectionism, since it is actually a euphemism to designate new forms of quantitative restrictions" (Sachwald 1995, 179), which encompassed import restrictions, license struggles, non-tariff trade barriers (Hughes 2001, 52), and, last but not least, an unpleasant and sometimes racist rhetoric of accusation and defamation (News Week 1991). This first stage of replies was followed by a set of policy responses on a European level, which eventually led to "The Single Market" action of 1992 (though its implementation is a different issue). Given that situation, "a common external policy and more open markets were the most important prospective consequences of the Single market for the car industry" (Sachwald 1995, 81). By that, the Japanese threat – like the American threat two decades before – strongly correlates with the Community's Member States' 1992 milestone to collaborate and to unify more closely than ever before. In that sense Lehmann argues: "To revitalize, to re-industrialize and to regain global competitiveness, the creation of the single market was presented as the solution" (Lehmann 1992, 41). Since a functioning and trustful domestic market can be the precondition for mutual innovation, quality and economic success, the Community's aim was to establish an expanding single European market. Competition as well as technology and R&D cooperation were "the overriding objective[s] to regain economic dynamism and international competitiveness" (Hager 1992, 17).

In short, the fear of the European industries pushed the Europeans once more "to recognize the need to coordinate more fully their economic, political and security interests". In doing so, the Japanese threat "had an indirect and ultimately positive effect upon progress towards European integration" (Hughes 2001, 57).

Proposing new dark scenarios for today

The concept of decline seems to be a constant element of the past debate for the European transport industry, although the decline itself was avoided for many sub-sectors. Such a historical trend and its controversial issues was a clue for implementing a foresight study about the future of European transport industry.

This was a task for RACE2050, a research consortium funded by the European Commission between 2012-2015, with the goal to investigate the competitiveness of the European transport industry up to 2050 and gathering six European research centres. The project viewpoint was to look into the next four decades up to 2050 in a reflective way, which takes into account the impact of foresight studies in the multifaceted world of overlapping layers of stakeholders. The case of the transport industry is naturally complex, encompassing a vast number of layers: industry representatives, EU and national policy-makers, workers, advocates and unions. Such a multi-layered realm must be multiplied by 12 sub-sectors of the transport industry, which often operate on a global scale, well beyond the old continent. Additionally, the European transport industry had (and has) a very relevant economic value, with high impact on the export balance. These elements make the sector a very sensitive topic, not just economically, but politically too. On the other hand, the project´s foresight task was not political *stricto sensu*, but had the target to assess winning parameters for the competitiveness of the European transport industry, which seems to be at the first look a very economical (or even numerable) issue.

Given these constraints, the project team developed a close analysis of the already existing scenarios available for the industry, naturally the ones accessible to the public. The investigation of those approximately 100 documents offered a landscape oriented to forecasting a sharp decline of the European brand, which resembled largely similar negative scenarios as presented in the past decades. Two elements have been depicted as main fears for the future: for many of the service sub-sectors (shipping, railway service, taxi etc.), the meagre financial results could lead to an even worse performance, and thus to a greater crisis (or bankruptcy (World Economic Forum 2012)). For many of the production industries, the rising competition from emerging economies is already challenging the dominant role of European producers, and some sub-sectors (as, for instance, the railway equipment industry) are feeling clear pressure, envisioning a medium-term strong decline (UNIFE 2010, 98). A further element, common in the large part of the scenarios and future analysis, was the impact of 2008 financial crisis, and its long-term effects, including its role as a turning-point for the mature economies, and thus for Europe too (European Commission 2012).

The project team discussed the 1960's-1980's threats and dark predictions for the European transport industry, and how those were transformed into many successful stories: Was, thus, yesterday's fear today's factor of success? The team agreed on this, and thus, the task became to identify and examine the past foresight strategies, particularly in the context of warning foresights. In other words, the aim was to better understand how dark outlooks mobilized the industry leaders and policy makers to enhance competitive resilience and change business models. With the help of those historical examinations, the objective of the project was to present a well-grounded and careful analysis of the scenarios already on the floor, and to use those outcomes to feed RACE2050's scenario making process and to recommend strategic measures for strengthening the European transport industry's global position for 2030 and beyond (Ritchey 2013). Therefore, the project faced the question of the foresight's didactical power. The final report of the research did not aim to present clear measurable and quantitative impacts of foresight studies, but to present evident correlations between warning foresights and European industrial and political responses. So the final target was presenting the on-going debate (largely oriented to assess a declining role for Europe), openly claiming a gloomy future, but in order to mobilize the distinct sub-sectors of the industry. To achieve this goal, we have shaped our "dark" scenario, which was fairly general, long term oriented, strategic and policy orientated (Dienel, Kellermann & Moraglio, 2014).

This was the combination of two levels:

1. How dramatic transport foresights made industry change, learn, adapt and keep competitiveness. In short, how threat foresights had positive effects and how the dramatic foresights did support the preparedness in the transport industry to modernize, change and speed up.

2. At the same time, the project also analysed the outline and impact of positive, stimulating and envisioning foresights and leitmotifs for clear and reachable goals for the European transport industry.

The final report was thus conceived not as a neutral foresight, but as giving clear messages of necessary change to industry, politics and society at large. The project scenarios needed to be powerful enough to reach a multitude of stakeholders, fragmented in many different sub-branches, with different if not conflicting agendas.

The project developed two sets of scenarios. Those two sets were used for two time-frames, one 2030, showing the nadir of the European industry; and one for 2050, showing the resurgence of the industry. The intrinsic goal is to better depict the negative (negative for Europeans) trends, and possibly to avoid them as a "no-go" path, moving directly to the "go-this-way" path of the 2050 bright scenario. So, a first set of three scenarios was focused to the 2030 time-frame and amplified the current debate, containing thus a very *dark* message, in which the European transport industry lost its competitive advantages, declining dramatically. This 2030 set dark scenarios actually went further, claiming how the social polarization of the European society had a strong spill-over effect in the transport realm, and due to budget constraints, Europeans reduced their movements (which worsens the situation of the industry). Such a threat forecast had – intrinsically – a didactical function, which had the goal to reach the different actors involved in the discussion, including lay-people. As said before, such a message needed to be rather general, but not generic, and as it was for past dark scenarios, the aim was to be credible for the experts, but nevertheless able to "rattle-the-cage". The real challenge was to develop a dark scenario indeed able to "threat" but also to be realistic; and this not just for one sub-sector, but for the whole industry. A scrutiny to the current situation offered two elements over-crossing the sectors, which could be leveraged for the purpose of the research.

The first one was the 2008 financial crisis, which effects and deepens the already critical situation of the European "domestic" market, weakening it further. So the RACE2050 team claimed how the European Union internal market has become so feeble to "threat" the European industry in its very basis. This is affecting European companies both in term of decreasing shares of market; but also, considering the "allure" of many European products, such a gloomy perspective is making, in a more subtle way, the European productions less appealing. The second element was the rising performance of emerging economies′ industrial peers, which are showing a robust development and a growing quality. While the European "domestic" is smaller, other markets are nowadays more and more crowded, and the competition is running not only in terms of final cost, but also in terms of quality, political pressure and end-to-end offers.

The combination of those elements, already largely present in the current debate, was submitted to a mixed audience of stakeholders (policy-makers, users′ advocates, industrial representatives from different sub-sectors) aiming to get a (negative) picture able to have the right ingredients of a dark scenario. Surely, a central element for the credibility of this foresight exercise was a correct time frame: envisioning a 2030 collapse was indeed fitting the expectations. If 2030 is the nadir, there is hope in a didactical 2050. To balance such a bitter outcome, the project developed also a set of three "bright" scenarios for the time-frame of 2050. The goal, in the latter case, was twofold. First, in a more trivial way, to offer "a blade of light at the end of the tunnel", describing a revival after the turbulence of the 2020's. Secondly, the project team analysed the current trends, potential business and social drifts, which could have the role to subvert the gloomy suggestion of the dark forecasts. In particular, the main element of counter-trend was a scrutiny to 2040-2050 social and demographic trends in today's emerging economies. This shows how the European ageing society, lack of skilled labour force, and awareness of environmental and social externalities related to transport activities will become common features also for China, India and so on. As the Europeans are the first in the line to cope with those elements, and with the need to develop innovative concept and business models, this should offer a strong comparative advantage.

Here, the didactical function has been even stronger, considering this positive future a sort of back-casting, inviting the stakeholders, and the citizens, to discuss alternative paths and even radical alternative ways of thinking of the transport industry as a whole. In this set of positive scenarios, the concept of security has been central in assessing the role of energy. The weakness of Europe in grasping fossil energy sources is a pushing factor (as for the Chinese industry) in developing energy-saving devices as well as alternatives to the fossil-fuel based engines. In this case, feebleness can become a selling point for the 2050 global market.

Conclusion

It has been written that, unfortunately,

> "in regard to the various functions of foresight, so far little is known in terms of impact assessment. While the policy-informing function is generally acknowledged (though little hard evidence is provided), the policy-counselling and -facilitating functions are still comparatively novel concepts, and have thus not yet been subject to deeper investigations." (Havas, Schartinger & Weber, 2010, 92).

Facing this lack of knowledge, we have offered here a long-term assessment, focusing on the European transport industry, scrutinizing previous foresights as well as their impacts. With this long-term assessment, we noticed how some dark predictions had the ability to act as a counter-trend, calling for action which, eventually, lead to avoid the outcomes proposed by the predictions themselves. We have also depicted some main features of those horror forecasts, which have been used in a current foresight research.

In the paper we had two sets of questions: i) what made those dark foresight exercises so largely discussed and ii) how the predictions failed, letting the European transport industry avoid its "inevitable" collapse.

Concerning the first question, we noticed how three elements have been crucial:

1. A gripping narrative, which encompassed statistical data, a general but not generic display of elements driving toward the decline, and the ability to be credible and shocking at the same time;

2. An already on-going debate on the decline;

3. A perfect timing of the forecast, e.g. not too early and not too late, able in other words to be rooted in current discussion, but also capable of escalating its main features.

The second question, e.g. why those dark predictions failed, can be answered mainly through two elements.

The first is the large impact in the public debate, *which was reaching layers beyond the experts*. Such a large, social discussion created a sort of common background, an "idem sentire", which alerted the stakeholders (at very different ranks) about the new industrial landscape, and, considering the extreme power of the challenge, to give extreme answers, definitely moving out of the *status quo*.

The second element was the presence of a supranational agency, e.g. the European Union, as a potential alternative, which offered a viable substitute to the traditional business model. In other words, considering the "inevitability" of the collapse, even the less EU-friendly sentiments (like e.g. in the United Kingdom during the 1960's) were dropped in favour of a European action, like Airbus or the EU automotive agreements. Facing dramatic dark predictions made it possible – beyond the industrial leadership – to overcome national boundaries, develop European responses, enhance competitive resilience, modernize technologies, change business models and re-structure strategic goals.

As mentioned, our investigation about dark predictions and gloomy scenarios aimed at feeding the discussion about the impact of foresight exercises, in order to better tune the current activities. Additionally, such a scrutiny offers also a long term perspective, rooting the on-going research into a historical path. But, we think that an analysis of "dark" scenarios can also offer further elements of understanding. This is particularly the case when we consider the public debate on some relevant issues, which are often embedded in gloomy or even horror forecasts. In very recent times, it has been pointed out how climate change debate has been developed also under the viewpoint of apocalypse (Skrimshire 2014). Here we have an intriguing case study, in which – on the contrary to our outcomes regarding the European transport industry – the presence of dark predictions has not (yet) activated counter-actions.

The same can be said, to some extent, about the field of security, in which we can also identify horror predictions and forecasts in great numbers. More particularly, we argue that further analyses of historical and present dark scenarios in the field of security studies should be scrutinized, in order to detect similarities and differences against the present essay. It can be true that security (foresight) studies are usually focused on threats and therefore "dark" scenarios naturally play a decisive role there. In contrast to other fields, horror, threat, warning scenarios are in this field the usual, accepted form of foresight, and perhaps therefore intellectually not so shocking. Nevertheless, we see also in security studies the need to analyse the didactical awareness, motivation and impact of horror scenarios. Security studies here are conceived in a wider sense, which is not limited to security threats (see, for instance, the case of FESTOS and ZIF projects′ scenarios as presented in this volume), but includes studies on surveillance, privacy, data protection and governmental control. Looking at the past, such dark predictions were Aldous Huxley′s "Brave new world" (Huxley 1946 [1931]), Herman Kahn′s "On Thermonuclear War" (1960), the report "Limits of Growth" of the Club of Rome (Meadows et al. 1972) or scenarios on the dying of the woods (Waldsterben) and the Brandt-Report (1981) and Samuel Huntington′s "Clash of Civilizations" (1993).

Here, we claim how an investigation on those reports, articles and books can help us understand the cultural debate on such an issue, and additionally to better frame the policy-makers and citizen reactions to those dark foresights. Indeed, Huxley′s and Orwell′s claim of a dictatorship control over citizens, or Huntington′s statement about the civilisations′ clashes provoked a large and endless discussion about the inevitability of those foresights, which produced, among other outcomes, also counter-arguments and counter-actions. A long term scrutiny could be indeed beneficial, offering valuable clues to assess the present situation and to better shape the future, keeping in mind this strong didactical function (made consciously or not by the authors).

References

ACEA (2012). *The Automobile industry Pocket book 2012*. Brussels: ACEA.

Altshuler, A., Anderson, M., Jones, D., Roos, D. & Womack, J. (1984). *The Future of the Automobile*. Cambridge: MIT Press.

Brandt, W. (1981). *Das Überleben sichern: Der Brandt - Report. Bericht der Nord - Süd - Kommission*. Berlin: Ullstein.

Da Costa, O., Warnke P., Cagnin C., & Scapolo F. (2011). *The Impact of Foresight on Policy-Making: Insights From The Forlearn Mutual Learning Process*. Sevilla: Institute for Prospective Technological Studies, Joint Research Centre / European Commission.

De Cugis, C. (1969). A Commentary on Jean-Jacques Servan-Schreiber's book The American Challenge. *Business and Economy History*, *1* (5), 123-145.

Dienel, H.-L., Kellermann R. & Moraglio, M. (2014). Projektbericht ACE2050. Entwicklung einer innovativen und verantwortungsvollen Agenda für die Wettbewerbsfähigkeit der europäischen Transportindustrie bis 2050. *Zeitschrift für Zukunftsforschung*, *3* (1), 48-60.

European Commission (2012). *Car 21 final report*. Available at: http://ec.europa.eu/enterprise/sectors/automotive/files/cars-21-final-report-2012_en.pdf [30.05.2013].

European Commission (1976). *Future of the European Automobile Industry*. Brussels: European Commission.

European Commission (1970). *Report to the Council and the Commission on the realization by stages of economic and monetary union in the Community*. Luxembourg: European Commission. Available at: http://ec.europa.eu/economy_finance/emu_history/documentation/chapter5/19701008en72realisationbystage.pdf [08.06. 2013].

European Commission (1984). *The Community and the car industry*. Brussels: European Commission.

European Parliament (1969). *Fact Sheets on the European Union.* Available at: http://www.europarl.europa.eu/factsheets/1_1_2_en.htm [08.06. 2013].

Giesecke, S. (2012). *From Transport Forecasting to "Mobility Science".* EFP Brief No.220, European Foresight Platform.

Hager, W. (1992). EC 1992 and Japan. In T. Leuenberger & M. E. Weinstein (Eds.). *Europe, Japan and America in the 1990s (*17-37). Berlin: Springer.

Harper, J.C. (2013). *Impact of Technology Foresight: Compendium of Evidence on the Effectiveness of Innovation Policy Intervention.* Manchester: Manchester Institue of Innovation Research.

Havas, A., Schartinger, D. & Weber, M. (2010). The impact of foresight on innovation policy-making: recent experiences and future perspectives. *Research Evaluation, 19* (2) 2010, 91–104.

Hedberg, H. (1969). *Die japanische Herausforderung.* Hamburg: Hoffmann & Campe.

Hughes, W. C. (2001). Japan in Europe: Asian and European perspectives. In G. Hasegawa, & Harukiyo, D. H. (Eds.) (2001). *Political Economy of Japanese Globalization* (52-64). London: Routledge.

Huntington, S. (1993). The clash of civilizations?. *Foreign Affairs, 72* (3), 22-49.

Huxley, A. (1946) [1931]. *Brave New World.* New York: Harper & Row.

Jones, D.T. (1981). *The Maturity and Crisis in the European Car Industry.* Sussex: Sussex European Research Centre, Univ. of Sussex.

Könnöla, T., Scapolo, F., Desruelle, P. & Mu, R. (2011). Foresight tackling societal challenges: Impacts and implications on policy-making. *Futures, 43* (3), 252-264.

Kahn, H. (1970). *The Emerging Japanese Superstate: Challenge and Response.* Englewood Cliffs: Prentice-Hall.

Kahn, H. &A. Wiener. (1967). *The Year 2000: a framework for speculation on the next thirty-three years.* New York: The Macmillan Co.

Kahn, H. (1960). *On Thermonuclear War.* London: Oxford University Press.

Kenney, M. & Florida, R. (1993). *Beyond Mass Production: The Japanese System and Its Transfer to the U.S.* Oxford: Oxford University Press.

Lehmann, J.-P. (1992). France, Japan, Europe, and industrial competition: the automotive case. *International Affairs, 68* (1) 1992: 37-53.

Lehmann, J.-P. (1982). Mutual Images. In L. Tsoukalis & White, M. (Eds.). *Japan and Western Europe* (14-30). London: Frances Pinter.

Meadows, D. H., Meadows, D. L., Randers, J. & Behrens III, W W. W. (1972). *Limits to Growth: A Report to The Club of Rome.* Available at: http://www.clubofrome.org/docs/limits.rtf [05.03.2013]

News Week (1991). "The Rise of Japan." *News Week Japanese Edition, May 1991.*

Plowden, E. N. P. & Britain, G. (1965). Report of the Committee of Inquiry into the Aircraft Industry, appointed by the Minister of Aviation under the chairmanship of Lord Plowden.

O'Leary, S. D. (1994). *Arguing the Apocalypse: A Theory of Millennial. Rhetoric.* New York: Oxford U. P.

Ritchey, T. (2013). *D7.1 – Scenario Development. Synopsis of the Current Scenarios on the EU Transport Industry.* Available at: http://www.race2050.org/fileadmin/files_race2050/Reports/RACE2050_D7.1_FINAL.pdf [03.11.2014].

Sachwald, F. (1995). The Automobile Industry: The Transplantation of the Japanese System Abroad. In: Sachwald, F. (1995). *Japanese Firms in Europe – Studies in Global Competition*, 169-210. Luxembourg: Harwood Academic Publishers.

Servan-Schreiber, J.-J. (1968). *The American Challenge.* London: Hamish Hamilton.

Shepherd, G. (1981). The Japanese Challenge to Western Europe's New Crisis Industries. *The World Economy*, *4* (4), 375-390.

Skrimshire, S. (2014). Climate change and apocalyptic faith. *Wiley Interdisciplinary Reviews: Climate Change*, *5* (2), 233–246.

Stoltenberg, G. (1968). Die amerikanische Herausforderung - ABENDLANDS UNTERGANG (II)? *DER SPIEGEL*, *11*, 154-157.

Tilly, S. & Triebel, F. (2013). *Automobilindustrie 1945-2000. Eine Schlüsselindustrie zwischen Boom und Krise.* München: Oldenbourg.

Timms, P., Tight, M. & Watling, D. (2014). Imagineering mobility: constructing utopias for future urban transport. *Environment and Planning A*, *46* (1), 78–93.

Union des Industries Ferroviaires Européennes (2010). *World Rail Market Study. Status quo and outlook 2020.* Brussels: UNIFE.

Van der Gießen, E. & Marinelli, A. (2012). The Value of FLA for Strategic Policy Making. In S. Giessecke, A. Van der Gießen & S. Elkins (Eds.) (2012). *The role of forward-looking activities for the governance of Grand Challenges* (22-31). Paris: European Foresight Platform.

Womack, J. P., Roos, D. & Jones, D.T. (1990). *The Machine That Changed the World: The Story of Lean Production.* London: Simon&Schuster.

World Economic Forum. (1971). *A partner in shaping history*. Available at: http://www3.weforum.org/docs/WEF_First40Years_Book_2010.pdf [08.06.2013].

World Economic Forum (2012). *Outlook on the Logistic & Supply Chain Industry 2012*. Available at: http://www3.weforum.org/docs/WEF_SCT_GAC_OutlookLogisticsSupplyChainIndustry_IndustryAgenda_2012.pdf [22.05.2013].

Zimmermann, H. (2000). Western Europe and the American Challenge: Conflict and Cooperation in Technology and Monetary Policy, 1965-1973. *Journal of European Integration History*, 6 (2) 2000: 85-110.

II. Scenarios in Practice

The Use of SWOT Analysis for Future Scenarios: A Case Study of Privacy and Emerging Technologies

Liisa Luoto, Annika Lonkila

Abstract

This paper presents a SWOT analysis for future scenarios, which can be used as a tool for the detailed analysis of scenarios in a more transparent and systematic way. This method was developed by using the original future-oriented SWOT method[1] in order to analyze scenarios that examined the future relationship between privacy and emerging technologies. Based on researchers' experiences from the use of the original method, two limitations were identified. Therefore, this paper presents suggestions for tackling these identified limitations and, as a result, presents a practical and comprehensive tool: SWOT analysis for future scenarios to analyze scenarios in a more detailed manner.

Introduction

Scenario planning is a method originating from strategic planning and future studies that explores alternative future paths within a certain timeframe (Schwartz 1991). Scenario planning stands out in its ability to capture a whole range of possible and desired futures by identifying basic trends and uncertainties (Masini & Vasquez 2002, Durance & Godet, 2010). As scenario planning creates alternative paths to the future, it helps decision makers to spot the key trends, drivers, emerging issues, uncertainties, and possibilities leading to a certain future image within a certain time frame (Schoemaker 1995). Herman Kahn began to develop scenario planning in the 1950s, and since then it has played an important role in strategic thinking in the field of business (Kahn & Wiener, 1967).

[1] Meristö et al. (2007) have presented the future-oriented SWOT method, which combines SWOT analysis and scenario planning in order to achieve a better and more comprehensive strategic planning for organizations.

R. Peperhove et al. (Eds.), *Envisioning Uncertain Futures*, Zukunft und Forschung 6, https://doi.org/10.1007/978-3-658-25074-4_7

A scenario describes alternative future developments of the subject matter in the contexts of different general frameworks. In this paper, we used a broad technology scanning (report on different technology trends with potential privacy impacts) (Hauptman 2011) and the results of 55 qualitative expert interviews that were carried out in six different countries as material for the scenario process. The objective of the scenarios was to identify how emerging technologies and their convergence might affect the societal perceptions and conceptions of privacy and the fundamental individual and structural values in Europe in 2030. As a result, five scenarios for privacy and emerging technologies were constructed.

Originally, SWOT analysis was developed as a tool for strategic planning and has been most commonly used by business policy academics and organizations for the design of new strategies (Hill & Westbrook, 1997). The goal of the SWOT method is to identify strengths and build on them, eliminate weaknesses, exploit opportunities and find a way around threats (Dyson 2002). In this paper, we present an adapted SWOT analysis for future scenarios. We present the use of the original future-oriented SWOT method presented by Meristö et al. (2007) and its results at a workshop in Belgium in 2012. Based on the feedback collected from this workshop and researcher's experiences from use of the method, we were able to identify two limitations that needed to be overcome in order to present more transparent and systematic SWOT analysis for future scenarios. As a result, this paper describes a tool (= SWOT analysis for future scenarios) that can be used for detailed analysis of scenarios in such a manner that it will be easy to duplicate in the future.

This article comprises of seven chapters. In chapter 2, the scenario process, including material and methods used in the process is presented. In chapter 3, five scenarios for privacy and emerging technologies are briefly described. In chapter 4, the theoretical background and the implementation of the original future-oriented SWOT method are presented. In chapter 5, identified limitations and improvement suggestions for the future-oriented SWOT method are described and, as a result, SWOT analysis for future scenarios is presented. A discussion can be found in chapter 6 where the pros and cons of SWOT analysis for future scenarios are reflected upon and in chapter 7 conclusions of the research are presented.

Scenario Process

Material

We will present an example case of the scenario process that was originally constructed during the PRACTIS research project[2] (See chapter 3). A broad technology scanning (report on different technology trends with potential privacy impacts) (Hauptman 2011) and the results of 55 qualitative expert interviews were used as material for the scenario process. The main objective of technology scanning was to carry out a long-range scan of the technology landscape and horizon, emphasizing potential privacy aspects. Additionally, the aim of the technology scanning was to map emerging technologies with the objective of assessing their potential privacy risks. The report on technologies with potential privacy impacts (Hauptman 2011) presents a preliminary review of emerging technologies that may have an impact on privacy. The report covers technologies from five different fields: 1. Information and communication technologies (ICT), 2. Biology and biometrics, 3. Nanotechnology and new materials, 4. Robotics and 5. Converging technologies (the convergence of nano-bio-info-cogno technologies). We acknowledge that the use of the term 'emerging technologies' is problematic, as it covers all fields of technologies. In this article, however, the term addresses only the presented five technology fields as defined in the report by Hauptman (2011).

Expert interviews were carried out with 7-13 experts per country in six different countries in order to explore the key issues related to privacy perceptions and their changes due to the emerging technologies over time. In total, three categories were discussed with experts. The first category was the perception of privacy including, for example, the questions on the definition of privacy and the expert's view on the possible change of the privacy perception in the future. The second category included the technological trends (in the five previously defined technology fields: 1. ICT, 2. Biology and biometrics, 3. Nanotechnology and new materials, 4. Robotics and 5. Converging technologies) and their potential impacts on privacy. The third category was ethical issues and future legal frameworks for privacy. In total, 55 interviews were conducted. Figure 1 illustrates the percentage

[2] We want to thank all the members of the PRACTIS research team, who made this article possible. For more details: PRACTIS homepage or CORDIS homepage.

distribution of the experts' countries of residence and figure 2 illustrates the percentage distribution of the professional background of the experts.

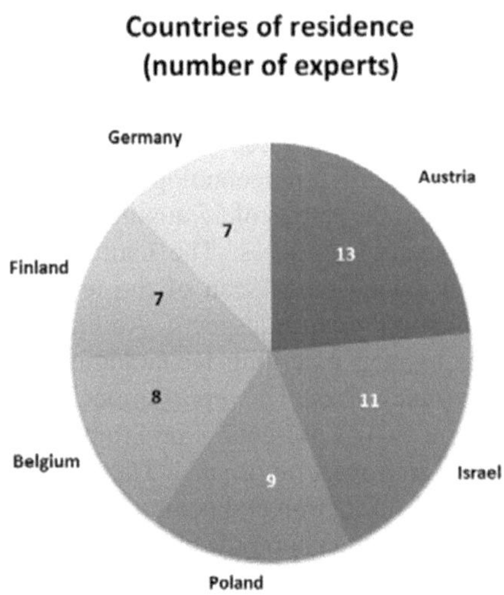

Figure 1: Countries of Residence (Number of Experts, total 55)

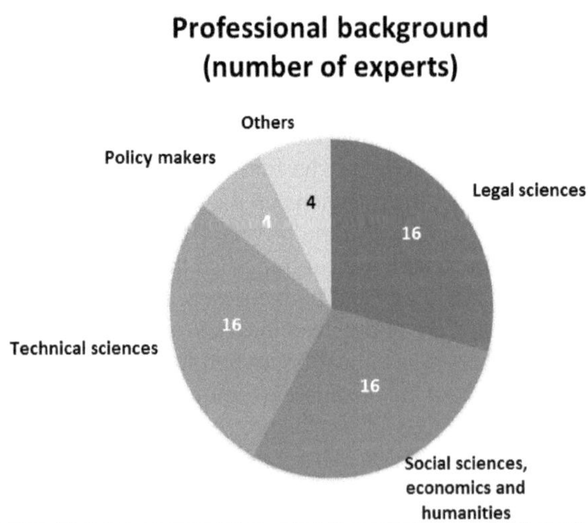

Figure 2: Professional Background (Number of Experts, total 55)

The interviews were conducted in the experts' native languages in each country during the summer/autumn of 2010. The transcripts were translated into English (Bach et al. 2011). The authors of this paper received translated transcripts from Austria, Belgium, and Finland and summaries from Israel and Germany. All coded citations and analyses were made with MAXQDA software. The summaries, detailed interviews, and the coded analysis built the basis for a content analysis for examining the most important and interesting issues related to the research topic. The scenarios are based on an analysis of the results of these expert interviews and the previously presented technology scanning (Hauptman 2011).

Method

The following method, which consists of four steps, was used to construct five alternative case scenarios: **The first step** was to identify the research problem and the timeframe (Peterson et al. 2003). In this study the research problem was defined as follows: What kind of new possibilities for privacy concepts and perceptions in the context of emerging technologies might evolve in 2030? **The second step** was to identify alternative directions of development **(Step 2a)** and drivers **(Step 2b)** that would be the most influential for the chosen research problem (Masini & Vasqúez, 2002). These alternative directions of development were based on the criteria of how technology will impact privacy and change people's behavior and perception of privacy. The process of the identification of these alternative directions of development is described below.

At the beginning of **Step 2a**, the most important issues relating to the research topic were identified from the expert interviews using the content analysis method. Additionally, the report on different trends of technologies with potential privacy impacts (Hauptman 2011) and the European Commission scenario report *The World in 2025* were utilized by the research team. These documents were used as an impulse for constructing ideas in the brainstorming session to follow. The objective of the future-oriented brainstorming sessions was to stimulate creative and 'out of the box' thinking. This was very important, as scenario planning requires intellectual courage (Schoemaker 1995). The following five alternative directions of future developments were identified in the first brainstorming session: 1. Increased collection of information about all human beings, 2. Integration of humans and machines, 3. Vanishing of the border between public and private space, 4. The virtual world replacing the physical world as the main space for human interaction and activities and 5. People regaining control over their personal data.

The second brainstorming session was held to identify four to five alternative sub-trends[3] within each alternative direction of development. Below we present, as an example, the four sub-trends that were identified within the integration of human and machine.

- Decision making transferred to robotics – technology no longer a mere tool but increasingly an independent actor.
- Unification of biological and non-biological medical technology and the human body, creation of a 'perfect man' without disabilities.
- The implant/machine collects information and sends it to a centralized data bank.
- People wholly dependent on technology.

All the five alternative directions of development were evaluated in the second brainstorming session. Four to five alternative sub-trends were identified within these alternative directions of development and gathered in the coherent "tables" presented above.

The scenario process continues with the identification of the key drivers (**Step 2b**). Drivers are understood as key issues or forces, and they have a major impact on how a certain scenario will develop (Wack 1985; Wollenberg et al. 2000; Oudshoorn et al. 2011). In this scenario planning process, key drivers that would be the most influential for the research problem were identified from the following fields of society: social, legislation, economic, political, and values **(SLEPV)**. This approach for choosing certain fields of society was modified from the STEEPV method (Loveridge 2002). The first working phase was to describe the present state of the drivers before we were able to analyze them further. Each driver from the different fields (social, legislation, economic, political and values)

[3] The term sub-trend is understood here as a part of a main direction of development. In this article, we will use the term "sub-trend", when we speak about alternative "sub-directions" of a development. We realize that even though we call them sub-trends, not all of them are trends in the sense "trend" is understood in the traditional way. However, we use this term, as the option would have been to use the term "sub-direction", which is linguistically problematic and incorrect.

was described according to present valid EU documents[4]. The aim was to form a loose framework of drivers and use them as a starting point for scenario planning. As an example, these valid EU documents described the *economic field* in the following way; the EU's guiding principle for the establishment and enhancement of a single market that is 'a highly competitive social market economy' striving for 'full employment' and 'social progress'[5] (European Union 2010).

The third step was to describe briefly three potential manifestations of each driver. For example, we differentiated the following three manifestations from the economic field: 1. Liberal market economy, 2. State regulated market economy, and 3. Planned economy. We then selected a suitable option from the three different manifestations for each alternative sub-trend. We acknowledged that in reality these options would not occur as such, but for scenario work it was necessary to select one of the different extremes of each driver in each alternative sub-trend. One of the sub-trend tables within identified drivers is presented in Table 1.

Table 1: Unification of Biological and Non-Biological Medical Technology and the Human Body, Creation of a "Perfect Man" without Disabilities (Auffermann et al. 2011).

Field of society, which is seen as a key driver in respect to how they will develop in the future.	Suitable option out of three different manifestations of how the current field of society might occur in the future.
Social (S)	Liberal state
Legislation (L)	In favor of business
Economic (E)	Liberal market economy
Political (P)	Democracy
Values (V)	Openness towards technologies; high equality (people become more alike) and low human dignity

[4] For instance, documents such as the European Council 1993, European Parliament and the European Council 1995: *Directive 95/46/EC on the protection of individuals with regard to the processing of personal data and on the free movement of such data*, European Union 2010: *Consolidated version of the treaty on European Union*, European Union 2010: *Charter of the Fundamental Rights of the European Union 2010/C 83/02*, and European Commission Economic and Financial Affairs 2011: *EU economic situation were used.*

[5] Please notice that the example is only a short version, which was a part of the complete description from one dimension out of five.

The fourth and final step in the scenario planning process was to combine the identified alternative sub-trends together into a framework. We grouped each sub-trend into five categories according to their common features. In the categorization phase, we used the key drivers to identify similarities within the sub-trends. In addition, the impacts of these alternative sub-trends on privacy and its perception were considered when grouping them. After the grouping was made, the final brainstorming session was held to analyze the results of the grouping and construct scenarios.

Five scenarios for privacy and emerging technologies

As the result of this scenario process, we present short descriptions of five scenarios in relation to privacy perceptions in the context of emerging technologies in Europe and neighbouring countries in 2030 (Auffermann et al. 2011). The scenarios are written as historical developments or as continuities in chronological order.

Scenario 1: "Privacy has faded away"

Certain goods and services (for example, effective health care) have become more vital than privacy, and the majority of people are ready to make trade-offs in favor of these goods and services. This development is the result of long-term change in the value system of society and in people's ways of thinking. Privacy is still valued, but people have started to sell their "morality" moral valuations for money. This change has happened smoothly, and privacy has slowly faded away. People have acknowledged that they can also be observed at home and that there is always someone (or something) watching them. This is possible, for example, at home, where household robots or robots employed as social actors constantly collect information with the help of wireless sensor networks. Other technologies that are widely used are for example "mind reading" commercial gadgets and intelligent medical implants. (Auffermann et al. 2011.)

Scenario 2: "People want to maintain as much privacy as possible"

In this scenario, a large amount of information is exposed to the public, but people have preserved a certain amount of their privacy. The private sector cannot take maximum advantage of this increased amount of private information as it is scattered in different databases. However, the majority of people are worried about the collection of information into one database covering different areas of life. In order to avoid the creation of such a database, the state controls the use of information. Due to progressive change in prevailing social norms, a majority of people have started to oppose the "big brother phenomenon". The situation has escalated to a point where people have no urge to expose their private lives to the media or to other people. In contrast, they want to maintain as much privacy as possible. Another, more extreme, development path can be imagined. People may revolt for privacy more aggressively and extensively. There is a possibility that most people will organize extensive demonstrations, riots, and strikes in order to press decision makers. Either way, people have become more aware of the possible privacy threats posed by new technologies. This does not mean that they do not use these technologies anymore, but they do not accept them as easily as before. (Auffermann et al. 2011.)

Scenario 3: "People have lost their control of privacy"

In this scenario, the majority of people have treated new technologies with great openness for a long time and the path of development has remained relatively unchanged. New technology applications were continuously developed. Along with these new applications, people had to disclose increasing amounts of information. As stated in the expert interviews, at first, people were seduced into giving more and more private information in exchange for different games and other on-line applications. Plus, in this scenario they even use brain-to-brain communication applications. People practically "sleep walked[6]" into a world without privacy, without noticing anything and suddenly they had no choice but to live in it. Eventually, people started to fear database unification. After this, most people started to treat emerging technologies with increasing skepticism. This was followed by a public debate concerning the risks of new technological applications. Despite the debate, the situation did not change much, and technological development continued as before. Over time, people forgot their "fears" and got used to being monitored and stopped worrying about losing their privacy. Either the state or the private sector started to constantly monitor the private life of an individual, with the help of new technological applications like Smart Carts, which could persuade people to buy goods or services. Medical services are an example of technology applications to which people have become highly dependent. (Auffermann et al. 2011.)

[6] The term *sleep walked* is referring to a situation where people were not aware of current development and suddenly they "woke up" and understood what has happened.

Scenario 4: "Segmented privacy"

In this scenario, social inequality has increased drastically, both between different social groups and in geographical dimensions (north-south). The prevailing state of society is reflected by the fact that many producers have made two different versions of their gadgets – one with high privacy settings and a higher price, and another with low privacy settings and a lower price. For example, elite schools can offer better privacy settings for virtual-reality teaching environments than public schools. Due to this, privacy possesses an increasingly important market-value when new technology applications are marketed and sold. For example, if you want to use social media for free you have to settle for low privacy settings. All privacy-enhancing applications have additional charges. There are significant differences in people's quality of life. Also, the perception of privacy differs amongst different social classes. Past developments have led to a situation in which income inequality is extremely high and society is very prone to conflicts. This has increased the tension between different social classes. (Auffermann et al. 2011.)

Scenario 5: "Tailor-made privacy"

In this scenario, technology enables people to achieve tailor-made privacy. Each individual understands privacy differently. People's freedom to choose and make decisions for themselves, as well as transparency in society, is highly appreciated. As stated in the expert interviews, people know how the information gathered about them is used and for what purposes. Through the development of education, people have become more aware of the possibilities and disadvantages of emerging technologies. The majority of people remain open towards new technologies, since they are perceived to offer major benefits, and people do not have to worry about their privacy risks. For example, traceless biometrics has become popular. However, people always have the opportunity to choose which technological application to use and to what extent. In this scenario, regulation guarantees that, for example, automatic systems are developed in a way that they cannot violate users' privacy. Privacy enhancing technologies are available to everyone, so people can enjoy the benefits of the latest technological applications without having to worry about losing their privacy. (Auffermann et al. 2011.)

Future-oriented SWOT method

The following subchapters describe the theoretical background of the SWOT method and its implementation, how the future-oriented SWOT was used as a tool to further analyze scenarios. At first, the theoretical background is described and discussed at length in order to demonstrate the article's contribution to methodological discussion. The second subchapter describes in detail how the future-oriented SWOT method was conducted.

Theoretical background

The development of the SWOT method

SWOT analysis is a method used for evaluating the Strengths, Weaknesses, Opportunities and Threats of an organization or a project. SWOT analysis was initially developed as a tool for strategic planning and has been most commonly used by business policy academics and organizations when they design new strategies (Hill & Westbrook, 1997). The goal of the SWOT method is to identify strengths and build on them, eliminate weaknesses, exploit opportunities and find a way around threats (Dyson 2002). As the method has been used in relation to business organizations, the strengths and weaknesses are usually seen as related to the organization's internal affairs, whereas the threats and opportunities are used to portray attributes of the external environment, covering political, economic, social and technological contexts (Mintzberg 1998.)

Weihrich (1982) presented his TOWS matrix that compiles all four SWOT factors together and systematically matches them. The TOWS matrix (Table 2) is often used to identify four different strategies in order to provide a business strategy for an organization. These different strategies are: maxi-maxi (strengths/opportunities), maxi-mini (strengths/threats), mini-maxi (weaknesses/opportunities), and mini-mini (weaknesses/threats) (Weihrich 1982; Ghazinoory et al. 2011).

Table 2: TOWS Matrix (Weihrich 1982)

	Strengths	Weaknesses
Opportunities	SO (maxi-maxi) strategy	WO (mini-maxi) strategy
Threats	ST (maxi-mini) strategy	WT (mini-mini) strategy

The future oriented element has always been a part of SWOT analysis, because it is most often used to plan new strategies. Kurttila et al. (2000) combine the SWOT analysis method and the decision analysis method Analytical Hierarchy Process (AHP) in order to improve the usability and effectiveness of SWOT analysis in strategic planning. Additionally, Kangas et al. (2003) link the Multiple Criteria Decision Support (MCDS) with SWOT analysis in order to elaborate on the analytical priorities for SWOT factors and make them more commensurable. Kangas et al. (2003) also combine the methods as one hybrid method, S-O-S, with the aim to create a more comprehensive tool for supporting the strategic decision-making process. In addition to these studies, several other articles combine SWOT analysis with decision-making support methods in order to improve SWOT analysis in various strategic planning situations (See for example: Kajanus et al. 2004; Leskinen et al. 2006; Kajanus et al. 2012).

Meristö et al. (2007) describe how SWOT analysis and scenario planning can be combined in order to achieve a better and more comprehensive strategic planning for organizations. This approach is called the future-oriented SWOT method. In their study, changes (threats and opportunities) of the environment are examined from a future perspective. The organization's weaknesses and strengths are evaluated with the aim of developing a strategy where the organization is able to grasp or avoid the challenges (opportunities or threats) in the future. Additionally, Dyson (2002) has argued that the SWOT analysis method and scenario building can enhance one another.

This article builds on these theoretical concepts in order to develop a tool, SWOT analysis for future scenarios, for a more detailed, transparent and systematic analysis of scenarios.

Critique of the SWOT method

Even though SWOT analysis is well known and often used as a tool for strategic planning, critical arguments have also been presented. Mintzberg (1998) argues that the SWOT method is too restricting as it simplifies the process of planning and providing strategies. Mintzberg (1998) has written at length about the challenges of SWOT analysis, and his main concern is that the method places too much emphasis on descriptions and lists. In other words, strategy formation is seen as a process of conception rather than as one of learning; "the thinking" is separated from "the doing". This means that the results of SWOT analysis are often not implemented, as Hill & Westbrook (1997) also discovered in their study. According to Dyson (2004), SWOT analysis might be outdated in some cases, but he appreciates its usefulness of focusing simultaneously on the internal and external factors. Contrary to Dyson, Hill & Westbrook (1997) who disapprove the implementation and how the method separates the external factors from the internal.

This critique is worth considering, but not all of it applies to this study and our case example of privacy and emerging technologies, where the objective was not strategic planning. In our case, the original future-oriented SWOT method was used as a content analysis method to further analyze scenarios in order to construct an analytical generalization of the changes in privacy climates[7]. In relation to the lack of implementation of the results, the future-oriented SWOT aims to move past this criticism and adapt the results of SWOT analysis into policy recommendations. In this case study, the results of the future-oriented SWOT method offered an important input in order to accomplish the next step in the research project PRACTIS, which worked as an input for the final stage of the project, drafting policy and legal recommendations.

Overall, the future-oriented SWOT is used to further analyze scenarios at a specific angle in order to gain a better understanding about an issue. With respect to this, the critique presented by Hill & Westbrook (1997) does not apply to future-oriented SWOT analysis, because the objective is not necessarily to implement the results of SWOT analysis or move from "thinking" to "doing". What needs to be remembered is that the results of SWOT analysis are not goals in themselves, but can provide important instruments for strategic planning. However, as Hill and Westbrook (1997) have argued, the SWOT method must move beyond simple description and constitute some type of analysis. In this study, the future-oriented SWOT method was used specifically for analytical purposes, for constructing an analytical generalization of the changes in privacy climates.

Implementation: How to use future-oriented SWOT analysis as a tool to further analyze scenarios?

The objective was to use the future-oriented SWOT method as a content analysis (e.g. Krippendorff 2004; Hsieh & Shannon, 2005) method in order to further analyze scenarios. Content analysis was carried out by identifying the potential impacts on privacy in the scenarios and by constructing an analytical generalization of the changes in privacy climates. In this chapter, we describe the

[7] The term *privacy climate* is a project (=PRACTIS) specific term and it is understood in this article as a combination of the state of the privacy (how is it valued, respected and implemented in society), and how people perceive and treat their privacy.

implementation steps of the future-oriented SWOT method in such a manner that it will be easy to duplicate in the future.

As mentioned earlier, the future-oriented SWOT method in this study did not have a predetermined objective in the same way as strategic analysis has. The point was merely to achieve a deep understanding of the potential impacts of the scenarios on ethical principles. There arose a need to pay close attention to the objective of what categorizes the attributes as a strength, weakness, threat or opportunity– defining the potential impacts – and this was based on the personal values of the research project's consortium members. However, in order to avoid biased views we invited all consortium partners to take part in the future-oriented SWOT process. Partners were asked to evaluate the strengths, weaknesses, opportunities, and threats (SWOT) for each scenario in relation to privacy. They were also asked to imagine that they lived in the world described in the scenario, and to analyze which attributes in this world were beneficial (strengths and opportunities) and detrimental (weaknesses and threats) to their privacy and the ethical principles of the contemporary world. The instructions guided participants to write down all the strengths, weaknesses, opportunities, and threats, even though they were not exclusively related to privacy, as they can still be part of the larger concept, "privacy climate". In the end, five consortium partners provided answers for the analysis, by filling in the factors for each scenario. They analyzed the scenarios' impacts on privacy using the Social, Technological, Economic, Ecological, Political and Value-based (STEEPV) framework as a guideline.

After receiving the results of the future-oriented SWOT analyses from partners, the next step of the process was to combine the answers into a comparable form. To achieve this, a quantitative and qualitative evaluation was completed. First, we counted the times each attribute was mentioned under each category and awarded the attribute one point for each time they were mentioned. The highest possible number was then 5, and the lowest was 1. The exact wording of attributes was not important, as we looked more at the general idea behind the answer. Then, we combined the attributes and created simple sentences that captured the main point of the mentioned strength, weakness, opportunity or threat. The goal of the point system was merely to indicate the importance of certain attributes as impacts on the ethical principles. For example, an attribute mentioned four times was not twice as significant as an attribute with two points. Several attributes were only mentioned once, but there were similarities between the attributes too. In many cases, the same attributes were mentioned under opposite categories, and in some cases even in all four of them. After the point system was completed, we further analyzed results in relation to ethical principles. The combined attributes of the future-oriented SWOT analysis of the first scenario "Privacy has faded away" can be seen below (Table 3). It is presented as a case example of how the results were combined into comparable and categorized tables.

Table 3 The SWOT Analysis of Scenario 1. The number in brackets symbolizes the number of answers given for each attribute (Auffermann et al. 2011).

STRENGHTS	WEAKNESSES
• More transparency / less fraud, corruption & lying (3) • Geographical distance • does not matter (3) • Increased equality (2) • Services become cheaper (2) • Technological advances (2) • Robots make life easier (2) • Enhanced self-responsibility(1) • Collectivity in society increases (1) • "Safe" world (1)	• No privacy / significant decrease in it (3) • Equality turns into inequality (the rich will find ways to bypass the system; some people have no access to social media and are excluded from society) (2) • Loss of physical contact (2) • Loss of privacy changes • Human mentality (2) • Lower innovativeness (2) • No "second chances" or • social mobility (2) • End of the individual (1) • Dependency on technological systems (1) • Decreased respect to democratic system and national/international laws (1) • Human beings are treated as objects not subjects / total control of people (1)
OPPORTUNITIES	**THREATS**
• Advanced technological development (4) • Greater efficiency; lower costs (2) • More customized products (2) • Capitalism re-evaluated (2) • Safer environment(1) • Economic growth (1) • Easier to socialize (1) • Easier to form social movements and groups (1) • Minorities accepted (1) • Fair and equal economic system (1) • The amount of knowledge increases (1) • Overload of information = information is useless (1) • Absolute honesty (1) • Democratization of societal structures • within private space (public = private) (1)	• Social exclusion and polarization (3) • Commodification of the individual (3) • Total government control; end of democracy as we know it (2) • Loss of human interaction (2) • Minorities persecuted (difficult to express deviant opinions) (2) • Misuse of technologies (1) • Increased amount of knowledge (1) • Capitalism re-evaluated (1) • The reinforcement of the market and • marketing (1)

Limitations and improvements

This chapter will present two identified limitations to the original future-oriented SWOT method, based on which we developed our tool for scenario analysis. Additionally, it will describe the means of how to tackle these limitations in order to analyze the scenarios in a more detailed manner and to gain more transparent, systematic comprehensive and qualitative results. As a result, SWOT analysis for future scenarios is introduced. We presented the use of the original future-oriented SWOT method and the results achieved at a project workshop in Belgium in 2012. Project partners and external experts commented and discussed the method and the results, and according to the collected feedback researchers were able to identify the limitation number one: *invalid results* (chapter 5.1.). The second limitation: *biased selection of participants and external experts* (chapter 5.2.) was also identified based on researcher's experiences from the use of the method.

Limitation number one: Invalid results

The first mentioned limitation had been that the results were less valid because the number of participants who conducted the future-oriented SWOT analysis was too low. In the workshop, an expert suggested that the number of the participants should be increased in order to tackle this limitation. However, after discussion, the research team concluded that this would not be the best solution, because of the complex and impractical task of combining answers into a comparable form and categorizing them into the tables (See pages 19-22). Additionally, if the participants who conduct the SWOT analysis for future scenarios are properly selected, as we present later in chapter 5.2., additional attributes are not achieved at this point of the study. Therefore, it would not solve the problem, even though the number of the participants would be higher and theoretically it seems that the results would be more valid, but in practice this would not be the case.

Instead, we follow Dyson's (2002) argumentation in his article and suggest a slightly modified solution to overcome this limitation. Dyson (2002) describes conducted SWOT analysis at the University of Warwick at length in his article. According to him, after identifying the different attributes as strengths, weaknesses, opportunities and threats, they made a follow up questionnaire where participants were asked to score each attribute on a scale from 1 to 5. Our suggestion, slightly modified from Dyson's model, is that the follow-up questionnaire is sent to the original participants who conducted the SWOT attributes and also to external experts[8]. In Dyson's model the follow up questionnaire was sent only to the original participants who constructed attributes for SWOT analysis, but in SWOT analysis for future scenarios it is, additionally, sent to the external experts.

This scoring system will realistically tackle the problem of less valid results due to the increased number of respondents evaluating the SWOT attributes. Although in Dyson's (2002) paper the highest score of five represents an opportunity not to be missed, this article suggests that the researcher or the research team implementing SWOT analysis for future scenarios is the one who will decide on the definition of numbers and, therefore, the evaluation angle for SWOT attributes. However, the definition needs to be in line, of course, with the research problem in order to use SWOT analysis for future scenarios as a tool to examine the answers for the research problem.

Limitation number two: Biased selection of participants and external experts

The biased selection of participants who conducted the original future-oriented SWOT analysis is identified as the second main limitation. In the case study of the research project, the participants who conducted the future-oriented SWOT were consortium members of the project. In addition to us, five international consortium partners conducted the future-oriented SWOT analysis. In this case, the selection was acceptable, because the partners covered a wide range of expertise from the studied field: future studies, law (especially legislation related to privacy and human rights), ethics, emerging technologies, sociology and social sciences. Even though the selection of participants was quite comprehensive in this case, it still needed some improvements to be valid and to overcome the limitation of biased selection. Furthermore, the process needed to be more transparent and systematically described in order to meet the requirements for a well-structured SWOT analysis for future scenarios.

In future studies, selection of the "right" expert or participant has been under discussion for some time now (Welty 1972; Galanc & Mikus, 1986; Tichy 2004). Different approaches are presented in order to tackle the challenges with biased selection of experts and participants (Delbecq et al. 1975; Moldrup & Morgall, 2001; Von der Gracht & Stillings, 2013; Warth et al. 2013). Co-nomination is commonly used approach in future studies in order to construct

---

[8] The term *external experts* is used in this article to define the group of experts who will score each SWOT attribute on a scale from 1 to 5.

reliable expert or participant panel. Within this method researchers identify the most important experts or participants for the studied issue and then these chosen experts suggest more participants, for example, into the Delphi panel (Tapio 2003; Varho & Tapio, 2005). Essential risk with this method is that the chosen experts suggest additional participants who share similar school of thought as themselves (Tapio 2003). Additionally, researcher's ability to follow and control the construction of the panel, in order to reach desirable coherence regarding the background information of the experts, is very small.

The "information-oriented selection" is also used approach for selecting reliable experts or participants (Flyvbjerg 1991, Moldrup & Morgall, 2001). Various criteria, based on assumptions what kind of knowledge or information different expert's hold, are used to choose reliable experts or participants (Moldrup & Morgall, 2001). These different inclusion criteria are for example: area of expertise, level of expertise or organization. They are well argued, but nevertheless they don't tackle the challenge to follow the background information of the chosen experts or participants. To overcome these described challenges above, the predefined frame, which is transparent and it enables for researchers the opportunity to follow the structure of the participants regarding the field of expertise and background information, is the most suitable approach in this study.

As a result, we follow the model called *expert matrix*. Chosen approach is originally developed for selection of the experts for Delphi studies. (Kuusi et al. 2006; Rikkonen & Tapio, 2009; Tapio et al. 2011, Varho & Tapio, 2013.) The selected approach is well founded because the objective of the Delphi study is to exploit expert knowledge in order to study alternative futures (Bell 1997). In addition, it aims to study how probable or desirable these alternative futures are (Amara 1981). Because both of these studies (Delphi and the future-oriented SWOT method) explore the future with the same preconditions and constraints, it is justified to use the same selection method to choose participants and external experts for the SWOT analysis for future scenarios than what is used to compile a Delphi panel.

Table 4 presents a hypothetical and simplified example of the expert matrix.

Table 4: Hypothetical and Simplified Expert Matrix (See Kuusi et al. 2006; Rikkonen & Tapio, 2009; Varho & Tapio, 2013)

Experts	**Expert A**	**Expert B**	**Expert C**	**Expert D**
Expertise in:				
Future Studies	x			
Technology		x		
Law			x	x
Privacy	x	x		x
Level of education:				
High school				
University of Applied Science		x		
Master in University	x			
PhD			x	x
Age:				
20-29	x	x		
30-39				
40-49				
50-59				x
60-69			x	

With the help of the expert matrix, the research team is able to monitor whether the selection of the experts is balanced or not. It is likely that some of the categories are more represented than others, but the basic rule is that the matrix should be mainly in balance and no empty spots remain. (Kuusi et al. 2006; Rikkonen & Tapio, 2009; Varho & Tapio, 2013.) Basic background information should be in balance when selecting participants and the external experts. At least, addition to the field of expertise, gender, age, and nationality should be added into the expert matrix before the SWOT analysis for future scenarios begins (Tapio 2003; Kuusi et al. 2006; Varho & Tapio, 2013). Additionally, for example, the field and level of education can be added into the expert matrix (Varho & Tapio, 2013) if it gives more value to the study.

However, the objective of balance does not apply in all cases. For example, if the SWOT analysis for future scenarios is implemented clearly in a female- or male-dominated professional field, the gender-variable will be imbalanced for a reason. Participants and external experts can be co-nominated by their colleagues, but the risk is that they nominate only those whose thinking is similar to theirs (Tapio 2003). A mixed approach, where researchers select part of the panel of external experts and ask external experts to co-nominate additional participants, could be the best approach. In both cases, the most important criterion is the studied matter.

In future-oriented research, the exact number of the respondents for achieving a representative sample is hard to define. For example, in the Delphi study, statistical representativeness is not necessarily required or even desirable. This is because Delphi studies explore the future, which is the concept of time that has not yet realized. Therefore, we do not have facts about it. (Tapio et al. 2011) Overall, the objective is to get a good coverage of well-argued views (= SWOT attributes) rather than a random sample (Varho & Tapio, 2013). Using the same logic in the SWOT analysis for future scenarios, the number of the respondents is not the most critical criterion for making the results more valid.

Additionally, Rikkonen & Tapio write:

> "A good operating principle in Policy Delphi studies in our experience is that the collected opinions should saturate during the process, that is when new respondents are included and no new views emerge anymore" (2009, 981).

This is also a very applicable rule for testing whether the coverage of participants providing SWOT attributes is completed. After the attributes are collected and inserted into the tables, saturation[9] can be tested by adding one or two respondents, or, alternatively, presenting the results at a conference. If new views are not presented, the research team can continue to the next phase and send the questionnaire to external experts.

[9] The term *saturation* means here that no additional SWOT attributes appear even though one or two additional experts conduct the SWOT analysis for future scenarios.

Discussion

In this paper, we have presented a SWOT analysis for future scenarios, which provides a tool for the detailed analysis of scenarios in a more transparent and systematic way. The method has many merits, but there are also some dimensions of it that may profit from further development. We will analyze both features here in discussion.

The greatest merit of SWOT analysis for future scenarios is its aim to provide decision-makers with transparent results and due to them the best possible tools for making decisions. Systematically selected experts are asked to evaluate the scenarios by assessing them based on their personal values and visions. The SWOT attributes enable this **value-based analysis** and help to take analysis one step further. The task of the research team is to assist in the categorization of results and to present them to decision-makers. The goal is not to rate the scenarios, for example, from the least preferred to the most preferred, but to determine which scenarios, according to external experts, contain the highest risks or greatest possibilities – related to the chosen specific context. These may well be manifested in the same scenario, and this is why it is important to not see the process as a simple scoring method for determining the best scenario – because "best" has no significance here and is no distinct category.

The method aims to contribute to a more transparent and systematic analysis process, as the use of the expert matrix to choose the participants and external experts contributes significantly to transparency. SWOT analysis for future scenarios is also useful for companies as they can use the method in strategic planning. In this case, the specific context for analysis is created according to the company's needs. Additionally, SWOT analysis for scenarios is especially helpful when scenarios need to be analyzed in regard to a specific question or issue within a certain context. Any well-built scenario may be analyzed in a more detailed manner with the SWOT analysis for scenarios, but broad and extensive, *complex*[10] scenarios (Van Notten et al. 2003) are especially useful in this way.

There are some methods that have evaluated scenarios from a slightly different perspective, but we came to the conclusion that there is a need for a

[10] Van Notten et al. 2003 describe the complex scenarios in the following way: "Complex scenarios are composed of an intricate web of causally related, interwoven, and elaborately arranged variables and dynamics."

method that provides a value-based evaluation of scenarios. For example, multi-criteria decision analysis methods (e.g. MCDA, AHP, and PMCA) combined with cost benefit analysis (CBA) have been used to evaluate scenarios in order to support decision-making in complex situations (Diakoulaki & Karangelis, 2007; Harries 2003; Kowalski et al. 2009; Ram & Montibeller, 2012). In these processes, scenarios are evaluated against policy goals or an organizational strategy defined by the decision-makers. The evaluation criteria as well the preferences of the decisions makers are predefined. Therefore, the results will reveal the most preferable or the best-case and worst-case scenarios from the studied object. The goal is to make the decision-making process more objective, well informed, and legitimate (Diakoulauki & Karangelis, 2007; Ram & Montibeller, 2012; Kowalski et al. 2009; Harries 2003).

The aforementioned decision analysis methods are quantitative analysis tools for evaluating, for example, environmental or economic impacts, from scenarios against predefined policy goals or organizational strategies, whilst SWOT analysis for future scenarios is a tool for qualitative analysis with no predefined criteria set by the decision-makers. The experts produce the results in SWOT analysis for future scenarios, which guarantees the use of the best knowledge and objectivity available. This approach works best when the policy goals or organizational strategies are in the drafting stage and expert knowledge is needed.

One of the limitations of SWOT analysis for future scenarios is that the process may prove to be quite a heavy task for the research team if the number of the participants and external experts is high. The method requires careful selection of experts, which is a laborious task. There is certainly room for development in creating a better mechanism for choosing external experts. One possibility would be to select the external experts through a random sample. This would increase the number of external experts and eliminate the possibility of biased selection because the research team does not directly participate in the selection of the respondents. This procedure also has it disadvantages. SWOT analysis for future scenarios is a value-based analysis, which means that the selection of the external experts influences the results greatly. It is very important that the external experts are determined by focusing solely on the research questions. This problem might be best solved by a pre-selection by the research team and taking a random sample of this pre-selected pool.

It is also important to note that in some cases the scenarios are so explicit and focused that there is not necessarily a need to analyze them in more detailed manner. However, this method also provides a possibility for the research team to examine some other perspective than the objective of the initial research process, which might lead to innovative new research results. All in all, this method works best in projects where extensive general scenarios are created and there is a need to analyze them further with a more narrowed-down research problem in mind. Van Notten et al. (2003) use the terms complex and simple scenarios. The latter are limited in scope while the former are "composed of an intricate web of causally related, interwoven, and elaborately arranged variables and dynamics". Both can be well constructed and useful in different contexts, but complex scenarios are much better suited for use in this type of detailed analysis with SWOT analysis for future scenarios. It is also important to note that the future-oriented SWOT is especially equipped for analyzing future images or scenario "snapshots", not pathways to a certain future.

Conclusions

SWOT analysis for future scenarios is most useful in research projects where analysis is aimed at supporting the decision-making process and strategic planning, whether in companies or governmental institutions. The method helps to increase the transparent and systematic nature of the analysis through making value-based assessments of its essence. Decision-makers are provided with the expert evaluations of the strengths, weaknesses, threats and opportunities of scenarios, so that they have all the necessary tools for making well-rounded decisions. In SWOT analysis for future scenarios, external experts provide the evaluations, which can increase the objectivity of the study. The method works best when the policy goals or organizational strategies are in the drafting stage and the best possible expert knowledge is needed.

References

Amara, R. (1987). The futures field: searching for definitions and boundaries. *Futurist, 15* (1), 25-29.

Auffermann, B., Luoto, L., Lonkila, A. & Vartio, E. (2011). *Report on potential changes in privacy climates and their impacts on ethical approaches.* Available at: http://www.practis.org/docs/PRACTIS,%20D4.2_Report%20on%20potential%20changes%20in%20privacy%20climates%20and%20their%20impacts%20on%20ethical%20approaches%20_Final%20version%2013.2.12_.pdf.

Bach, N., Köhler, M., Dienel, H., Horvath, L., Schmidt, M. & Pohoryles, R. (2011). *Report on Changing Perceptions of Privacy and the Changing Role of the State*. Available at: http://www.practis.org/docs/D3%204_final_report_20110725.pdf.

Bell, W. (1997). *Foundations of Futures Studies. Human Science for a New Era. Volume I: History, Purposes, Knowledge*. New Brunswick and London: Transaction Publishers.

Cuhls, K. (2000). *Reasons for a new foresight approach—The FUTUR process in Germany*. Paper presented at the conference "The Quest for the Futures: a Methodology Seminar", Organised by the World Futures Studies Federation (WFSF) and Finland Futures Research Centre, Turku, Finland, June, 2000.

Diakoulaki, D. & Karangelis, F. (2007). Multi-criteria decision analysis and cost-benefit analysis of alternative scenarios for the power generation sector in Greece. *Renewable & Sustainable energy Reviews, 11* (4), 716-727.

Delbecq, A. L., Van de Ven, H. A. & Gustafson, D. H. (1975). *Group Techniques for Program Planning: A Guide to Nominal Group and Delphi Processes*. Glenview: Scott Foresman.

Durance, P. & Godet, M. (2010). Scenario building: Uses and abuses. *Technological forecasting and social change,* 77 (9), 1488-1492.

Dyson, R. G. (2002). Strategy, performance and operational research. *Journal of the Operational Research Society, 51*, 5-11.

Dyson, R. G. (2004). Strategic development and SWOT analysis at the University of Warwick. *European Journal of Operational Research, 152*, 631-640.

European Union (2010). Consolidated Version of the Treaty on European Union and the Treaty on the Functioning of the European Union. *Official Journal of the European Union C 83, 53*. Available at: http://eur-lex.europa.eu/LexUriServ/LexUriServ.do?uri=OJ:C:2010:083:FULL:EN:PDF [15.3.2011].

Flyvbjerg, B. (1991). *Rationalitet og Magt*. (Rationality and Power). Bind 1. Copenhagen: Akademisk Forlag.

Galanc, T. & Mikus, J. (1986). The Choice of an Optimum Group of Experts. *Technological Forecasting and Social Change, 30* (3), 245-250.

Ghazinoory, S., Abdi, M. & Azadegan-Mehr, M. (2011). SWOT Methodology: A State-of-the-Art Review for the Past, a Framework for the Future. *Journal of Business Economics and Management, 12* (1), 24-48.

Harries, C. (2003). Correspondence to what? Coherence to what? What is good scenario-based decision making? *Technological forecasting and social change, 70* (8), 797-817.

Hauptman, A. (2011). *Report on technologies with potential privacy impacts.*

Hill, T. & Westbrook, R. (1997). SWOT analysis: It´s time for a product recall. *Long Range Planning, 30* (1), 46-52.

Hsieh, H-F. & Shannon, S. (2005). Three Approaches to Qualitative Content Analysis. *Qualitative Health Research, 15* (9), 1277-1288.

Kahn, H. & Wiener, A. J. (1967). *The year 2000: A Framework for speculation on the Next Thirty-three Years.* New York: MacMillan.

Kajanus, M., Kangas, J., & Kurttila, M. (2004). The use of value focused thinking and the A'WOT hybrid method in tourism management. *Tourism Management, 25* (4), 499-506.

Kajanus, M., Leskinen, P., Kurttila, M. & Kangas, J. (2012). Making use of MCDS methods in SWOT analysis – Lesson learnt in strategic natural resources management. *Forest Policy and Economics, 20,* 1-9.

Kangas, J., Kurttila, M., Kajanus, M. & Kangas, A. (2003). Evaluating management strategies of a forestland estate – the S-O-S approach. *Journal of Environmental management, 64* (4), 349-358.

Kowalski, K., Stagl, S., Madlener, R. & Omann, I. (2009). Sustainable energy futures: Methodological challenges in combining scenarios and participatory multi-criteria analysis. *European Journal of Operational Research, 197* (3), 1063-1074.

Krippendorff, K. (2004). *Content Analysis: An Introduction to Its Methodology. Second edition.* Thousand Oaks: Sage.

Kurttila, M., Pesonen, M., Kangas, J. & Kajanus, M. (2000). Utilizing the analytical hierarchy process (AHP) in SWOT analysis – a hybrid method and its application to a forest-certification case. *Forest Policy and Economics, 1* (1), 41-52.

Kuusi, O., Kinnunen, J., Ryynänen, O-P., Myllykangas, M. & Lammintakanen, J. (2006). Suomen Terveydenhuollon tulevaisuudet. *Terveydenhuollon tulevaisuus, Eduskunnan kanslian julkaisu 3/2006.* [The futures of health care, in Finnish.]

Leskinen, L. A., Leskinen, P., Kurttila, M., Kangas, J. & Kajanus, M. (2006). Adapting modern strategies decision support tools in the participatory strategy process – a case study of a forest research team. *Forest Policy and Economics,* 8 (3), 267-278.

Loveridge, D. (2002). *The STEEPV acronym and process – a clarification. Ideas in Progress. Paper Number 29.* Manchester: The University of Manchester. Available at: http://php.portals.mbs.ac.uk/Portals/49/docs/dloveridge/steepv_wp29.PDF [07.10.2011].

Masini, E. & Vasquez, J. M. (2002). Scenarios as seen from a human and social perspective. *Technological Forecasting and Social Change,* 65 (1), 49-66.

Meristö, T., Molarius, R., Leppimäki, S., Laitinen, J. & Tuohimaa, H. (2007). Laadukas SWOT. Työkalu pk-yritysten innovaatiovetoisen tulevaisuuden menestyksen turvaamiseksi. [High quality SWOT. A tool for innovation driven small and medium-sized enterprises to guarantee their success in future, in Finnish]. Turku: Corporate Foresight Group CoFi / Åbo akademi. Available at: http://virtual.vtt.fi/virtual/proj3/innorisk/LAADUKAS_SWOT.pdf [27.06.2012].

Mintzberg, H., Ahlstrand, B. & Lampel, J. (2005). *Strategy Safari: A Guided Tour Through The Wilds of Strategic Mangament.* New York: Simon & Schuster.

Moldrup, C. & Morgall, J. M. (2001). Risks of future drugs: A Danish expert Delphi. *Technological Forecasting and Social Change,* 67 (2-3), 273-289.

Oudshoorn, F., Sørensen, C. & de Boer, I. (2011). Economic and environmental evaluation of three goal-vision based scenarios for organic dairy farming in Denmark. *Agricultural Systems, 104* (4), 315-325.

Peterson, G., Cumming, G. & Carpenter, S. (2003). Scenario Planning: a Tool for Conservation in an Uncertain World. *Conservation Biology*, 17 (2), 358-366.

Ram, C. & Montibeller, G. (2013). Exploring the impact of evaluating strategic options in a scenario-based multi-criteria framework. *Technological Forecasting and Social Change, 80* (4), 657–672.

Rikkonen, P. & Tapio, P. (2009). Future prospects of alternative agro-based bioenergy use in Finland – Constructing scenarios with quantitative and qualitative Delphi data. *Technological forecasting and Social Change, 76* (7), 978-990.

Schoemaker, P. (1995). Scenario Planning: A tool for Strategic Thinking. *Review of Sloan Management,* 36 (2), 25-40.

Schwartz, P. (1991). *The Art of the Long View*. New York: Doubleday Currency.

Tapio, P. (2003). Disaggregative Policy Delphi Using cluster analysis as a tool for systematic scenario formation. *Technological Forecasting and Social Change, 70* (1), 83-101.

Tapio, P., Paloniemi, R., Varho, V. & Vinnari, M. (2011). The unholy marriage? Integrating qualitative and quantitative information in Delphi processes. *Technological Forecasting and Social Change, 78* (9), 1616-1628.

Tichy, G. (2004). The over-optimism among experts in assessment and foresight. *Technological Forecasting and Social Change, 71* (4), 341–363.

Van Notten, P., Rotmans, J., van Asselt, M. & Rothman, D. (2003). An updated scenario typology. *Futures, 35* (5), 423-443.

Varho, V. & Tapio, P. (2005). Wind Power in Finland up to the year 2025 – 'soft' scenarios based on expert views. *Energy Policy, 33* (15), 1930-1947.

Varho, V. & Tapio, P. (2013). Combining the qualitative and quantitative with the Q2 scenario technique – The case of transport and climate. *Technological Forecasting and Social Change, 80* (4), 611–630.

Von der Gracht, H. A. & Stillings, C. (2013). An innovation-focused scenario process — A case from the materials producing industry. *Technological Forecasting and Social Change, 80* (4), 599–610.

Wack, P. (1985). Scenarios: Shooting the rapids. *Harvard Business Review, 63* (6), 139-150.

Warth, J., Von der Gracht, H. A. & Darkow, I. L. (2013). A dissent-based approach for multi-stakeholder scenario development — The future of electric drive vehicles. *Technological Forecasting and Social Change, 80* (4), 566-583.

Weihrich, H., 1982. The TOWS Matrix A Tool for Situational Planning. *Longe Range Planning 15* (2), 54-66.

Welty, G. (1972). Problems of Selecting Experts for Delphi Exercises. *Academy of Management Journal,* 15, (1), 121-124.

Wollenberg, E., Edmunds, D. & Buck, L. (2000). Using scenarios to make decisions about the future: anticipatory learning for the adaptive co-management of community forests. *Landscape and Urban Planning, 47* (1-2), 65-77.

The Future of Water Use: Scenarios for Water Management in Telangana - Strengthening Local Governance in the Minor Irrigation Sector

Angela Jain, Sascha Dannenberg

Abstract

Water management in Telangana (India) is a complex issue: Water scarcity and related resource conflicts in the former federal state of Andhra Pradesh (India) have been linked to the perception of regional discrimination and finally caused state-bifurcation. Today's transition situation bears great opportunities to develop visions and action plans for future development of the new Telangana state.

In an expert workshop ("Salon") on Future Scenarios for Governance and Participation in the Telangana Region (Hyderabad 2012) a visionary process was initiated in order to consult decision makers and to integrate the perspectives of experts, civil society and the private sector into the possibly upcoming process of state re-organisation.

Background of the project

In the Telangana region, which was part of the South Indian federal state Andhra Pradesh until June 2014, separation demands have arisen from time to time ever since the creation of Andhra Pradesh in 1956. Water scarcity and related resource conflicts at the inter- as well as intra-state level are linked to the perception of regional discrimination and as such have been among the core issues in the statehood debate. In December 2009, the Government of India announced that the state assembly of Andhra Pradesh would consider the process for the formation of a Telangana state upon a separation statement. The Government of India constituted a committee headed by Justice B. N. Sri Krishna. This committee evaluated the situation and submitted a comprehensive report in January 2011 (Sri Krishna Committee 2011). In June 2014 the independent state of Telangana was finally declared.

In such a situation of political transition, in which Telangana still finds itself, it is necessary not only to look at the political debate and whether the demand for separation is justified or not. As studies show (e.g. GIGA 2010),

R. Peperhove et al. (Eds.), *Envisioning Uncertain Futures*, Zukunft und Forschung 6, https://doi.org/10.1007/978-3-658-25074-4_8

separate statehood can actually bring economic development forward and improve the social infrastructure. However, in experiences from some of the newly created states in India (in 2000) a high level of political instability (frequent strikes, fragmented landscape of political parties) can continue (e.g. Beck, Destradi & Neff 2010). Therefore, it seems recommendable to try to tackle some central problematic issues of the local situation and governance that need to be improved irrespective of a separation of the state.

To address at least some of the critical issues, it was suggested that a visionary dialogue should be organised, resulting in scenarios to discuss and finding solutions for infrastructure governance.

Water is one of the major conflicting issues in this context as agriculture is still the main source of income for 75 per cent of the population. Major water projects, e.g. the extremely controversial construction of the Povalaram dam, have received extensive political and media attention (e.g. Janyala 2011). In contrast, the focus of this dialogue-orientated project was on the tank irrigation system that is rather neglected in the debate on water issues, but bears great potential for the future of agriculture in Telangana (e.g. Gujja 2009).

Water management in Telangana is an extremely complex issue for many reasons. Therefore a few distinct characteristics of the region have to be considered: First of all, the people do not have easy access to natural water bodies as the region is geographically located on the Deccan Plateau, whilst the two rivers in this area, Godavari and Krishna, flow on a much lower level. Hence, their water can be used for irrigating the fields in Telangana only by means of sophisticated pump techniques or big dam projects. Additionally, a great share of the water is taken by the metropolitan area of Hyderabad, which has a rising demand for water due to a growing population, whilst, at the same time, it produces huge amounts of wastewater. The farmers of the Telangana region, thus, suffer chronically from insufficient water resources and are mainly dependent on rainwater as well as groundwater for agriculture.

Another important characteristic of the region is the traditional tank irrigation system for storing rainwater, which is not unique to Telangana but plays a distinct role in the region. It is a relatively simple system of catching rainwater in the village in a body like a pond from where the fields are irrigated through sluices or small canals. They were often connected to other tanks through canals so that whole areas were covered by a net of interconnected tanks. This tank system was constructed and maintained to great extent in the time of ancient kingdoms when culture centred on "tank and temple" serving as an independent economic base (Ibid.). Later the system experienced a major spurt in the period between 1875 and 1940 when tank irrigation grew ninefold, whilst total irrigation in Telangana multiplied sevenfold. However, the system has been entirely ignored and mistreated for the past fifty years (Ibid., 125).

Instead, in the last decades the use of private bore wells has increased extremely causing a chain of dramatic problems for nature and humans, predominantly through a drastically decreasing groundwater level. In an extensive analysis of the groundwater situation Jain et al. established alarming findings. In 5096 villages and 111 Mandals (an administrative unit between village and district) in Andhra Pradesh the groundwater basins are estimated to be over-exploited (Jain et al. 2009, 10). Thus, there is a natural limit to the availability of groundwater, but the quality of the water becomes a problem much earlier. As 85 per cent of the domestic water supply in rural areas is also achieved by ground water (Ibid., 8) the effects of bad quality are felt directly. The most disastrous effects on people's health are probably caused by a high content of fluoride, which came to the surface for example in the Nalgonda district, where the groundwater level has decreased extremely after people started building bore wells (Ibid., 10).

Other problematic side effects of the trend to construct bore wells are related to the situation of electricity supply and the indebtedness of many people through investments in private wells. In fact, the trend to construct wells for which electricity is needed is supported by the policy of the state government, to provide highly subsidised electricity for agricultural use for seven hours per day (since 2004). Excepting the bad quality (e.g. high voltage fluctuation) and unreliability of this power there are other negative consequences of this scheme, such as hidden costs, for instance, if machines are damaged through voltage fluctuation.

Against this backdrop the Berlin based nexus Institute for Cooperation Management and Interdisciplinary Research conducted a project on behalf of the German political Foundation Friedrich-Ebert-Stiftung (FES) in which challenges as well as future options for minor irrigation management in Telangana have been examined within the framework of an expert dialogue. Controversial debates about concrete issues among all concerned stakeholders that lead to fair compromises are the pillars of a functioning and social democracy. However, too often compromises seem to be impossible because of vested interests causing political polarisation. How to overcome policy deadlocks? How can all stakeholders be included in public deliberation processes in order to open up new perspectives? How to develop socially just policies? How can we ensure that these policies are implemented and actually strengthen the capabilities of those, who were previously marginalised?

The overall idea of the project was to assess the current situation and problems concerning infrastructural sectors that are at the core of statehood demand and create visions and concrete action plans for future governance and development of the region. In a preparatory study on governance issues the thematic fields of water management, energy supply and education were analysed regarding main problems, challenges and possible future improvements. Based on this research narrative Scenarios were developed and discussed. The overall goal was to develop future visions and strategies that can lead to a socially just water distribution for those who depend on it for their livelihood. By applying the innovative "Salon-Method", participants were encouraged to explore policy alternatives beyond entrenched policy- and thinking patterns.

The Salon method

The Salon method was developed and applied by the nexus Institute for Cooperation Management and Interdisciplinary Research. Historically, the Salon method derives from the intellectual salon of the 17th to 19th century in Europe, which was a place of profound discourse taking place in a relaxed atmosphere such as a club. The ´modern` Salon combines these characteristics with the particular aim of developing solutions for current problems and devising realisable options for forward-looking action. By applying creative techniques such as used in the World Café or the Future Workshop (e.g. Kuhnt et al. 2006), the Salon method offers a novel, stimulating environment for a temporary and creative think tank that combines the pleasure of intensive, controversial exchange with tangible results (Dienel & Legewie, 2005). In the context of the project mentioned above, the pleasant atmosphere as well as the scientific setting of the Administrative Staff College of India (ASCI) in Hyderabad provided the ideal atmosphere for this think tank, convening several experts with profound academic or on-the-ground experience in the areas of water management, governance and participation.

In general, the Salon method comprises five steps and is usually scheduled over two days (Dienel & Legewie, 2005). For organisational reasons the main working sessions of this particular Salon were confined to only one day and complemented by a presentation and discussion of the results targeting a wider public on the second day. As the following remarks will focus on the application of scenarios in the Salon method, see Jain et al. 2012 for an in-depth description of the salon and its results for the project „Scenarios for the Future of Governance and Participation in the Telangana Region".

In general, the Salon is initiated through the submission and presentation of an initial conceptual paper. It is not the form of this paper that matters, i.e. whether it is in form of controversial statements, statistical data or visionary plans, but its general function of introducing the main issues and different aspects of the Salon's topic as well as encouraging initial discussions amongst the participants. For this particular Salon the application of explorative-narrative scenarios was decided upon.

The second step of the gathering is designed to discuss the problems in greater depth and rank them according to their importance and impact. Therefore, this session of complaints not only aims at detecting the most challenging issues from the point of view of the participants, but it also has the effect of relieving the mind from addressing a problem over and over again. Furthermore, raising concerns guarantees a simple entry point, as all experts have critique that they can bring forward here.

In the next step, participants are asked to put aside all constraints and barriers regarding the possibility of realisation and envision a perfect situation in the future. In order to develop these visions, the participants are randomly grouped in pairs and asked to have a walk in an adjacent garden or park while being engaged in a bilateral discourse on their preferable futures concerning the issues discussed. This method is linked to Aristotle's peripatetic school of philosophy (lat. peripatetic = itinerant, wandering, meandering, or walking about) that combines physical activity with intellectual exchange and intensive dialogue by offering a pleasant and enticing atmosphere.

Subsequently, the visionary statements of each group are collected and collaboratively condensed into several core visions. These core visions form the basis for the next phase, in which each participant commits himself to one core vision. The resultant two or more groups are then requested to determine short and medium term goals as well as necessary actions for the realisation of their visions. The central purpose of this phase of the Salon is the elaboration of realisable pathways for transition connecting the vision to the present situation. By applying the back-casting approach (Höjer et al. 2000), the participants are asked to reverse their perspectives. In particular, participants engage as a kind of historian, looking back from their visionary future and identifying certain milestones up to today. In effect, possible and realisable pathways are identified which form a kind of roadmap to transform the present situation by describing central sub-goals to be reached as well as possible constraints to be dissolved for their realisation.

Finally, the Salon concludes with an exclusive dinner. This occasion gives every participant as well as the facilitators the opportunity to reflect and discuss the results of the day in a relaxed atmosphere. In order to enhance the dissemination of the results and the participant's commitment to realisation, the occasion is used to encourage the participants to deliver short speeches as a kind of toast on the fulfilment of their visions. This brings the Salon up to a round figure and should leave every participant with pleasant memories of the occasion and its intellectual output.

Using scenarios in the Salon method

Thinking about future developments is inevitably linked to our past experiences. This kind of extrapolation or "continuity of change" (Bezold 2011, 13) was never as difficult as it is today. In times of an accelerating speed of change it is probably not only the uncertainty about the 'shape' of the future as such which is worrying, but the certainty that the future will look different from what we know now. Therefore, by thinking about the future and about preferable changes it is necessary to not only extrapolate present times into the future by changing some of its conditions, but also to consider alternative developments to broaden the intellectual horizon for plausible and preferable future conditions. In order to enrich the development of visionary governance models by depicting possible alternative futures, this particular project was based on a three-step approach of conceiving visions. First of all, an environmental assessment was conducted in order to identify central issues in the area of governance structures concerning minor irrigation, education and energy supply and the link to governance (Jain & Bonaker 2011). The results of this preparatory study formed the initial basis for the development of narrative scenarios, which explore and depict alternative future developments. Finally, visionary programs were developed in the Salon through a participatory approach in Hyderabad, India.

As Mietzner and Reger point out, scenario is "a fuzzy concept that is used and misused, with various shades of meaning" (Mietzner & Reger 2004, 50), which indicates that there is no consistent and common theoretical substantiation for the scenario method so far. Notwithstanding, research and application of the scenario method seem to be based on a more implicit understanding. This generally perceives scenarios as a description of possible alternative futures, constructed through the identification and alternative adjustment of certain driving forces (Kosow & Gaßner, 2008). What is more, scenarios combine the three crucial ways of understanding the relationship between past, present and future. On one hand, scenarios generally presume the possibility of describing certain conditions of the future on the basis of present knowledge. But at the same time, scenarios also urge the uncertainty of future developments by describing possible, but alternative futures. The link between these partially contradicting views is the general consciousness that future developments are not generally predetermined as such, but will be - more or less - shaped by present actions (Kosow & Gaßner 2008).

Overall, the application of scenarios has several functions, which can be summarised into four main goals: knowledge generation, communication, goal-setting and strategy development (Kosow & Gaßner, 2008). Using scenarios in the Salon method can theoretically meet all these goals. In the particular Salon described above the application was more or less focused on the first two goals, diverting the goal-setting function and strategy development to the subsequent visionary process.

Knowledge generation most of all refers to the structuring, focusing and substantiation of present knowledge, taking into account the conditions and crucial influences for the central issue. What is more, the examination of present conditions also discloses interdependencies, which generally help to conceive future developments in a systemic way (Kosow & Gaßner, 2008). Therefore Bezold argues that scenarios are a "consistent type of learning" (Bezold 1999, 467) through stimulating imagination and creativity. As such scenarios used in visionary processes are to be seen as a cognitive trilogy of understanding, choosing and creating (Bezold 1999).

Furthermore, identifying and describing uncertainties concerning future influences, interdependencies and developments generally support the learning process. Wilkinson and Eidinow argue that scenarios help to tackle these uncertainties by defining and exposing "wicked problems“ (Wilkinson & Eidinow 2008, 1) of the issues concerned. These problems are as such difficult to define because they tend to be circular in respect to their definite end and influence other factors heavily as well as being influenced from different developments additionally themselves. By exposing these uncertainties, alternative developments can be conceived and a common discourse on necessary actions can be integrated into a comprehensive strategy (Wilkinson & Eidinow, 2008).

Using scenarios in visionary processes as a tool of communication refers to different levels. On one hand, the creation of scenarios can be seen as a communicative process, which not only stimulates discourse but ideally creates a common understanding of the issues concerned. From this point of view scenarios constitute a tool to inform participants (Kosow & Gaßner, 2008). On the other hand, scenarios help to find what could be called a common language. As Lindgren and Bandhold point out, scenarios help to find a common ground on which to place discussion between participants who may lack appreciation or interest in the others domain. Through the presentation of descriptive and simplified futures, those scenarios not only focus on the main issues but also facilitate discussion on common ground between different groups (Lindgren & Bandhold 2003). This function was particularly important in the case of the Telangana Salon, which was conducted in times of fervent discussions about the secession of the Telangana region from the federal state of Andhra Pradesh. The project's aim was not to decide whether the demand is justified or not but rather to envision solutions and actions for some central problematic issues of the local situation irrespective of the present or future political conditions. To prevent the Salon being a single-minded separation discussion, the initially presented scenarios helped participants to focus on these central issues and create a common understanding on what should be discussed in the Salon and what and what should be left aside.

References

Bezold, C. (1999). Alternative futures for communities. *Futures, 31*, 465–473.

Bezold, C., Peck, J., Bettles, C. & Olson, B. (2009). Using Vision in Futures. In J. C. Glenn (Ed.). *Futures research methodology. Version 3.0.* Washington, D.C.: The Millennium Project (CD-Rom).

Dienel, C. & Legewie, H. (2005). Methodik und Ablauf der Zukunftskonferenz Wörlitz 2005. In C. Dienel (Ed.) (2005). *Vision Sachsen-Anhalt 20-xx Zukunftsperspektiven für nachhaltiges staatliches Handeln* (8-10). Magdeburg: Friedrich-Ebert-Stiftung.

Beck, G., Sandra D. & Neff, D. (2010). Neue Bundesstaaten in Indien – eine Gefahr für die nationale Einheit? *GIGA, Focus Asien, 9,* 1-7.

Glenn, J. C. (2009). Scenarios. In J. C. Glenn (Ed.). *Futures research methodology. Version 3.0.* Washington, D.C.: The Millennium Project (CD-Rom).

Gordon, T. J. and Glenn, J. C. (2009). Environmental Scanning. In J. C. Glenn (Ed.). *Futures research methodology. Version 3.0.* Washington, D.C.: The Millennium Project (CD-Rom).

Gujja, B., Dalai, S., Shaik, H. & Goud, V. (2009). Adapting to Climate Change in the Godavari Basin of India by Restoring Traditional Water Storage Systems. *Climate and Development, 1* (3), 229-240.

Höjer, M. & Mattsson, L.-G. (2000). Determinism and backcasting in future studies. *Futures, 32,* 613-634.

Jain, A. & Bonaker, A. (2011). *Study on Governance and Participation in the Telangana Region. With special emphasis on local governance in the areas of water and energy management, and education.* New Delhi: Friedrich-Ebert-Stiftung.

Jain, A., Bonaker, A. & Dannenberg, S. (2012). *Scenarios for the Future of Governance and Participation in the Telangana Region: With Special Focus on the Minor Irrigation Sector.* New Delhi: Friedrich-Ebert-Stiftung.

Kosow, H. & Gaßner, R. (2008). Methods of Future and Scenario Analysis. Overview, Assessment, and Selection Criteria. *DIE Studies, 39.* Bonn: Deutsches Institut für Entwicklungspolitik. Available at: https://www.die-gdi.de/uploads/media/Studies_39.2008.pdf.

Kuhnt, B. & Müllert, N. R. (2006). *Zukunftswerkstätten verstehen, anleiten, einsetzen. Das Praxisbuch zur sozialen Problemlösungsmethode Zukunftswerkstatt.* Frankfurt am Main: AG SPAK Bücher.

Lindgren, M. & Bandhold, H. (2003). *Scenario Planning: The link between future and strategy.* New York: Palgrave Macmillan.

Mietzner, D. & Reger, G. (2004). Scenario-Approaches: History, Differences, Advantages and Disadvantages. In *Proceedings of the EU-US Scientific Seminar: New Technology Foresight, Forecasting & Assessment Methods.* Seville, Spain, 3-14 May 2004.

Srikrishna, S. (2010). Committee for Consultations of the Situation in Andhra Pradesh – Report. Available at: http://techdows.com/2011/01/download-srikrishna-committee-report.html [03.02.12].

Wilkinson, A. & Eidinow, E. (2008). Evolving practices in environmental scenarios: a new scenario typology. *Environmental Research Letters, 3,* 1-11.

The Future of Water Use: Construction of Scenarios in the Project

Sascha Dannenberg, Angela Jain

The construction of the particular scenarios for water governance was based on the so-called explorative-narrative scenario technique. Following the approach of intuitive logics to integrate not only the data available, this method focuses mainly on expert's estimations and expectations (Kosow & Gaßner 2008, 48). The group of experts contributing to the scenario development consisted of Germany based researchers who are concerned with issues of minor irrigation, water management or governance in Andhra Pradesh whose point of views were subsequently commented upon by dedicated Indian researchers via Email.

By and large, the development of explorative-narrative scenarios is guided by the same basic principles as other scenario techniques except that it is less formalised (Kosow & Gaßner, 2008). First of all, an environmental assessment (or environmental scanning) was conducted. 'Environmental' in this context refers to conditions – material and immaterial – having influence on a core issue. As such they shape this core issue, influencing and changing it (Gordon 2009, 2-3). Therefore, the core issue as well as its environment had to be identified and defined first. An intensive literature review was conducted initially to identify the central problems regarding governance and participation. Three core issues were identified in this research; water management (especially minor irrigation), education and energy supply.

Following the identification of the core issues, on-site empirical research was conducted in the Telangana region. This phase included expert interviews as well as visits to the rural site of the region. In interviews information and the perspectives of 22 people who can be considered experts on at least one of the core issues was gathered. Amongst those experts are authors of recent articles or books related to the subjects, a member of the Sri Krishna Committee (which evaluated the Telangana statehood demand), heads of civil society organisations, non-governmental organisations (NGOs) as well as staff members of the Irrigation Department. Moreover, four interview partners were master or PhD students who focus in their dissertations on topics related to the core issues (Jain & Bonaker, 2011). Having identified the situation and factors that influence developments in the focus areas water, energy supply and education, the results formed the basis for the development of alternative scenarios. Although the findings concerning the

R. Peperhove et al. (Eds.), *Envisioning Uncertain Futures*, Zukunft und Forschung 6, https://doi.org/10.1007/978-3-658-25074-4_9

situation in the educational sector also reveal a strong need for empowerment of local bodies, it was decided that the focus of the Salon was to be on water management as the most urgent issue. Considering the above-mentioned regional conditions and the situation of the tank irrigation system, a concentration on governance structures seemed especially interesting and relevant.

The next step contained the identification of influential factors by using the so-called STEEP scheme (Social, Technological, Economical, Ecological and Political). These factors were further substantialised through the assessment of past developments in the Telangana Region and assessed by the expert panel mentioned above subsequently. Using the so-called cross-impact analysis (Glenn 2009) they identified interdependencies between the conditions in a first step. Furthermore the uncertainty concerning the expected developments of the factors had to be assessed. The expert panel identified seven key factors, which can be considered driving forces for future developments because of their huge influence on other factors and their unpredictability or uncertainty. These factors crucial for developments in the minor irrigation sector are the following:

- patterns of seasonal rains affected by climate change
- groundwater levels
- use of specific irrigation devices
- crop patterns
- legal regulations concerning irrigation and institutionalization
- commitment through local opportunities of participation
- sense of responsibility of local authorities.

For each of these key factors the project team subsequently conceived several alternative developments. Furthermore, these alternative developments were condensed into consistent scenarios, resulting in a set of three explorative-narrative scenarios[1]. For the compilation of scenarios the creative technique of narrative short stories was used, describing not only possible conditions in Telangana in the year 2025 but also conveying the dynamics leading up to that future. In fact, the scenarios describe a broad variety of possible future

[1] For more information, please see Gaßner & Steinmüller, pp. 37-48 in this volume.

developments in Telangana and are thereby focused on different possible dynamics of aspects mentioned as crucial by the expert panel. Based on the on-site empirical study and its expert interviews, the three scenarios could be described as worst-case (scenario 1), business-as-usual (scenario 2) and best-case scenario (scenario 3).

These scenario "stories" together with the overview of main developments constructed for key factors were sent to the invited participants in advance of the Salon. The aim was to offer examples of how the future could look and encourage them to think in terms of alternative future developments. Therefore the scenarios can be seen as a preparation for the subsequent visionary process, facilitated through the Salon method. It helped to prevent the Salon from being a narrow-minded, single-tracked discussion on statehood separation[2], but instead created a common understanding on the subject matter to be discussed in the Salon.

Scenario 1 "Unlimited cash crop agriculture" [3]

Heavy-hearted farmer R. climbs into the lorry, and takes himself and his family to the city of Warangal[4]. Of the few things still belonging to them, they only took with them what was worth transporting. For a long time he had postponed this decision, still hoping for things to get better - but they did not... Unable to feed his family anymore, either from the little crops he sold or cultivation for subsistence purposes, his choices were now limited: Stay here – on the land that had belonged to his family for generations – facing further hardship, disease and probable famine? Or move to the city, trying to earn at least some rupees as a construction worker? He does not like the thought but he knows that some of the people of his community have found jobs on a construction site and they would try to help him. If that doesn't work out he would at least find a place where his family could stay with their relatives and he could try to get a daily-wage job as agricultural labourer on one of the large-scale farms near the city...

Looking at the countryside as the lorry moves on, he knows that there is no alternative. How should he go on cultivating on soils like this, with no sufficient and secured water access? How, if most of the land has to be left fallow because of salinisation and declining groundwater levels, so deep that the wells dug do not

[2] For more information, please see Jain & Dannenberg, pp. 133-142 in this volume.
[3] Alva Bonaker contributed to the narration of the scenarios.
[4] All places mentioned in the scenarios are existing villages, towns or districts of the federal state Andhra Pradesh.

reach it anymore? How could he afford investments in deeper tube wells if he is not even able to pay for seeds anymore? He had already taken out a loan for that and was unable to pay back even the interest rates as the last harvest had failed. How was this land of his childhood, once able to feed the people of his village, now in such a horrific condition? Passing by the entrance sign of the large-scale farm "Warangal Cotton Inc." he knows that people do not value natural resources anymore.

Over the last decades the farmers of Telangana dedicated themselves to the global slogan of sustainability - Glocality: Acting globally, thinking locally! Unfortunately, the slogan has been interpreted only economically and the implications were different from what was initially deliberated. By trying to satisfy the global demand for rice, cotton or organic oils, local conditions have been changed dramatically, resulting in an almost mono-culture agriculture in many parts of Telangana. R. remembers these days very well, when many of his fellow farmers switched from cultivating diverse food grains to rice or cotton only. Today – he knows – 66% of the cultivated area in Warangal, for example, and 65% in the adjacent district of Nalgonda is used for planting cotton and rice respectively. But what is more, in the end these changed planting habits have affected the patterns of landownership. Enlarging revenues by planting more cash crops was one thing; irrigating these mainly water intense crops the other. The cynicism, R. knows very well, lies in the deliberate process of over-exploitation of groundwater basins. He and his people knew that this was not a sustainable way of irrigation and they could almost second-guess the implications. But as he is assuring himself further and further, there has been no alternative for them – faced with the need to feed a family and left alone to cope with ever declining groundwater levels due to decreasing rainfalls and further over-exploitation of groundwater resources. Because tanks for irrigation purposes have been relinquished step by step and even shallow tube wells in many parts of Telangana did not reach the groundwater anymore, his fellow farmers invested in loans in digging and maintaining deep tube wells. Or, as he did, resorted to drawing water from existing deep tube wells by paying high fees. In effect, both paths led into further indebtedness for those like R., forced in the end to sell his house and land or further amplify the process of salinisation and deteriorating harvests. Today, more than 25% of all groundwater basins in Telangana are over-exploited and almost 40% in critical use. A condition that can not only be seen in the fields left fallow, but also in the steady deterioration of the health of the rural poor. Two of R.´s children died because of kidney dysfunction in their early childhood, triggered by steady malnutrition and contaminated drinking water.

However, by passing by the large-scale farm of "Warangal Cotton Inc." R. is once more assured that there are not only losers, but also people who profited from the developments of the last years. Those who had already owned deep tube wells in the early 2010s became those who were able to accumulate financial power. On one hand, by giving loans and, on the other, by collecting fees for using water from their wells. Unable to pay back the loans or even the high interest rates, R. and many of his fellow farmers had to sell parts of their land to them. In the end, those owning deep tube wells enlarged their farms tremendously. But what was worse for people like R. was the further focus on cultivating water intense cash crops on these farms, amplifying the vicious circle of over-exploited groundwater basins and further salinisation even more, making even small-scale farming on their remaining fields impossible.

R. still fails to understand why this kind of unsustainable farming has never been restricted for the sake of nature and future livelihoods. In fact, there are no legal regulations to stop this exploitation of groundwater reservoirs and small farmers respectively. There is no law to restrict the extraction of groundwater or regulate the access to water in general. To R. it seems as if the government just does not care to intervene. On the contrary, he knows how much corruption controls the whole system. Even if there were regulations, he is quite sure that no one would bother to adhere to them as there are no effective control mechanisms. The administrative institutions are full of corruption and long bureaucratic procedures.

On the village level the situation doesn't look any better. There has been a range of village bodies responsible for different areas of village life such as the Water User Associations (WUA) taking care of local irrigation management. But those organisations have never had enough power to be effective and have today become mere skeletons. Nobody sees any use in participating in village organisations anymore as the interests and power structures have become very different and farmers try to find other ways of managing their affairs. This absence of any well-functioning village organisation in which people could voice concerns has, as R. is sorely aware of, led to a complete marginalisation of the poor rural population. It has hit the economically weak parts of society, most of all minorities such as Scheduled Castes and Scheduled Tribes. Thus, completely excluded from any power these farmers have to depend on the rich landowners who, with their control over water access, also possess all decision-making powers.

As conflicts between frustrated farmers and big landowners have started in some villages, R. and some of his fellow farmers have seen a little hope again and initiated a small revolt against the exploitative landowners of their area. They have just taken the water they needed from wells and refused to pay the high charges. This was reason enough for the landowners to fight back with brutal methods. The injuries he sustained during the attack were not severe but his family has been threatened and he realised that it was not safe for them to stay any longer. At this point his ultimate decision to abandon village life was clear – he had no other choice but to give up. These thoughts and memories of how life has turned into a struggle for survival haunted him while he tried hard to look forward to their uncertain future in the city.

Scenario 2 "Local crisis and central planning"

Looking at the Cultivation and Irrigation Plan for the year 2025 the officer had just handed over to him, the Sarpanch is concerned. Again the plan confines the cultivable land to an even smaller area and again they are not allowed to plant more cash crops. How should he explain this to his community, which had great trust in him to negotiate the new plan with the central authorities in the district office of Nizamabad? After spending uncountable hours in the overcrowded office, this is all he achieved for his people: a sheet of paper, designed by bureaucrats and issued by the Ministry for Irrigation and Water Issues in Hyderabad, describing exactly where his community is allowed to plant what kind of crops and which area they are confined to for extracting groundwater for irrigation purposes. This sheet of paper determines future harvest outcomes but doesn't have much to do with the current needs of his community. What once seemed to be a promising reform of the irrigation sector has now turned into an obscure bureaucratic procedure...

Faced with an economic disaster caused by ecological crisis and an apparently ineffective legal framework, calls for radical reform of the irrigation sector gained popularity in the late 2010s. Badly funded and supported by manpower, local organisations such as Water User Associations (WUA) were quickly marked as scapegoats, unable to break the vicious circle of increasing need for food of a growing population, on the one hand, and deterioration of groundwater basins and exhausted soils, on the other. In trying to cope with the declining groundwater levels the farmers – unhindered by legal regulations or local institutions – resorted to digging even deeper wells, exploiting the groundwater basins even further. As a result, in 2018 the groundwater level plunged down to an average of 18 mbgl (meter below ground level) in may, making irrigation through dug wells and shallow tube wells for many farmers impossible. As tanks and other devices for rainwater harvesting have been neglected over the last decades, those farmers have been confronted with an existential crisis. What is more, those farmers who were still able to irrigate the lands through deep tube wells further exhausted their soils in the first place through the exaggerated need for food grains and secondly by amplifying the process of salinisation. In the end the cultivable area steadily declined from about 4800 lakh ha in 2010 to only 4000 lakh ha in 2018. The effects have been rather palpable in those years: abandoned or fallow farmlands and an increasing number of the urban poor.

For those politicians pleading for more institutional centralisation and restrictive regulation of water access and use, these conditions provided a fruitful atmosphere. The populist rally, based on a radical reform of the irrigation sector, proved successful. The government that was elected in 2018 promised to solve these problems through radical change in the structure of the system. In order to make the system more effective and clear they had done away with all parallel institutional structures. In fact, all powers have been centralised in one ministry responsible for all aspects of irrigation in the federal state. It has been widely believed that central regulation and strict laws that have been introduced on water use in general and groundwater extraction in particular would provide a good framework for a positive rural development.

Along with the introduction of strict regulations on water use and cultivation, an important role has been assigned to the Sarpanch. In fact, the task to achieve cultivation permissions for farmers – in form of the plan that he now holds in his hands – has been introduced as one of the central duties of a Sarpanch in 2018. This was meant to simplify the communication between the central authority and the population. All farmers have to adhere to the yearly regulations of water use and cultivation and it is the task of the Sarpanch to collect the new Cultivation and Irrigation Plan from the district office as well as to submit the plans and suggestions for local irrigation from his village. Initially, the farmers believed that the decision makers in the ministry would actually take the plans and suggestions they worked out in the villages into account. Now that a few years have passed by and the initial euphoria about the new system has faded, the expectations of the farmers have not been fulfilled. The Sarpanch, as a kind of middleman between the administration and his village people, has soon discovered flaws and disadvantages of the system. He has been the elected Sarpanch of his village for almost three years now and he had realized soon enough that whatever he submits from his village, the Cultivation and Irrigation Plans the ministry prepares do not reflect their suggestions but are simply created according to their criteria.

After all, the Sarpanch is well aware that there is no scope in the system to consider the local concerns in the bureaucratic procedures of the administration. All laws and regulations are created in the centre which is distant from the everyday reality of farmers and all the matters they come up with take a very complicated and time consuming path through the central authority. This has led to widespread frustration and many people have found other ways to manage their affairs. And how should the centre control all unofficial practices such as rice plantations in places where they were not permitted and the use of wells that have been constructed without official permission? But what options do the farmers have as the applications are often pending for months or even years if they do not have the money to bribe the officer in charge? Even here in this office many things happen this way. If you know how, getting a few small changes completed on paper is not impossible. He, too, sometimes makes use of his position for his own benefit and is more or less forced to try his best for a few influential people in his village who would not re-elect him otherwise. But all this doesn't make a big difference, he thinks. Everybody plays his role in the system, that's how it works. He had fulfilled his task and would show the paper to his people, how they would implement it was another question.

Scenario 3 "Community empowerment"

The press conference hall in the Ministry of Ground Water Development is packed with journalists, both national and international, who impatiently await the presentation of this year´s "Annual Groundwater Report 2024-25 for Telangana". The tremendous public interest is justified with some rumors that have leaked through informal networks, about the minister himself attending the press conference to announce something sensational. And truly, the way the honourable minister enters the room smiling, accompanied by the minister for minor irrigation and the minister for water resource management respectively confirms all the expectations of the journalists that something special must have happened. And indeed it has! As the minister proudly proclaims, Telangana and its people have accomplished a historical achievement: No over-exploited groundwater basins in Telangana any longer and less than 10% in a critical condition! This achievement cannot be cheered enough, as the minister points out, looking back at the disastrous conditions of many groundwater basins one and a half decades ago. Furthermore, the minister continues, the people of Telangana had to face the implications of global climate change, affecting foremost seasonal rainfall in Southern India. Therefore, the steady decrease of annual rainfall from a former 800mm in 2011-12 to only 600mm in 2024-25 had to be dealt with, confronting many farmers mainly in Nalgonda, Medak and Warangal with insufficient water access for irrigation purposes and further salinisation of their soils in these years. The minister himself remembers those times as Telangana standing at the crossroads: A steadily growing population, both urban and rural, with rising demand for food and enhanced living standards, constituting a further threat for groundwater resources. Fortunately, the year 2012 marked a turning point in water politics, resulting in a widespread consensus for reform and sustainable water management.

As the journalists listen carefully, eager to learn more about how the change from such dramatic conditions to the present announcement of recovered groundwater basis could have happened, the minister reports on how the whole governance in the field of minor irrigation has witnessed a major change over these years. Farmers had increasingly claimed more power for local institutions. There had been a lot of such institutions, but generally ineffective because of a lack of financial as well as human resources. In fact, the Participatory Irrigation Management (PIM) was not working at all effectively in those days and could only be turned into a functioning scheme through a strengthening of the local institutions. Have they not heard about reforms like this before, some journalists start to murmur – and how often had these turned out to be pure tokenisms? Something seems to be different here... Not only the farmers, but also the government at this time has seen a need for a radical reform, the minister continues. The institutional set up has been re-organised to create a much more transparent, well-structured system. On the village level all organisations, including the Water User Associations (WUAs), have been made sub-organisations of the Gram Panchayats. Through clearer division and regulation of competencies and at the same time closer cooperation between the different village bodies they can nowadays work more effectively within their set of responsibilities. On the other hand, to ensure just and appropriate allocation of funds to local organisations, bureaucratic processes have been shortened and open access to budget allocations has been introduced as a control mechanism. This new regulation tied in with the core ideas of the Right to Information (RTI) Act of 2005. As it is effectively used by the population, it has brought the level of corruption down drastically. Now, that the members of the WUAs know that they receive the funds that are needed for construction, maintenance and management of irrigation systems, WUAs have become important local institutions. But how exactly, mainly international journalists start to interrogate the minister, could the re-organisation of governance structures on village level lead to this astonishing success? The minister, who was waiting for this question to crop up, starts to explain one of the main changes that was introduced ten years ago through legal regulations.

In fact, after the region had faced the already mentioned dramatic climate changes, there was a need to re-think the whole concept of water management. The consensus of that time was that over-exploitation of water resources could be most effectively fought through seeing water as a common good that has to be taken care of and shared by everybody. Only that could allow equal access and control over the use of water. Consequentially, private construction of bore-wells or other water extracting systems for private purposes has since then been forbidden per law. All access to water, whether canals, tanks, wells or systems for rainwater harvesting, is controlled by the community, which is organised through WUAs. The restriction of water access resulted in the increased use of tanks for minor irrigation, which account for almost 50% of the net-irrigated area in Telangana in 2025.

As their meetings and decisions have become highly important to the whole community, farmers now feel much more encouraged to participate in the decision making and allocation of water resources. In contrast to the former regulation which allowed membership in WUAs only to land owners and tenants, now everybody who uses water for any purpose is automatically a member and responsible for the functioning of the organisation. For some tasks they work in close cooperation with the staff of the Irrigation Department, this is e.g. the collection and re-allocation of water tax and the assessment of which crops can be grown on which land according to the water capacities available. In both these areas new regulations have been introduced following the general aim to make water use more responsible and just. As far as the tax system is concerned, a volumetric taxation of water has been implemented which allows for much more transparency than the earlier system. Regarding the cultivation of crops, regulations have become much stricter, in order to avoid cultivation of water-intense crops when there is not enough water available for their irrigation. Every year before the sowing season the capacity of all water bodies, including groundwater, are assessed and on this basis WUAs decide on the kind of crops that can be cultivated by farmers and which area is eligible. As a result, the minister announces, the total area cultivated in Telangana could constantly be increased to satisfy, on one hand, the growing demand for food and, on the other hand, the economic interests of cash crop producers.

References

Gordon, T. J. & Glenn, J. C. (2009). Environmental Scanning. In J. C. Glenn (Ed.). *Futures research methodology. Version 3.0.* Washington, D.C.: The Millennium Project (CD-Rom).

Jain, A. & Bonaker, A. (2011). *Study on Governance and Participation in the Telangana Region. With special emphasis on local governance in the areas of water and energy management, and education.* New Delhi: Friedrich-Ebert-Stiftung.

Kosow, H. & Gaßner, R. (2008). Methods of Future and Scenario Analysis. Overview, Assessment, and Selection Criteria. *DIE Studies, 39.* Bonn: Deutsches Institut für Entwicklungspolitik. Available at: https://www.die-gdi.de/uploads/media/Studies_39.2008.pdf.

"Peace Operations 2025": From Shaping Factors to Scenarios

Björn Theis, Stefan Köppe

Abstract

"Peace Operations 2025" identified 14 pertinent factors that will likely shape the global security landscape in the future and the international community's crisis management responses. This chapter outlines the various steps of this scenario process, summarizes the four distinct scenarios for peace operations in the year 2025, and provides some lessons learned and insights into working with a diverse, multi-disciplinary group using the applied methodology.

International peace operations by the United Nations, the European Union, the Organization for Security and Cooperation in Europe (OSCE), and other regional organizations have been an instrument commonly used by the international community in de-escalating conflicts, monitoring cease-fires, helping communities emerge from conflicts to build lasting peace, and even preventing conflicts.[1] In the last decades, the world of peace operations has changed tremendously in terms of scope, mandates and actors involved. It will certainly continue to evolve further. Thus, there is a lot of uncertainty about the future character and the future requirements of peace operations. However, this field has been a rather reactive one, being driven by conflicts and the imperative to react to them and with a strong focus on operational issues of day-to-day business.

The Center for International Peace Operations (ZIF)[2] sought to provide an impulse for more pro-active engagement and room to taking a longer perspective on the issues at hand. Some of the main organizations in the field are, of course, engaged in contingency planning, but ZIF wanted to set up a foresight process for the community and provide inspiration and as well a specific product to work with and challenge our thinking of today. This process was conducted

[1] For an overview of the various instruments and actors in this field, see: Major, C. et al. 2013.

[2] The Center for International Peace Operations (ZIF) was founded in 2002 by the German Federal Government and the Bundestag (German parliament). The Center's core mandate is to recruit and train civilian personnel and to provide analysis and advice on peacekeeping and peacebuilding issues. ZIF works closely with the German Federal Foreign Office and is responsible in particular for Germany's civilian contributions to EU, OSCE and UN missions.

R. Peperhove et al. (Eds.), *Envisioning Uncertain Futures*, Zukunft und Forschung 6, https://doi.org/10.1007/978-3-658-25074-4_10

under the project "Peace Operations – Fit for the Future" which was endorsed and financed by the German Federal Foreign Office.

In recent years, there has been no shortage of reports and publications about future global challenges in the wider security policy field (e.g. the National Intelligence Council "Global Trends" series and the annual "State of the Future" report of The Millennium Project). However, when the project started, ZIF could not identify a similar, full-fledged scenario approach to the field of peace operations, and therefore partnered with Z_punkt[3] to facilitate a process that provides credible outcomes.

A simple question marked the beginning of the project: "What do we have to expect from the future?" In order to give some answers to that question, it was necessary to conduct a fully-fledged scenario process (e.g. Fink & Siebe, 2006; Schwartz 1991; Van der Heijden 1996; Wilms 2006) that includes all relevant factors and actors and thus to generate alternative future options for global conflict management. Therefore, ZIF and Z_punkt chose an explorative as well as participative scenario approach (Fig. 1). Explorative scenarios (also called projective scenarios or trend scenarios) involve the extrapolation of challenges, trends and other shaping factors (or influencing factors) and explicitly consider uncertainties. Inconsistencies between individual trends are taken into account through interdependency methods (morphological box, cross-impact method, trend-impact method) or computer simulations.

[3] Z_punkt is a leading strategy and foresight consultancy, operating internationally and focusing on strategic future issues. Z_punkt is specialized in corporate foresight – the translation of findings derived from trend and future research into practical advice to assist with strategic management.

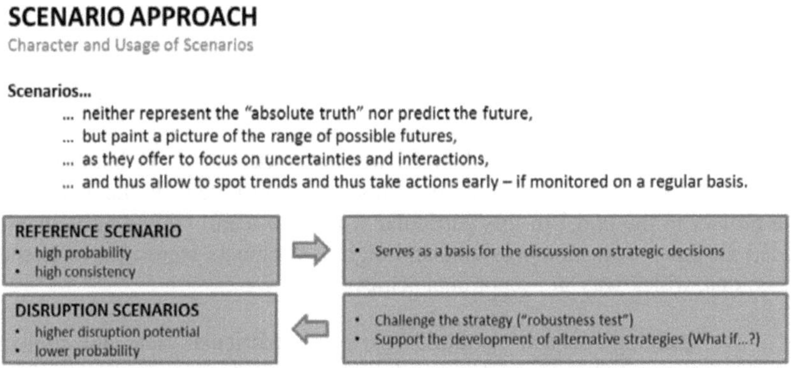

Figure 1: General Character of Explorative Scenario Approaches

The main difference between explorative and normative scenarios is that an explorative approach takes a variety of possible future developments (different projections) into account, while a normative scenario describes only one picture of the future, most of the time a best-case scenario. Therefore, one can think of such scenarios also as a goal statement. Based on that vision, a normative scenario approach tries to answer the question: "What must be done to make that vision come true?"

In contrast to normative approaches, in an explorative one, all scenarios are seen as equally important and valuable. Even "negative" or "worst-case" scenarios with all their disagreeable aspects (and perhaps some attractive ones) deliver insights on risks and opportunities, options and strategies. Viewed from this angle, negative and positive scenarios provide the basis for reflection on long-term oriented policy measures. In short, the focus of an explorative scenario process is on the conclusions taken from scenarios and, based on these, to find answers to the question: "How could/how should we act to be ready for the uncertainty of the projected alternative futures?"

Due to the high complexity of the field of peace operations it was clear from the beginning that the in-depth knowledge of an interdisciplinary team was needed. This team had to consist of experts and practitioners working in this area but also non-insiders to the world of peace operations that could challenge some of the conventional wisdoms and perspectives of the community. Gathering the right people for the process is a crucial step and we – the organizing team from ZIF and Z_punkt – aimed to include a broad spectrum of views. However, it was not possible to satisfy all criteria at once. We wanted to represent all major regions of the world, the various components of today's multi-dimensional peace operations (military, police, civilian), an adequate gender mix, a good balance of academics vis-à-vis practitioners and decision-makers, and also foresight experts and futurists. Bearing all these considerations in mind, one would have easily ended up with an unmanageable group size. In the end, we worked with just more than 30 colleagues, never more than 25 in one workshop. It is important to establish a certain "core group" of participants who contribute from the beginning of the project to the end.[4] In this particular workshop team, twelve participants attended all three workshop sessions, and eight participants were able to attend two sessions, which was an exceptional achievement.

By applying scenario methodology to this particular field, the project "Peace Operations 2025" aimed to contribute to the international reform debate and conceptual evolution of peace operations, to start an innovative form of dialogue amongst experts and decision-makers and a systematic transfer of knowledge to the policy community. An interactive workshop series, which engaged various experts and their in-depth knowledge in scenario generation, seemed to be the appropriate format. We designed a five-stage scenario process with three expert workshops (Fig. 2).

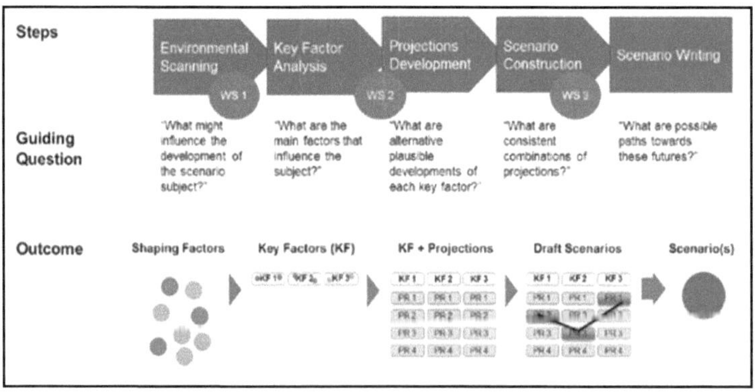

Figure 2: Overall Process Design

[4] The reason for this is twofold: i) knowledge transfer – the group develops a deeper understanding of the applied methodology and meaning of the intermediate steps in such a foresight endeavor, the same holds true for the discussed content, so that previous results will not be constantly challenged in the next phase of the project; ii) over the course of the project, participants create a sense of ownership for the process and ultimately for the final product, increasing the chances that they will use it for their daily work and act as multipliers.

Workshop 1 – Environmental Scanning

Many scenario processes are based on "key factors" – factors that characterize and determine the future development of the topic, irrespective of whether the key factor is seen as a cause (e.g. as an external parameter) or whether it describes its main effects. The concept of "key factors" is used to classify and assess the large number of parameters (actors, challenges, trends etc., where applicable also key actors' options for action) in order to reduce complexity, make things more manageable and select the most pertinent factors in the end. Hence, the objective of a key factor analysis is to create an easy-to-handle set of factors for the scenario design.

To do so, a broad collection of parameters, so called "shaping factors" or "influencing factors" – had to be identified, systemized, and clustered. This was done through an "environmental scanning" as an intuitive approach to create a first "mind map" of the whole field of the future of peace operations and to map all relevant aspects systematically. To structure this approach, it has proven useful to discuss thoughts and ideas in the so-called STEEP sectors: Society, Technology, Economy, Ecology and Politics.

Accordingly, we "deployed" all experts to work stations on the individual STEEP sectors on the first day. We asked them which developments, trends, and actors in the respective sector are relevant for the future of peace operations. As food for thought we presented some initial ideas that were derived from a preparatory workshop we had held before.

On the first day of the workshop, 102 shaping factors were identified (Fig. 3). On the second day, these factors were evaluated according to the four criteria "impact on peace operation," "uncertainty," "reach" and "salience." The "impact" refers to the expected degree of change that the specific shaping factor entails, while "reach" can be understood as an indicator for the scale and/or area of influence. This area of influence can be geographical or actor-specific, ranging from 1 (only local relevance or relevance for single parties) up to 5 (relevance for the whole world, all actors in peace operations). "Uncertainty" reflects the rating of participants on how sure they are about the future outcome of the development of this shaping factor: from very certain (1) to highly volatile/highly uncertain (5). "Salience" reflects the relative prominence, and exciting character of the issue from the personal perspective of the participants, mirroring the individual interests and "gut feeling" to a certain extent. In addition, all shaping factors were grouped into 16 clusters according to their commonalities. In that process 13 wild cards[5] were identified and described.

In order to profit as much as possible from this interdisciplinary group, we established so-called "walking groups." These small teams were mixed as much as possible for maximum diversity and each team had the chance to visit every group workstation and comment on the work done by previous groups (the facilitators remained stationary, moderated the discussions and briefed subsequent groups). This principle was followed in all three workshops, so that participants had the opportunity to run through all content-related modules instead of being confined to e.g. one STEEP sector or one particular scenario later on (see below).

Intermediary Processing: Key Factor Analysis

The results of the second workshop were then further clustered and refined by Z_punkt and ZIF in a two-stage method of analysis which consisted of a computer-based cross-impact analysis (using the software Parmenides EIDOS[6]) and an additional "impact-uncertainty analysis" of the redefined clusters, in order to reduce complexity further and to identify the most influential factors or clusters of factors, the so-called "key factors" (Fig. 3). It is in the nature of foresight that they are always uncertain, but the degree of uncertainty may differ between individual factors. Demographic development, for instance, can be characterized by comparatively low uncertainty within the given time frame. Economic factors, by contrast, are often subject to sizeable volatility. In this scenario project, we worked with twelve key factors with considerable uncertainty (i.e. several possible future projections of the individual factors have to be considered for scenario construction) and two factors with low uncertainty (i.e. only one or very few parameters have to be considered for scenario construction). Since the development of these factors can be projected over a long period of time and are grounded on solid scientific models, they are also called "given factors,"

[5] Wild cards can be described as „future development[s] or event[s] with a relatively low probability of occurrence but a likely high impact on the conduct of business." (BIPE Conseil et al. 1992; Steinmüller & Steinmüller, 2004, 19) The mentioned 13 wild cards emerged during the clustering and evaluation of the shaping factors and were considered to be too important to be left out of the scenario project.

[6] The Parmenides Eidos Suite is a software toolbox designed to foster strategic clarity for complex decision-making. It allows planners to visualize relationships and outcomes, and to develop, compute, and visualize the relationships between the many variables involved in implementing strategies. For more information see:
http://www.parmenides-foundation.org/application/parmenides-eidos/
Z_punkt uses this software suite for scenario development and monitoring, and the subsequent development of strategies.

demographics and climate change in our case. These final key factors were the basis for the scenario construction and the focus of the second workshop (see Table 2).

Table 1: Glossary

GLOSSARY: Different Kinds of Factors in a Scenario Process

Shaping Factors:
The concept of "shaping factors" is used to compile an exhaustive collection of parameters (actors, challenges, trends, etc.; where applicable also key actors' options for action) in order to create a first overview of the environment of the research subject. Often, the collection of factors will begin with an intuitive approach, e.g. a "mind map" of all possible factors.

Key Factors:
Key factors are parameters that characterize or significantly determine the scenario's topic and its future development. The concept of "key factors" is used to assess, classify, cluster and systemize the large number of shaping factors in order to reduce problem complexity and make scenario construction more manageable. They are factors with a high impact on the future development of the research object and considerable uncertainty. Therefore, they might show several different future alternative "projections", all of which should be taken into consideration for scenario construction.

Projections:
The term projections refers to the different possible future developments of a key factor. For example, the key factor "National Interest versus Global Interdependence" has three different projections: "Golden Age of Global Cooperation," "Temporary Coalitions of the Willing," and "New Unilateralism." As this example shows, projections should be formulated to be mutually exclusive (minimal overlap between two future developments).

Givens:
In contrast to key factors, givens are factors with a low uncertainty. Therefore there is only one projection that has to be considered for scenario construction. Nevertheless, they are factors with a high impact on the future development of the research object. Demographic trends, for instance, are characterized (with the sole exception of migration) by comparatively low forecast uncertainties.

Participants were provided a "Key Factor Report" as documentation of the first and in preparation of the upcoming second workshop. The report comprised a short outline of the methodology, descriptions of the identified key factors (consisting of a brief definition, a summary detailing some aspects, a small collection of facts & signals – i.e. current specific examples of how this factor is already affecting peace operations – and first indications of possible areas of impact), and an annex with an overview of all factors and their rating scores.

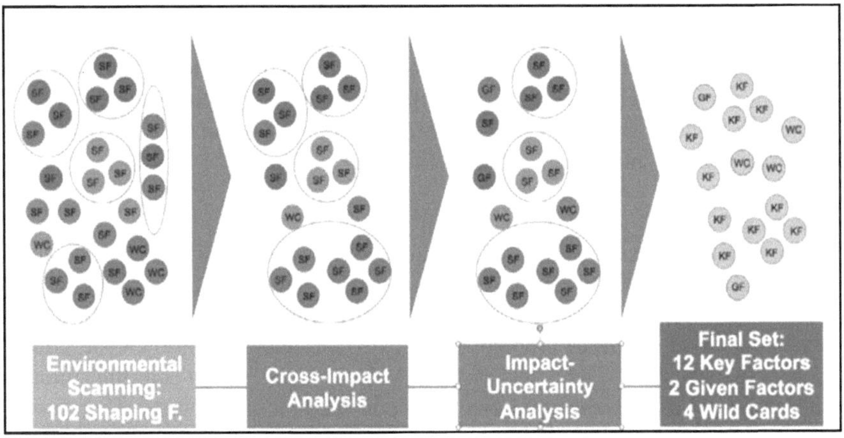

Figure 3: From Shaping Factors (results workshop 1) to Key Factors (starting point workshop 2)

Table 2: Identified Key and Given Factors [7]

Key Factors

- National Interest versus Global Interdependence
- State of the Global Economy
- Economic and Political Power Shifts
- Norms and Values
- Evolution of International Organizations
- State Fragility
- Organized Crime
- Resource Scarcity
- Migration, Refugees, Diasporas
- New Technologies
- New Media
- Private Security Companies

Given Factors

- Demographics
- Climate Change

Workshop 2 – Projection Development

The second workshop aimed at defining various possible future projections for each key factor, i.e. how might the key factors develop or which alternative occurrences might they have at the end of the study's time frame in the year 2025. These projections ought to be exhaustive, meaning that all relevant and plausible alternatives have been considered, and are mutually exclusive. So we did not look for the most probable development path only, but rather sought for all possible ones.

To fulfil this task, we chose a two-stage approach. On the first day of the workshop, we asked the participants to gather in four working groups – each dedicated to three factors – and to discuss and describe relevant projections for each key factor. Since these projections described possible developments of key factors on a more general level – for instance "Rise of Regional Power Centers"

[7] The final key factors are quoted from the ZIF publication "Peace Operations 2025" (Von Gienanth & Hansen & Köppe, 2012, 5) Please refer to this document and pages 9ff. for more detail: http://tinyurl.com/peace-operations-2025.

as a projection of the key factor "Economic and Political Power Shifts" – we asked participants to describe the specific impacts of each projection on peace operations on the second day. Overall, 33 projections and their impacts on peace operations were described.

Again, we compiled a "Key Factor Projections Report" as an intermediate product.

Intermediary Processing: Identifying the Raw Scenarios

Once all key factors and their projections had been described, the next major step in the construction of scenarios was a consistency analysis, which identified conflicts and synergies between the projections along the twelve key factors. Each set of consistent projections of different key factors forms a raw scenario.

The basic idea of a consistency check is that projections of different key factors occasionally dovetail, but may also clash violently. The number of possible raw scenarios (projection bundles) will grow very rapidly mirroring the number of key factors and their projections. Hence, the reduction of complexity is again crucial.

For "Peace Operations 2025," we used two methodological approaches for the analysis of the interdependencies between key factors, the reduction of complexity and the consistency check of raw scenarios. The first approach is the so-called morphological box (see Fig. 4) which lists all key factors and their projections. Here, we look for consistent (or even synergetic) combinations of projections amongst key factors. Consistencies were determined in a dialogue between Z_punkt and ZIF. This discussion collected and weighed arguments for and against the compatibility of specific projections.

TOOL: Morphological Box

What are possible alternative future developments of each shaping factor that are

- **exhaustive (all relevant & plausible alternatives),**
- **mutually exclusive (no overlap)?**

Project Overview

Final List of Key Factors and Projections (Morphological Box)

Evolution of Inter. & Reg. Organizations	Organized Crime and Corruption	State Fragility	National Interest vs. Global Interdependence	Economic Stability and Inequality	Global Migration and Role of Diasporas	Role of Private Security Services	Evolving Global Norms and Networks	Shifts in Economic and Political Power	New Media	Competition for Natural Resources	Cyber Security & Surveillance Technol.
Status Quo – "Muddling trough"	POs Combat Organized Crime and Corruption	Fewer Failed States	Golden Age of Global Cooperation	Extreme Instability and Fluctuations	Decrease in Migration	Diminishing Role of PSCs	Global Consensus on Values & Norms	Rise of Regional Power Centers	New Media Decrease Conflicts	Resource Scarcity Triggers Conflicts	Global Spread of CS and ST
Decline of Int. & Reg Organizations	Global Drive against OC and Corruption	State Fragility Fatigue	New Unilateralism	Uneven Recovery	Status Quo in Migration	"PSC Blue Helmets"	Clash of Norms and Values	Disintegration and Decline of the West	New Media Increase Conflicts	Scarcity Triggers Innovation & Cooperation	Asymmetric Spread of CS and ST
Strengthening Int. & Reg. Organizations	OC & Corruption Flourish	More Failed States	Tempor. Coalitions of the Willing	Broad Economic Recovery	Major Increase in Migration	Status Quo		Integration of Emerging Powers			
Rise of Reg. & Private Actors											

Figure 4: Morphological Box

Secondly, we used a software-based approach, the Consistency Matrix and Clustering. All pairs of projections of different key factors are given "consistency values" (1 = fully inconsistent; 5 = strong mutual support) which describe their individual compatibility.[8] The software RAHS (Risk Assessment and Horizon Scanning)[9] that was developed by Z_punkt for the German Bundeswehr identified those combinations of projections which achieved the highest consistency scores.

[8] For example, the projection that resource scarcity triggers widespread international cooperation in the development of resource-efficient technologies and the free access of these new technologies, does not go particularly well with the projection of another key factor that describes a new unilateralism with nations focusing on narrowly defined self-interests.

[9] RAHS (Risk Assessment and Horizon Scanning) is a software suite that provides knowledge of methods and tools for strategic future analysis (inter alia for scenario construction, or roadmapping).

Usually, after this computation, there is still a fairly large number of projection bundles. The next step is hence an (automatic) clustering based on similarities (number of common projections) between projection bundles. These clusters form the raw scenarios.

The final number of scenarios in such a project should arise from the process as such. However, it is obvious that a too-small set of scenarios will at best provide a sketchy vision and will not cover the full scope of possible futures, whereas a large number may lead to confusion and may not be distinguishable enough and intellectually manageable. Therefore, the final choice of quantity should be based on the distinctiveness and substance of the projection bundles. General criteria for scenario selection are therefore that each scenario includes a projection of each key factor, a high overall consistency of each scenario, the maximum distinctiveness of scenarios, and, most importantly, that each chosen scenario possesses intrinsic sense and provides a specific insight.

Stemming from these criteria, we could identify four raw scenarios, roughly characterized as a positive, a negative, a "business as usual" scenario, and finally one that displays strong features of regionalization with a decline of existing multilateral fora in favor of emerging strong regional organizations.

Workshop 3 – Scenario Construction

The four raw scenarios were the point of departure for the third workshop. The overall aim was to enrich previous work and create four consistent scenarios. When raw scenarios are further enriched, assumptions about the causalities or underlying "logics" are crucial. By mapping out credible trajectories towards these scenarios, denser descriptions of these pictures of the future unfold. The guiding question was: "What actions and events must have occurred to make such a scenario possible?"

Again, we proceeded in two steps. On the first day, we asked participants to enrich the raw scenarios by describing relevant consequences of the raw scenarios for four crucial categories, namely i) peace operations in general, ii) the troop and police contributing countries, iii) host countries and iv) regional and international organizations with regard to the study's time frame. We asked participants to concentrate on more dramatic changes and developments. To

It is under development in cooperation of the Bundeswehr (armed forces of the Federal Republic of Germany), Z_punkt The Foresight Company GmbH, and Itonics GmbH and currently in a late development and testing phase.

emphasize such scenario-specific and consistent narration about the future of peace operations even more, the second day was dedicated to roadmapping.[10] In this step, the participants were asked to complete a "backcasting" of their raw scenario. This was conducted through a discussion of relevant societal, technologic, economic, ecologic or political events (STEEP) that may have led to that specific scenario. Finally, we asked the group to invent possible names for the scenarios. Scenario titles play an important role in communication. Vivid titles are more easily memorized, while overly concise or too general titles (such as "Boom") do not reveal the scenario's specific content. The title should always clearly express the scenario's basic idea. Cursory readers of the scenarios will often only really notice or memorize the titles. There were good proposals by the group. However, as the final shape of the narratives materialized much later, the titles where chosen by the authors. Initially, we have experimented with various allusions to – what the French would call – "la culture générale" (e.g. Shakespearean plays) but decided to stick to titles that are comprehensible and meaningful across cultures.

Scenario Writing – The Post-Workshop Phase

All three workshops provided an invaluable resource of ideas and thoughts about the future of peace operations that contributed to the last step – the elaboration of the final scenarios. This scenario writing and a visualization in the form of telling illustrations help to process the results in a suitable way for further dialogue with a broader audience of practitioners, policy-makers and scholars alike. So we distinguish between the proper scenarios, which are the combinations of twelve individual projections of the key factors, and the narratives which illustrate the scenarios and add storylines to them.

The challenge was to process the inputs of the previous workshops and come up with strong narratives based on the general premises of the scenario, i.e. the projections of all the key factors. The basic ideas were all laid out and the backcasting exercise was a very useful collection of thoughts. However, it was not possible to mold them into coherent narratives directly. Some "invented events" made more sense in combination with others; other results from the backcasting

[10] In general, the methodology of roadmapping is used to illustrate a future development path and to support strategic planning. We did not chart the map from the present to the future, i.e. a forecasting, but rather did it the other way around from the future state back to the present. Roadmaps are usually based on different projection methods (scenario planning, trend extrapolation or backcasting). In "Peace Operations 2025," the roadmapping was used as a backcasting of the raw scenarios, in order to check the consistency of each scenario and for the generation of further ideas and content for the final narratives.

were not on a linear and logical path. Although the four scenarios all had very different prerequisites, for our purposes they essentially evolve around conflicts and of how the international community responds to them. Since peace operations are only a small part of general foreign policy matters, the crises we wanted to be part of the narratives had to be embedded in a broader context and mood without being repetitive against the background of all four scenarios. So while writing, the storylines had to be revised continuously and the original path of proceeding chronologically soon gave way to a more thematically oriented approach.

Moreover, we thought that a common element appearing at the beginning of all scenarios would be a good way of setting the general tone before the narratives unfold in further detail. Therefore, the imaginary character of Grace Kimunya was introduced, a young Kenyan who started her international service career in the field of peace operations in 2012. At the dawn of the year 2025, she looks back to the beginning of her career and what had been achieved up until now. This element is meant to set the general mood, also in conjunction with the illustrations of each scenario, which pick up certain elements and provide quick visual access to the more detailed elaborations.

Brief Summaries of the ZIF Scenarios[11]

Erratic Progress

In this scenario, things are kind of so-so – in a familiar way. The stuttering engine of multilateralism is limping along through under-resourced initiatives towards poorly defined or unrealistic goals. New and powerful actors that could make a difference are still trying to find their place in the international system and have not yet translated their economic clout into decisive political action. A partial consensus on key norms and values is reflected in informal and minilateralist "club governance" structures. However, the UN remains the centerpiece of multilateralism. Peace operations are muddling through with occasional successes and frequent setbacks. After various shifts in strategy have failed to produce better results, there is not much appetite for investing in the stabilization of failed states. Uneven economic growth has done nothing to reduce global income inequalities. This continues to fuel conflict while keeping the resources for international crisis

[11] These summaries are quoted from the ZIF publication "Peace Operations 2025" (Von Gienanth & Hansen & Köppe, 2012, 15-16).

management efforts scarce. The overall outlook is not hopeless but somewhat messy.

National Interests

As the global economy is hard hit by the worst recession since the 1930s, an international climate of growing isolationism and unilateralism leads to the end of multilateral peace operations as we know them. Objectively, there is a strong demand for peace operations as many of the more fragile states relapse into violent state failure. Conflicts are also fanned by fierce competition for natural resources and the unchecked spread of organized crime – which in some cases has resulted in state capture by criminal networks. However, nations focus on economic survival and internal security at the expense of their international footprint. In addition, the rising powers fail to rally around shared values and agreed goals. A permanently blocked Security Council is yet another symptom of a growing divergence on basic norms and values and the prevalence of national interests. As a consequence, few operations are deployed and blue helmets are largely a phenomenon of the past. Where states do intervene in a crisis, ad-hoc and narrow coalitions of the willing prevail – usually not deploying their own boots but those of private security companies.

Regional Diversity

Regional organizations are clearly in charge – including of peace operations. Transnational challenges – from climate change to resource scarcity, organized crime, state fragility and violent conflicts – are increasing the need for functioning global governance structures. However, after the "rise of the rest" and the "decline of the West," existing multilateral structures failed to accommodate the new powers who in turn found ways to accommodate themselves – largely through a network of regional organizations. As a consequence, the UN has lost its role as the major multilateral player in this area and the Security Council is no longer the primary legitimizing body for such operations. While the regionalization of peace operations could have led to "regional solutions for regional problems," key actors alternate between cooperation, competition or mere co-existence without much consideration for each other. For peace operations, this to and fro is frequently getting in the way of sustainable successes. Fragile states remain a major challenge but state fragility fatigue limits reliable support and stabilization initiatives.

Global Cooperation

The golden age of global cooperation has finally arrived and the framework for peace operations is one of well-endowed multilateralism. These developments are underpinned by a broad global economic boom benefiting established and rising powers and even the least developed nations. With new actors on the stage, multilaterals have realized reform plans in order to better reflect the new realities. International and regional organizations across the board not only enjoy an adequate financial base but are also backed by a broad consensus on values and norms developed under the growing influence of advocacy groups, civil society organizations, mega-foundations, and social media. Peace operations have changed considerably but the main driver of change is innovation rather than resignation. As the number of conflicts and fragile states decrease, so too does the demand for peace operations. While fewer peace operations are deployed, those that are in the field are better resourced, benefit from advanced technology and, crucially, take a longer perspective on conflict resolution.

Some Lessons and Insights

Including preliminary thoughts and preparations, the entire process ran for the course of almost two years. Naturally, this involved continuous learning for both partners and all relevant steps in the process were thoroughly coordinated. Some of these experiences are shared below.

- The very first debate we had between Z_punkt and ZIF concerned the question of the project's time frame. Bearing in mind that we primarily aimed at a process and product for the peace operations community, we felt that 2100 or 2050 would be too far away and not yield the necessary insights for today's work. The year 2025 may not seem very ambitious. However, it was still 15 years ahead by the time we started with this project and looking back 15 years made clear that quite a lot had happened during this period and will happen in the future.

- Participants cherished the opportunity to discuss ideas in a rather uncommon format. We constantly asked the group to push the boundaries and invited the participants to take a look into the future detached from thinking in today's categories or merely extrapolating current trends, which remained a challenge. The difference between probability and plausibility was reiterated permanently. In the end, we managed to find middle ground and had a reasonable mix of trend-inspired thinking and "wilder" ideas. It is also good to be bold about some issues. The entire process is supposed to be somehow out-of-the-box, so there is no need for always looking for the least common denominator.

- Strong group cohesion and a concentrated way of working was facilitated by choosing slightly remote venues for our sessions on the outskirts of Berlin, Addis Ababa, and New York where the workshops took place. The atmosphere resembled that of a retreat and was very fruitful, not least because the informal talks after the official end of the working days proved to be a good occasion for rethinking the workshop's results and were therefore a very valuable source of additional contributions.

- Most foresight projects include people who are not used to the approach and methodology. We found that "icebreaker exercises" to start off each workshop were a good way to get participants into thinking about the future and stimulate a creative mood. For instance, at the beginning of the first workshop we asked them a series of question about future developments, e.g. "Will the US dollar still be the world's main reserve currency by 2025?", "When will we have the first hotel on the moon?", "Will green energy sources have surpassed fossil fuels by 2025?" or "When will a team of robots win the soccer world championship?" Consciously not posing questions from the realm of peace operations, we wanted to avoid extensive discussions at the beginning of the workshop, but rather to redirect the thoughts of the participants from the present to the future. Other "icebreakers" we used, were a game we called "Who wants to be a futurist?" that was inspired from the TV show "Who wants to be a millionaire?", or a short lecture on "Old Futures" that showed historical visions about the future.

- This scenario process was a very rewarding exercise with different stages and their benefits. The interactive workshop series with an outstanding group as a process in its own right was a success in itself, allowing participants to engage in a format of discussion they normally do not have. Gathering all the information and digging deeper into some of the current debates and making all the necessary connections and linkages amongst the driving forces of the field proved to be quite enlightening. The final product in form of the publication cannot cover the entire depth of the activities. However, it provides us with a vehicle to convey the main ideas. It should also inspire others to work with it, and to test some of their assumptions and planning procedures against these scenarios. In the end, it is meant to be a tool for the different needs of different audiences and we encourage people to use and adapt it for their purposes.

- The applied methods are now part of ZIF's own toolbox and provided new ideas and impulses for formats that are deliberately designed to be more than a regular panel discussion or roundtable.

- The project helped to identify some crucial issues worth exploring further and investing resources in for further content-related work.

- Although scenario processes are adaptable and scalable to the needs of the "customer" and can surely be done on a smaller scale and shorter period of time, it is important to stress the iterative character and importance of the intellectual work that was done in-between workshops. Time is one of the crucial resources in such an endeavor; time to reflect but also time to process all the inputs and necessary intermediate steps.

The book "Peace Operations 2025" was published in fall 2012, roughly four months after the last workshop. Since then it has been used for various other events: e.g. expert workshops to discuss the scenarios' operational consequences for today's work, or public book launches with discussions at various hubs of the peace operations community (inter alia in New York at the UN together with Mr. Hervé Ladsous, the UN Under-Secretary-General for the Department of Peacekeeping Operations (DPKO); at EU headquarters in Brussels, or at OSCE headquarters in Vienna). It will hopefully continue to inspire the thinking of colleagues and inform ongoing work on reforming global crisis management.

References

BIPE Conseil & Copenhagen Institute for Futures Studies (1992). *Wild Cards. A Multinational Perspective*. Palo Alto: Institute for the Future.

Fink, A. & Siebe, A. (2006): *Handbuch Zukunftsmanagement. Werkzeuge der strategischen Planung und Früherkennung*. Frankfurt/New York: Campus Verlag.

Major, C., Pietz, T., Schöndorf, E. & Hummel, W. (2013). *Toolbox Crisis Management. From Civilian Crisis Prevention to Peacebuilding: Principles, Actors, Instruments* (3rd edition). Berlin: German Institute for International and Security Affairs. Available at: http://www.zif-berlin.org/fileadmin/uploads/analyse/dokumente/veroeffentlichungen/ZIF_SWP_Toolbox _CrisisManagement.pdf.

Schwartz, P. (1991). *The Art of the Long View: Planning for the Future in an Uncertain World.* New York: Doubleday.

Steinmüller, A. & Steinmüller, K. (2004). *Wild Cards. Wenn das Unwahrscheinliche eintritt.* Hamburg: Murmann Verlag.

Van der Heijden, K. (1996*). Scenarios. The Art of Strategic Conversation.* Chichester: Wiley.

Von Gienanth, T., Hansen, W. & Köppe, S. (2012). *Peace Operations 2025.* Berlin: Center for International Peace Operations (ZIF). Available at: http://tinyurl.com/peace-operations-2025.

Wilms, F. (Ed.) (2006). *Szenariotechnik. Vom Umgang mit der Zukunft.* Bern: Haupt Verlag.

Anticipating New Security Threats: The FESTOS Project

Yair Sharan

Abstract

In this paper we briefly present some results of the Foresight study carried out within the FESTOS project within the framework of the EU security program between 2009-2012. In this research study, signals of change in the emerging space of technology were identified in terms of future technologies. These were further assessed in order to anticipate potential security threats which may evolve from several selected technologies. Threats were prioritized according to two different criteria developed in this project. Results are shown and later used as an input for scenario building presented further in this book.

Introduction

Technology is developing fast and giving rise to more and more emerging technologies, which may have future significant impacts on our society and our security. We are living in an era of increasing security concerns. The terror events of recent years in Europe, as well as in other parts of the world, have clearly demonstrated that terror groups are intent on threatening our society and causing great numbers of casualties. These events have also proved that such non-state actors are able to control complicated operations using innovative technological solutions in order to realize their plans. There is no doubt that such groups will continue to strive to acquire new technological capabilities and use them for their purposes. The terrorist of the future will be more "technological" and exposed to the latest scientific developments. Given this worrying potential, societies should be prepared in advance to cope with emerging threats. We follow in the steps of Winston Churchill, who lamented what he called the "confirmed unteachability of mankind". By that he meant the unfortunate reality in which decision makers and societies often slumber until danger takes them by surprise and finds them in a position in which it is almost impossible to make wise decisions. The legacy he wanted to bequeath was one of foresight and clear thinking about the future so as to avert emergencies ahead of time. With this in mind there is a need to try and foresee the development of future threats in order to be better prepared when they appear or, if possible, to diminish them. The space of S&T is full of weak signals for technological achievements and breakthroughs that may result in future

R. Peperhove et al. (Eds.), *Envisioning Uncertain Futures*, Zukunft und Forschung 6, https://doi.org/10.1007/978-3-658-25074-4_11

dangers and risks to society. Identifying these developments was an important objective of the foresight activity of the EU FESTOS research project. A final policy goal of this project was to assess preventive measures that might limit the proliferation of such valuable knowledge to malicious end users, thus increasing long-term security preparations in Europe.

The FESTOS Project

Recognizing the potential of future technologies to give rise to new threats the FESTOS project was launched under the research framework of the EU in their security program. FESTOS -Foresight of Evolving Security Threats Posed by Emerging Technologies- identified and assessed evolving threats with the aim to improve the knowledge of novel threats thus helping decision makers to assess alternatives for prevention and be more prepared for future security challenges. FESTOS was conducted by a consortium of five research centers from the EU and Israel, coordinated by the undersigned with the participation of leading researchers from partner institutes (Aufermann & Hauptman, 2012).

The goal of FESTOS has been thus to identify and assess evolving security threats posed by abuse or inadequate use of emerging technologies and new S&T knowledge, and to propose means to reduce their likelihood. Almost all such knowledge can be abused or cause damage through inadequate use. In a free society this should not hinder free generation and exchange of knowledge. As the pace of science-based development accelerates, there is a pressing need for continual scanning of the unfolding technology landscape for potential security threats.

Looking ahead to 2030, the foresight study realized in FESTOS scanned the technology horizon and sought out security threats that could stem from future technologies. Robotics, Information Technologies, New Materials, Nanotechnologies and Biotechnologies were some of the fields scanned in the project. (Hauptman & Sharan, 2013) The technologies identified and assessed were viewed as signals of change that would be able to impact the security environment. These were then evaluated and prioritized using several methods. FESTOS further stimulated "out of the box" anticipatory thinking and used the results achieved from the assessment and prioritization process to construct threat scenarios by analyzing the impact of the identified threats using the background of envisioned “security climates” (societal context of security issues). (See the paper of Roman Peperhove later in this book) An adequate mix of Foresight methods were employed. These include; horizon scanning, wild cards and weak signals analysis, expert surveys, STEEPV analysis, brainstorming, a "futures wheel", interactive scenario building and interviews. Key European stakeholders were addressed in the various project's phases.

Technology Signals of Change

The first step in the FESTOS project was to identify those future technologies which may, with relatively high likelihood signal the emergence of new security challenges. These signals will later inspire the scenario building to demonstrate the relevant anticipated developments.

Scanning the technology horizon yielded tens of potential technologies, which were further evaluated and filtered to create a list of 33 technologies which were prioritized according to various categories. The chosen emerging technologies originate from the six main fields studied in the project. These include: Information & Communications, Nanotechnologies, Robotics, Materials, Biotechnologies and Converging Technologies. In the following we detail this list including a very short description of the technology. (For more information see FESTOS D2.3; Hauptman & Sharan 2013).

A. Field 1-Information & Communication Technologies

1. Internet of Things (IoT), Ambient Intelligence (AmI), and Ubiquitous Computing – A network of everyday objects (food items, home appliances, clothing, etc.), as well as various sensors, addressable and controllable via the Internet.
2. Radio-frequency identification (RFID) and "RFID-dust".
3. Smart mobile telephone technologies mash-ups – New cellphones are equipped with video cameras, GPS, Internet connectivity, and more. As these capabilities are "mashed up" including "Augmented Reality" (AR) features, they turn the cellphone into an extremely versatile communications and surveillance device.
4. Cloud Computing – The provision of dynamically scalable and often virtualized resources as a service over the Internet.

5. Ultra-dense Data Storage.
6. Advanced Artificial Intelligence.

B. Field 2-Nanotechnology

1. Molecular Manufacturing – Assembling products "bottom up", molecule by molecule.
2. Self-replicating nanoassemblers – Uncontrolled "runaway replication" has been described in fictional/speculative scenarios of futuristic nanotechnology.
3. Medical Nanorobots – Could be one of the next steps in medical diagnostics and treatment.
4. Tailored nanoparticles – Designed for use in commercial products, can be hazardous to health.
5. Energetic nanomaterials – Enable powerful propellants and explosives.
6. Molecular sensors (sensors with molecular precision) – Will be able to detect where a person has been by sampling environmental clues. Advanced nanodiagnostics could make people "molecularly naked".

C. Field 3-Robotics

1. AI-based Robot-Human Interaction and Co-existence – "Social robots" with AI, with which people have emotional and even intimate interactions.
2. Autonomous & semi-autonomous mini robots: Toys and amateur objects.
3. Robotic artificial limbs.
4. Ethical Control of Robots – Ethical control becomes a new field in computer science. The application of autonomous systems in civilian environments will lead to the use of such ethical control systems.
5. Swarm Robotics – Coordination of large numbers of robots, inspired mainly by natural swarms. Based on the EU project I-SWARM, tiny (about 4 millimeter sized) robots could be mass-produced in swarms and programmed for a variety of applications.

D. Field 4-Biotechnology

1. Synthetic Biology – "programming living organisms like programming a computer".
2. DNA-protein interaction – One of possible ways to control DNA expression.
3. New gene transfer technologies – New devices/methods for transferring genes from one living organism to another.
4. Induced Pluripotent Stem Cells (iPS cells) – Turning ordinary cells into iPS cells, functionally equivalent to embryonic stem cells.
5. Bio-mimicking for fluids mixing on extremely small scales – Speeding up biomedical reactions by filling reservoirs with tiny beating rods that mimic cilia. Perhaps useful for preparation of toxic substances that need very small scale mixing and are harmful in micro quantities.
6. Multiplex Automated Genome Engineering (MAGE) – Quick creation of billions of unique gene strains for large-scale programming and rapid evolution of cells. Might be more useful than building genomes from scratch.

E. Field 5-New Materials

1. Metamaterials with a negative light refraction index – Could enable invisibility "cloaking", and creation of 'super-lenses‘.
2. Water catalyzing explosive reactions – In hot and dense environments water plays an unexpected role in catalyzing complex explosive reactions.
3. Programmable matter – Materials programmed to self-assemble, alter their shape and properties to perform a desired function, and then disassemble.
4. Personal rapid prototyping and 3-D printing machines – 3-D inexpensive printers able to self-copy and to use a variety of materials in order to print desirable systems.
5. Future fuels, processes and structural materials for nuclear technologies – Enable to determine the mechanisms of irradiation-induced swelling, predict the behavior of fuel elements in reactor cores, etc.

6. Crystalline polymers, polymer blends, multilayer assemblies – e.g. for gas separation, atmosphere control, reduction of gas permeability...

F. Field 6-Converging Technologies

1. Nanotechnology-enabled brain implant – "By 2035, an implantable information chip could be developed and wired directly to the user's brain. Information and entertainment choices would be accessible through cognition and might include synthetic sensory perception beamed directly to the user's senses".
2. Brain-to-brain communication ("Radiotelepathy") – Enabled by direct conversion of neural signals into radio signals and vice versa.
3. Cyborg Insects – Insects controlled through implanted electrical stimulators.
4. Brain-Computer Interface; "Mind Reading" commercial gadgets – Toy manufacturers plan to sell a game which involves players levitating a ball "using thought alone". Toyota has developed a wheelchair steered by brain waves.
5. Human enhancement/augmentation based on NBIC convergence – Unprecedented enhancement of human performance: alteration and augmentation of physical and mental abilities. Some envision that human and machine intelligence will converge over the coming century (the Cyborg vision).

Categorizing signals of change

Once the more significant technologies were chosen as a result of horizon scanning, a prioritization process was conducted using two main criteria, namely, the level of threat potential anticipated for each technology and the intensity of threat impact if realized. To derive these criteria for each technology, expert's opinions were elicited through an international online survey involving around 300 experts from various fields. Expert's estimates were questioned on the following three issues:

- The severity of the potential security threat posed by each technology (scale 1 to 5: 1=very low severity, 5=very high severity).

- The level of ease of malicious use of each technology (scale 1 to 5: 1=not easy at all, 5=very easy).

- Which societal spheres (people, infrastructures, economy, environment, political systems and values) would be mostly affected by security threats posed by each technology?

We define the potential of technology abuse (C) as the product of the ease of malicious use (A) with the severity of this threat once realized (B). The results regarding these criteria are presented in Table 1 for the ten technologies that are assessed as having a high potential for intended abuse. This enables us to prioritize the signals of change according to the first criteria, the potential of technology abuse.

Table 1: Severity of Threats, Ease of Malicious Use and Potential of Abuse (Top 10 Ranking)

Technology	*A: How easy will it be to use this technology for malicious purposes?*	*B: How severe is the security threat posed by this technology?*	*C: Potential of abuse (product of A and B)*
1. Smart mobile mash-ups	3.69	3.49	12.88
2. Internet of Things (IoT)	3.61	3.49	12.60
3. Cloud computing	3.29	3.53	11.61
4. Gene transfer	3.52	3.22	11.33
5. Advanced AI	3.21	3.43	11.01
6. Synthetic biology	3.16	3.40	10.74
7. Cyborg insects	3.33	3.08	10.26
8. Energetic nanomaterials	3.00	3.33	9.99
9. RFID	3.14	3.03	9.51
10. Mini-robots	3.36	2.83	9.51

Technologies stemming from ICT, Biotechnology and Robotics lead this list. The top 10 technologies in Table 1 have a relatively high potential of abuse (C>9) as they exhibit a rather severe threat potential and could be relatively easily used for malicious purposes. One should however pay attention also to other technologies which are relatively easy to implement (A>2.5) such as 3-D printing, Swarm robotics and AI-based Robot-Human Interaction.

A second way to prioritize is the STEEPV method. According to Kaivo-oja & Rikkonen (2005), the application of a structured analysis known as a STEEPV analysis provides a useful framework to assist management in considering the factors that have impact on the decision-making landscape. The meaning of using a STEEPV set-up is to better categorize topics connected to the changes in a social, technological, economic, ecological, political, and value environment. For the purpose of FESTOS the STEEPV scheme has been modified and developed further, and adapted to the needs of the analysis required by the project, namely the assessment of potential threats. Experts were asked to assess the impact of the potential threats posed by different technologies (the signals of change) on the following societal spheres:

- Economy (economic growth, markets, fiscal policies, taxation, industries, banks);
- Environment (biodiversity, materials, resources, climate, pollution, wastes);
- Infrastructures (energy, airports, communications, etc.);
- People (individuals, groups, mass populations);
- Political systems (structures, activities, leadership, power relations, stakeholders, policies);
- Values.

The following explanation of "values" was adopted by FESTOS: Human values tell people what is good/bad, desirable/undesirable, etc. Values are changing over time. Threats posed by new technologies might lead to a change of values. For example, omnipresent video surveillance or the control of individual behavior using RFIDs might lead to changes of values with respect to the democratic nature of society. Another example for changing values might be a political decision to use or NOT to use a specific technology which enhances security but limits personal rights. Specific future technologies could challenge the perception of what is "positive" and "negative" in such technologies – and consequently may lead to drastic changes of value systems with respect to technology (an example could be “swarm robotics” and its surveillance and control capabilities).

The impact of a threat on different societal spheres is presented as the percentage of respondents who opted for each sphere. Due to multiple choices the sum of percentages across each technology can vary between 0 and 600. We define the "overall intensity of a threat" as the integrative sum of all impacts. The results for this criterion are presented in table 2 with the right column presenting the overall intensity. One can thus prioritize the considered signals of change according to the second criteria, that of the overall intensity of threat. In Table 2 we detail the level of foreseen impacts of expected threats on different spheres of society.

Evidently some technologies potentially threaten several societal spheres while others affect fewer spheres. Broadly speaking, most technologies pose a significant threat to people. ICTs could also threaten the economy and infrastructure, new materials affect mainly the environment and infrastructure, nanotechnologies and biotechnology threaten mainly the environment, and converging technologies can also threaten political systems and values.

Interesting to note is the high impact on values of society of technologies such as human enhancement and brain-to-brain communications (70% and above) and even the risk to political systems expected in some cases. The impacts of these two spheres add in some cases significantly to the overall threat intensity.

Table 2 Threat Impact on Societal Spheres and its Overall Intensity (source) (Top 15 R28anking, source FESTOS D3.3 Integrated Security Threats Report, July 2011)

	Technology	*Economy*	*Environ-ment*	*Infra-structures*	*People*	*Political systems*	*Values*	***Overall Intensity of Threat***
1.	**Advanced AI**	67%	38%	76%	82%	51%	31%	**345**
2.	**Human enhancement**	38%	6%	38%	94%	69%	81%	**326**
3.	**Swarm robotics**	67%	67%	78%	78%	11%	22%	**323**
4.	**Cyborg insects**	42%	67%	92%	92%	8%	17%	**318**
5.	**Internet of Things**	66%	22%	80%	93%	24%	29%	**314**
6.	**Water catalyzing explosive reactions**	42%	58%	92%	83%	33%	0%	**308**
7.	**Fuels & processes for nuclear technologies**	25%	83%	83%	92%	25%	0%	**308**
8.	**AI-based robot-human interaction**	41%	41%	59%	88%	35%	41%	**305**
9.	**Cloud computing**	90%	10%	65%	81%	32%	19%	**297**
10.	**Programmable matter**	45%	64%	73%	73%	18%	18%	**291**
11.	**Brain-to-brain communication**	40%	10%	10%	100%	60%	70%	**290**
12.	**Molecular manufacturing**	50%	88%	38%	75%	25%	13%	**289**
13.	**Self-replicating Nanoassemblers**	55%	82%	55%	73%	18%	0%	**283**
14.	**Energetic nanomaterials**	25%	58%	83%	92%	25%	0%	**283**
15.	**RFID**	54%	9%	63%	91%	23%	31%	**271**

To sum up in Table 3 we present the 10 most significant technologies in both criteria. Four technologies appear in both lists of which three come from ICT and one – Cyborg Insects- comes from converging technologies. Results thus show that ICT and Robotics are a major part of these lists in both criteria. This could be related to the fact that these technologies are estimated to be realized in the near future and are more familiar to many security experts. However other fields are represented and appear to be very significant. These include: Materials, Biotechnology, Nanotechnology and converging technologies. These results could signal future dangerous potential. It has to be underlined that the experts were rather careful in their evaluations of the potential of technologies for malicious use and also cautious with respect to the intensity of the potential threat. They did not use in their assessments the highest values offered by the questionnaire, but moved slightly higher than the central field. Such lack of extreme views gives reason to interpret the views of experts as realistic and seriously concerned. This also justifies the use of two criteria for prioritization thus diversifying the signals of change considered, which will further influence the security scenario built to demonstrate the challenges in front of us.

Table 3: Categorization of Ten Potentially Threatening Technologies

Priority	Potential of a technology for malicious use	Intensity of the potential threat posed by a technology
1.	Smart mobile telephone mash-ups	Advanced Artificial Intelligence
2.	Internet of Things (IoT)	Human enhancement
3.	Cloud Computing	Swarm robotics
4.	New gene transfer technologies	Cyborg insects
5.	Advanced artificial intelligence	Internet of Things (IoT)
6.	Synthetic biology	Water catalyzing explosive reactions
7.	Cyborg insects	Future fuels and materials for nuclear technologies
8.	Energetic nanomaterials	AI-based robot-human interaction
9.	Radio-frequency identification (RFID)	Cloud computing
10.	Autonomous & semi-autonomous mini robots	Programmable matter

Another factor that could play a role when assessing relevant anticipated threats and when building a scenario based on these threats, is the time period in which they will be effective. Experts were thus asked about the expected time of maturity of various technologies. According to the results achieved the technologies under consideration can be roughly divided into four groups according to their estimated (median) time of maturity (Sharan & Hauptman, 2010, 2013):

Table 4: Time Horizon for Materialization of Future Technologies

Short term (now – 2015):
RFID, smartphone technologies mash-ups, cloud computing, tailored nanoparticles and new gene transfer technologies.
Near Medium term (2016 – 2020):
Internet of things (IoT), ultra-dense data storage, advanced AI, autonomous mini robots, robotic artificial limbs, energetic nanomaterials, molecular nanosensors, 3-d printers, synthetic biology.
Far Medium term (2021 – 2025):
Crystalline polymers, ethical control of robots, cyborg insects, AI-based robot-human interaction, molecular manufacturing, DNA-protein interaction, Induced Pluripotent Stem Cells, Brain-Computer Interfaces ("Mind Reading" commercial gadgets).
Long term (2026 - 2035) and beyond
Self-replicating nanoassemblers, medical nanorobots, Nanotechnology-enabled brain implants, Human enhancement based on NBIC (Nano, Bio Information and Cognition) technologies convergence, Programmable matter, processes and materials for nuclear technologies, water catalyzing explosive reactions, Bio-mimicking for fluids mixing, metamaterials and "optical cloaking", swarm robotics.

It should be noted that in many cases the level of consensus amongst experts is not high. Naturally, for many new technologies the uncertainty regarding their time of maturity is expected and therefore significant disagreement between experts is not surprising. We can see that technologies included in table 3 are distributed amongst all periods. Those stemming from the ICT field are mostly short range while those stemming from converging technologies are mostly long range.

From signals to scenarios

As presented earlier the selected technologies with their threat indications are considered as "weak signals" or signals of change hinting at future security challenges. These might be in the center of security counteraction efforts in the future. Some of them may signal "wild cards": which are defined as surprising low-probability high-impact events (Petersen & Steinmüller, 2009). The signals identified served, thus, as an input to a narrative scenario process carried out in the project. This process is described in detail in two papers in this book. The first of Roman Peperhove detailing the various stages needed to construct these scenarios and the second of Karl-Heinz Steinmüller describing the resulting scenario. Four different narratives were written

1. "Cyborg-insects attack!": Swarms of cyborg-insects (insects with implanted electronics) attack people, animals and agriculture crops.
2. "The Genetic Blackmailers": The DNA of human individuals is misused for extortion.
3. "At the Flea Market": Everyday, intelligent nanotechnology-based products are programmed to “self-destruct” with a wireless signal.
4. "We'll change your mind...": A terrorist group uses a virus to change the behavior of a portion of the population for a certain period of time.

All these narratives make use of combinations of the anticipated potential threats originating from the technologies considered. The narratives demonstrate possible realizations of these threats and are intended to raise awareness amongst decision makers to future security challenges and help security policy makers in better planning for such happenings once they are realized.

Conclusion

In this paper we presented highlights from the EU FESTOS research project, which resulted in the development of narrative scenarios. These narratives demonstrate various anticipated security situations with which society might have to cope with in the future. Looking ahead to the year 2030 technology space was scanned to identify technological developments, which may give rise to new security threats. FESTOS has been a foresight study which has exposed policy makers to future security challenges, the whole way from signals to scenario, to encourage early awareness to possible risks and consider relevant prevention measures. The scenario tool applied in this project helped translate future potential situations into an operational picture, assisting in the search for necessary preparation policy measures.

References

Auffermann, B. & Hauptman, A. (2012). FESTOS – Foresight of Evolving Security Threats Posed by Emerging Technologies. *European Foresight Platform, brief No. 225*. Available at: http://www.foresight-platform.eu/wp-content/uploads/2012/10/EFP-Brief-No.-225-FESTOS.pdf.

Auffermann, B. & Luoto, L. (2011). *FESTOS – Emerging threats. Integrated Security Threats Report.*

Hauptman, A. & Sharan, Y. (2013). Foresight of evolving security threats posed by emerging technologies. *Foresight, 15* (5), 375–391.

Hauptman, A., Raban, Y. & Katz, O. & Sharan, Y. (2011). FESTOS D2.3, Horizon Scanning - Final report on potentially threatening technologies. Available at: http://www.sicherheitsforschung-europa.de/servlet/is/14805/FESTOS%20Final%20report%20on%20potentially%20threatening%20technologies.pdf?command=downloadContent&filename=FESTOS%20Final%20report%20on%20potentially%20threatening%20technologies.pdf.

Kaivo-oja, J. & Rikkonen, P. (2005). Key issues for successful scenario planning perspectives on sustainable use of natural resources in agricultural sector. In A. Jalkanen & P. Nygren (Eds.). *Sustainable use of renewable natural resources— from principles to practices.* Helsinki: University of Helsinki, Department of Forest Ecology.

Petersen, J. L. & Steinmüller, K. (2009). Wild Cards. In J. C. Glenn (Ed.). *Futures research methodology. Version 3.0.* Washington, D.C.: The Millennium Project (CD-Rom).

Sharan, Y. & Hauptman, A. (2010). *Emerging Technologies and Evolving Security Threats.* In FFRC Security Conference, Security in Futures – Security in Change. International Conference in Turku/Finland, 3-4 June, 2010.

The Development of FESTOS Scenarios

Roman Peperhove

Abstract

In this paper I describe the process of developing scenarios in the research project FESTOS; which was funded within the framework of the EU security program between 2009 - 2012. Its focus was on an intended misuse of future technologies by terrorists and organized crime for attacks or felonies. The article describes the step by step procedure of the development process. The narratives include individual, societal, political and economic impacts. The article shows the approach, the completion and the validation of narrative scenarios and ends with a suggestion of how scenarios might be useful to identify indicators, as a monitoring instrument to assess the potential for similar events.

Introduction

As part of a research project, funded by the European Union as part of the Seventh Framework Programme (FP7), the project FESTOS scenarios was used as the means of choice to depict events with low likelihood but high impact. The acronym FESTOS denotes Foresight of Evolving Security Threats Posed by Emerging Technologies and focused on the potential misuse of upcoming technologies by terrorists and organized crime. Based on a list of technologies, which may be available within the next 20 years, narrative scenarios should be developed to give vivid descriptions of possible but unlikely events of an intended misuse and the impact it might cause in a future society.[1] Most of the technologies which were used in terrorist attacks so far can be described as low-tech. About 84 % of all attacks between 1970 – 2014 were carried out with simple weapons as firearms or explosives (GDT 2015). However there are a number of occasions and contexts in which terrorists or criminals have used high-tech already. The sarin attacks by Aum Shinrikyo are just one example (Dolnik 2009, Cragin et al., 2007) [2]. Another is the increasing use of high-end technologies by criminals inter alia in

[1] For more information on the project see Sharan, the FESTOS project in this volume.

[2] Aum Shinrikyo released Sarin nerve gas in the Tokyo subway system in March 1995, killing 12 people and injuring more than one thousand. The sect still exists but split into two groups under the name “Hikari no Wa” and “Aleph”.

R. Peperhove et al. (Eds.), *Envisioning Uncertain Futures*, Zukunft und Forschung 6, https://doi.org/10.1007/978-3-658-25074-4_12

the context of IT (Europol 2007) which is acknowledged by the European Union (Buono 2012).

It is very probable that the amount of high technology which people are going to use will increase in coming years. Technologies will become more sophisticated and easy to implement in different environments (e.g. home, work, public transport) as well as intertwined. Technologies, which were high tech a few years ago, are now implemented in everyday life (e.g. Global Positioning System – GPS). It is foreseeable that revolutionary technologies such as the 3-D Printer will be used broadly soon. As the importance of technology increases so does the potential impact it has on daily life if it fails.

In this article, the basic assumptions for the development of FESTOS scenarios are described as well as the reasoning behind the use of narrative scenarios. In the second part, the development of scenarios will be described including the preparation of a scenario workshop, its implementation and the results. The third and final chapter will consist of actual writing processes and finalization, using participants' feedback in an interactive feedback loop.

Basic challenges

As Kahn stated in the 1960's, scenarios "are hypothetical sequences of events constructed for the purpose of focusing attention on causal processes and decision points" (Kahn & Wiener 1967,p 6). Even though several descriptions of scenarios were produced to the present, it might be still the most precise one. This is true for near-term as well as long-term scenarios. Porters sketched it as "an internally consistent view of what the future might turn out to be - not a forecast, but one possible future outcome" (Porter, 1985). The scenarios which were developed in FESTOS were placed in a future 20 years from now and describe an intended misuse of then day-to-day technologies.

The FESTOS project aimed at the development of scenarios for two aspects, mainly: 1) to increase the awareness of the role of technology today and much more in the future in the context of an intended misuse, and 2) the severity of an intended misuse of technology; the impact people may face.

The project team concluded that it needs a specific kind of scenario to achieve both goals; to show experts and laymen alike the impact of a possible misuse and inspire a thought process on follow-up questions regarding development and the proliferation of potentially sensitive information on emerging technologies. The method of choice was *narrative scenarios* (e.g. Gaßner & Steinmüller, 2006, 2004; Burnam-Fink 2015).[3] Narrative scenarios were the best tool for several reasons and to fulfil the aforementioned goals of scenarios in FESTOS. Narrative scenarios enable immersion into the world of the described character and their environment. This allows us to "see" the event and the following impact from their perspective. Besides, experts are able to reassess existing security guidelines regarding the status of prevention of such events or reducing potential impacts and cascade effects. Scenarios provide a mixture of a detailed display of personal action, political and technical implications, as well as the challenges a future society might face if central technologies do not function properly any more.

The development of such scenarios in the project bore three practical challenges. Firstly, a misuse of a *future* technology takes place, in the future of course. The first challenge was to think about a framework in which the events should be placed. Since the scope of the project related to countries in the European Union, it was necessary to sketch out future European countries as a background. The second challenge was the interrelation between future technologies and a future society. There will probably not be single future technologies but combinations of technologies, new applications and converging technologies. A third challenge addressed the goal of FESTOS. One of the main objectives of the project was to raise awareness for potential technology misuse amongst technological experts, developers, security experts and administration alike. For this reason it was necessary to find a way in which it would be possible to make people aware of the potential threat of technology misuse.

The perception of an event or development as a risk is rather complex and difficult to generalize (e.g. Sjöberg et al., 2004; Slovic 2000; Adams 1995; Lupton 1999). However, it became clear, that risk assessment is influenced by a great number of aspects, like socio-cultural influences (e.g. Jacobs & Worthley, 1999; Douglas & Wildavsky; Beeman 2004; Nisbett 2004; Riley 1998) or cognitive biases (e.g. Heuer 1999)

The Background. When it comes to the perception of risks as well as to the reaction to incidents, a number of aspects might influence the result (biases etc.). Within the project team the concepts of *security climates* and *security*

[3] Please see also *Narrative Scenarios as an Analytical Instrument* by Karlheinz Steinmüller in this volume.

contexts were developed. In opposition to the weather, *climate* describes a long-term status and rather slow changes. Climates differ from country to country, from region to region. In context of scenarios it is how a society might perceive a situation based on historic experiences, cultural beliefs, the size of the country, the political situation, public opinion, an economic context and much more, the attitude toward risks differ significantly. That is why the project team sketched a number of characteristics for each security climate and background society to broaden perspective and enable a detailed impact analysis based on different characteristics. The *Security Context* on the other hand describe actors and drivers which influence the perception of a threat within a special context. Based on the concept of securitization (Buzan et al. 1998), it is not the existential risk alone, which defines the rules for action (e.g. "war" on terrorism), but the description of potential threats as well.

Future technologies. The first tasks of the FESTOS project were an international technology horizon scanning process and a Delphi survey which followed. The result of these two tasks was a list of 35 technologies, which were assessed by international technology and security experts regarding the time of their maturity and the potential of misuse (e.g. easiness of misuse, severity of impact). This list was the starting point for the development of wild cards (Steinmüller & Steinmüller 2004) during a scenario workshop Followed by a presentation of the results from the Delphi survey, the participants developed Wild Cards and potential attacks in a brainstorming session. The process was distilled as four wild cards were chosen, which became the nucleus of later scenarios.

The Scenarios

Narrative scenarios. Often, possible future developments are pictured as a funnel. It describes possible future developments, trends and settings in terms of a point on an imaginary real-time axis. Typically, scenarios show the best and worst case developments and explore trends ("business as usual"). In FESTOS however, the scenarios aimed at describing events with low likelihood and a high impact. These scenarios display potential situations after the misuse of future technologies – be it by a known perpetrator or with only vague suggestions.

By focusing on Wild Cards, the project team intended to surprise recipients and trigger an essential reflection on technology and its intended misuse in the future. This way, the scenarios have some similarities with counter-intuitive scenarios (Booth et al., 2009). The events are highly unlikely and difficult to anticipate and can be labelled as wild card scenarios[4]. Wild cards have the potential to influence the expected development significantly and suddenly – this is exactly what happens in the FESTOS scenarios.

Another characteristic is the style of the scenarios. They are narratives. At first glance, narrative scenarios appear to be thrilling stories, this is an intended effect. The effectiveness of a narrative scenario is based on this fact (Gaßner & Steinmüller, 2006, 2004; Burnam-Fink 2015). When inspected more closely, its usefulness for security issues becomes clear. The scenarios describe impact in a very sophisticated way and with minor details that are invented in the "stories". This way, scenarios stimulate the imagination and fantasy of a reader and encourage the reader to think alongside the plot. This makes it much easier to think about additional aspects (e.g. side and cascade effects, countermeasures) of the described situation intuitively. Readers assess the story with regard to stringency and potential areas of improvement. Professional and individual experiences serve as tools. The threat assessment, which is serious analytical work, becomes an entertaining task and produces new insights and results. The feedback we gathered from experts and readers confirmed that scenarios worked as they were intended to.

These effects do not only help to improve scenarios, but help to develop a methodology for identifying preconditions and indicators for an early warning system.

Methodological structure

The methodological approach which led to the final FESTOS scenarios was divided into seven consecutive steps (see Figure 1).

[4] Please see also *Anticipating New Security Threats: The FESTOS Project* by Yair Sharan in this volume.

Figure 1: Steps Towards Final FESTOS Scenarios

Figure 1 shows the schematic steps of the scenario development process including the preconditions (horizon scanning, threat assessment).

The **first** step was the identification of potential technological threats. Several single tasks were conducted to gain a comprehensive picture (e.g. horizon scanning, expert surveys, expert interviews). All information was edited and displayed in a number of detailed analyses (e.g. year of full development, ease-of-use, etc.). In a **second** step, the list of technologies was analyzed and assessed with regard to the threat potential of individual technologies. Their possible impact was evaluated, in the event of misuse. The **third** step consisted of the mentioned development of Security climates. This step led to the preparation of four different *security climates* and background scenario societies for the scenario workshop. These background scenarios emphasize different societal aspects and characteristics that help to differentiate expected impacts. The **fourth** step of the scenario development process was a two-day workshop in Berlin, Germany, with some 30 experts in technology, security and administration. It aimed at elaborating on the impact of technology misuse by terrorists or criminals in a future society. The **fifth** step involved writing scenario drafts based on the results of the workshop in the form of narratives. Each narrative was 4-5 pages long. The **sixth** step was to send these drafts to some 60 experts on security, technology and administration. Their feedback, reactions, ideas and comments were collected, analyzed and edited. The final and **seventh** step consisted of final adjustments to the scenarios. Feedback and suggestions were incorporated where possible and useful. The final narrative scenarios, as presented in this report, are results of these seven steps and are shaped by all of the experts and participants involved.

Scenario workshop

The heart of the scenario development process was the two-day workshop in Berlin in the summer of 2010. Experts from several technological fields, security experts and researchers as well as experts from administration, attended the workshop and collaborated closely with one another. The workshop lasted two days, as former experiences with such workshops suggested that on a second (or third) day, participants are more familiar with the subject as well as with other participants, making it easier for some people to contribute and discuss questions more openly.

All participants were familiar with the FESTOS project, its aim and scope as well as with the role of scenarios in it. Based on this input each participant was asked for a wild card - in terms of an intended technology misuse by terrorists or criminals - in a brainstorming session. Derived from the results a number of wild cards were combined, which were then used as the nucleus of the later scenarios.

The wild cards were connected to one of the background societies. Together both parts formed the framework in which the scenarios should be elaborated upon and play out. The intention was that the wild cards were developed without knowing background scenarios, since it was the aim of scenarios to display rare events which could theoretically happen everywhere – no matter what the underlying characteristics were. The basic assumption was that in 20 years most technologies will be available in all European countries and not only in some. However, the political agenda as well as size of the country and the degree of technologization are influential factors. It seems to be more reasonable that a country for example boosts a "green" technology if there is a common understanding that *green* is better and other countries does not. The project teams approach was a scenario development that triggers imagination and creativity by providing background societies (varying for example regarding political system, size, wealth, population density). A suppression of potential impacts through a too narrow framework had to be avoided. That is why wild cards and background societies were tied together randomly.

The process of scenario development was based on three concepts: 1) the world café method, 2) the idea of multi-level impact assessment, and 3) the assessment of potential impact within different socio-economic dimensions.

The **world café method**, within a project named the "Security Café" method, is based on a simple idea but works very well (Brown & Isaacs, 2005). The basic idea is simple: swhen people sit in a café and discuss something and want to explain something to the other(s) they may lack of paper and take the napkin or the cloth instead to draw ideas, pictures or notes on it. Therefore participants write on papery tablecloth. For the FESTOS workshop the idea was adjusted and combined with a Futures Wheel into the *Security Café*. The participants were divided into four groups (i.e. one for each of the four wild cards). In three rounds, participants described and discussed the possible impact of the wild card on future societies. This way, the method did not only support the brainstorming of new ideas and interrelations, but was also able to assess the impact in different societal and individual contexts.

The second idea of scenarios was a detailed analysis of the different levels of a potential impact. In this way, the assessment of a potential impact becomes more structured and the relationships between different impacts become more visible. Three levels distinguished impact: 1) direct impact, 2) indirect impact, and 3) cascade effects, starting with direct impacts (inner circle) and ending with cascade effects. Although it is not always possible to differentiate between the levels, the three-level-approach helps us to think about second level impacts that may be caused by the primal impact.

The third approach in this scenario development was the inclusion of several important socio-economic dimensions in the assessment. It seemed to be obvious to think about the impact of a technology misuse not only in terms of technology failure and technological implications, but also in relation to socio-political and socio-economic impacts on a medium and longer term. Close relations between technology, society, individuals, politics and economy makes it necessary to include them in impact assessment since they would be affected by an intended misuse of technologies (e.g. Silke 2003; Johnston & Nedelescu, 2006). Five dimensions were identified to cover the most important aspects of day-to-day life: *People/Society*, *Infrastructure*, *Political System*, *Economy*, *Environment* and *Value* based on STEEP analysis (e.g. Schwartz 1996) but enhanced by value, since values probably are influenced by an attack. These dimensions were intertwined with the level of impact and the wild card. This way a three dimensional framework for the development of scenarios appeared (Figure 2).

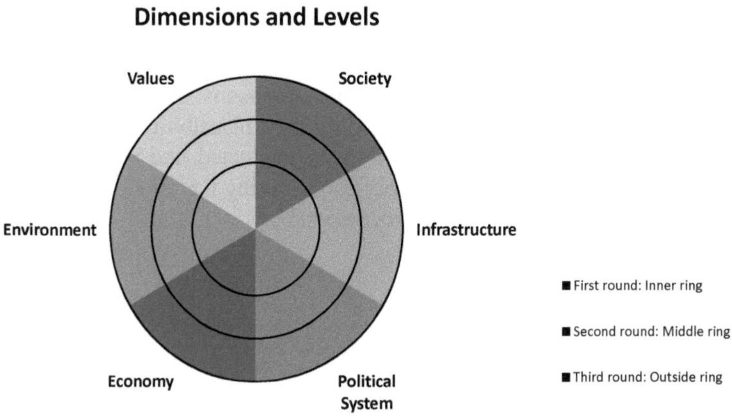

Figure 2: Security Café Approach for Scenario Development

Figure 2 displays the concepts and the methodological framework in which the scenarios were developed. Like the exemplary shown in the figure, tables were prepared in advance. Each wild card became the center of such a framework. The structure of impact analysis guaranteed the recognition of the several dimensions and the relationships between primal impacts and follow-up impacts.

Participants were divided into four groups to work on impact assessment in three rounds. In the first round, the direct Impact (e.g. mass panic) of the wild card was the focus of the group. Two more rounds followed: participants stood up, changed tables and participated in another wild card discussion. Round two identified indirect impacts (e.g. affect trust in the government) of the wild card. Round three identified cascade effects (e.g. impact on foreign investors). To facilitate the process and ensure it flowed smoothly, four members of the FESTOS team acted as table hosts. Their tasks were to supervise the table, motivate the participants and explain previous group input in the latter rounds.

There are at least three advantage of this procedure: Firstly, the input of the previous group was evaluated and validated promptly. Secondly, each group had to read former input and react to it. In this way the innovation process was constantly renewed. Thirdly, it was possible to involve more experts with different expertise in the development process.

After the first day, Karlheinz Steinmüller, author and futurist, sketched out the first outlines of scenarios. These outlines were presented on the second day to participants and were widely discussed. This chance to work on the scenarios on a second day was very useful for a number of reasons: 1) critical points were cleared up, 2) the stories were tested regarding their plausibility and consistency, 3) missing aspects were added 4) the stories were evaluated, and 5) the participants had the chance to speak about their experiences during the previous day and the concept of the scenario development process itself.

Finalization

Based on the results of the workshop as well as the input and comments of the participants on the second day, first drafts of the scenarios were written out. Due to this, the scenarios became much more detailed and vivid. The project team planned, right from the beginning, to have an additional feedback loop on the scenarios to improve them before they were finalized. Due to this the scenario drafts included a number of questions, which addressed the reader for additional ideas, comments and offered the chance for any criticism.

This feedback loop was conducted as an online survey for several reasons: 1.) The utilization of the input was easier, 2.) A greater community could participate and 3.) Otherwise, the drafts had been presented at workshops and discussed openly. Due to this, about 60 experts with different professional background were in involved in the feedback process.

Where possible and useful, additional input was implemented into the scenarios and critical parts were improved. The final scenarios, as they are presented in this volume, are the product of a close collaboration between the partners in the project team and Karlheinz Steinmüller, as well as the active participation of about 60 experts from security to technology.

Indicators as a strategic instrument for security improvement

For timely preparation, decision makers and analysts should try to anticipate the future a glimpse earlier than others. However, the future is of course unpredictable, but it may be possible to distinguish between different developments for orientation. To shorten the distance between desires and possibilities, indicators may be the means of choice. In economical and fiscal contexts, indicators are an appropriate tool to assess a development (e.g. stock dealing). Therefore, it seems to be possible to identify the most likely developments by developing indicators which display certain changes. These changes might hint at a certain future, which enables the analyst to adjust his strategy to be prepared for the things to come. In FESTOS, a similar approach was taken through the development of indicators. Indicators could be fruitful for security issues too. In security and intelligence "Nothing is more important in the world of intelligence than preventing surprise" (Hulnick 2005, 593). If indicators display changes in other environments and developments they could enable security experts not only to reduce the amount of surprises, but also to anticipate the future and initiate countermeasures to reduce the likelihood of their materialization.

Indicators and their strategic role

Indicators mark a change in a condition or development. They display that a certain point has been crossed. This is a rather general idea and not very useful without further definition. Indicators can be used for isolated issues like the increase or decrease of stock market value or for the changes in a whole market segment. It is enough to define the critical point to buy or sell a share for the former but it is much more complicated to develop indicators for the latter. To be able to develop indicators to assess the likelihood for a misuse of technology is challenging since a broad catalogue of aspects come into play: The perpetrator, the characteristics of the technology, its distribution and its security measures – to name only a selection. The project team tried to identify a number of aspects that may be potential indicators for an increasing likelihood of misuse. For this reason all results from the project, the scenario workshop, as well as the scenarios themselves were taken as sources. In an iterative process, three different contexts of indicators appeared: Technology, Background and Perpetrator.

Indicators in the **Technology** cluster are technological steps towards the complete development of a technology or parts of it. High-profile technological developments are usually completed either much sooner or much later than is initially expected. Besides, new technologies can appear as side effects of the main development. This is why indicators are broad enough to be used for all kinds of emerging technologies.

Table 1: Indicators for Technology

Condition	*Indicator of threat increase*
Competition	Monopoly-like
Security measures	Cracked
Countermeasure	Improper
Control/Development regulations	Decrease / lack of
Malfunction	Rare
Application	Remote controlled access possible
Dual-use	Possible/increase
All components developed	Technology developed

The second cluster of indicators represents the **Background** (i.e. social and economic conditions). These indicators describe attitudes towards technologies, their acceptance and use. The behaviour, (a lack of) the awareness of a potential misuse and (a lack of) security attitude increase the likelihood of surprise attacks or crime. Through awareness-raising and social, as well as technological assistance, the likelihood of crimes occurring is reduced (i.e. through alertness).

Table 2: Indicators for Background

Condition	*Indicator of threat increase*
Acceptance	Popularly accepted/increase
Price	Undercut the limit
Spreading	Non-regional
Handling	Easy
Availability	Obtainable everywhere/no regulations
Threat awareness	Decrease/non-existing
Interconnectivity	Connected with sensitive fields
Social cohesion	Decrease
Environment/lifestyle	Significant change of conditions

The third indicator group is the **Perpetrator** cluster. These indicators include early signs of actual misuse of a technology. Two stages can be distinguished here. It is possible to estimate (1) the technology-affinity of terrorist groups or criminals and the likelihood of use of new technologies and (2) the actual use or attempted application of an emerging technology.[5] A lot of technologies are on the shelf, but

[5] Dolnik 2007; Faria, JR 2006

only (surprisingly) few have been misused by terrorists or criminals so far and will be in the future.

Table3: Indicators for Perpetrator

Condition	*Indicator of threat increase*
Failed attacks	Occurred
Similar attacks	Occurred
Inspiring example	Appeared
Abuse	Information on ideas/plans
Perpetrator	Identified/Increasing number of potential perpetrators
Ideology	Fits the weapon/technology
Supporter	Abuse consistent with aim/ideology
Resources	High / Increasing

All three clusters of indicators combine multifaceted aspects of assessment of threats and vulnerability of technologies. They consist of social and technological aspects, as well as indicators for concrete possible perpetrators, for technology misuse or attacks. Since nothing like a list of indicators for the future misuse of a technology exists yet, the project suggested to start with indicators like these to develop a broad approach for an early warning of potential misuse of an emerging technology. It is a political and a strategical question of how to implement this in institutions which deal with early warning and according countermeasures.

The given indicators are not a closed list, which claim to be complete or perfect for each technology. There may be new and emerging technologies which cannot be monitored by the presented indicators.

Conclusion

The development and use of narrative scenarios in FESTOS was a multistage process. It encompassed the identification of threats, an assessment of possible impacts as well as possible perpetrators. "Scenarios will not provide all of the answers, but they help executives ask better questions and prepare for the unexpected. And that makes them a very valuable tool indeed." (Roxburgh 2009, p. 10). In FESTOS, this tool was used to challenge the expectations of tomorrow. Neither developers nor other experts dig too deep looking for vulnerabilities in future technologies and the consequences which may follow in such a case. Perpetrators, especially in organized crime, are very technology savvy and will use future technologies. The approach of describing the impact an intended misuse of a future technology may have, using the tool of narrative scenarios, was chosen due to a number of practical and theoretical reasons.

The scenarios had to include a host of different information which was rather difficult to unite: Information on future technologies, a potential perpetrator, a future society and various levels of impact of an intended misuse. Against this background a method had to be selected which enables simple access not only to individual information but also to open up the chance for intuitive access to the complex situation.

The main advantages of scenarios are their potential to support the communication process and the strategic planning process. Narrative scenarios are simple to understand and anticipate. At the same time, they are an adequate tool for transferring the complexity of a technological threat to a real life situation, twenty years from now. In addition to describing threat scenarios, narrative scenarios leave space for individual imagination and ideas that may emerge when reading the texts. They pose questions and challenge conventional approaches and expectations.

In contrast to the more mathematical and strategic scenarios, narrative scenarios are short stories that depict the impact of an event vividly and in detail.

A Precondition for the development and the use of scenarios is the openness of all involved participants in the method and the procedure. It is not necessary however, that everyone is euphoric, but a general willingness to deal with the method seems to be important.

References

Adams, J. (1995). *Risk.*

Barry Buzan, Ole Wæver, Jaap de Wilde: Security: a new framework for analysis. 1998

Beeman, W. O. (2004). The Concept "Risk", East and West. *Bulletin of the Royal Institute for Inter-Faith Studies, 6* (1), 29-45.

Booth, C., Rowlinson, M., Clark, P., Delahaye, A., & Procter, S. (2009). Scenarios and counterfactuals as modal narratives. *Futures, 41* (2), 87-95.

Brown, J., & Isaacs, D. (2005). *The world café: Shaping our futures through conversations that matter.* San Francisco: Berrett-Koehler Publishers.

Buono, L. (2012). Gearing up the Fight against Cybercrime in the European Union: A New Set of Rules and the Establishment of the European Cybercrime Centre (EC3). *New Journal of European Criminal law, 3*, 332.

Burnam-Fink, M. (2015). Creating narrative scenarios: Science fiction prototyping at Emerge. *Futures, 70,* 48-55.

Douglas, M. & Wildavsky, A. (1982). *Risk and Culture: An Essay on the Selection of Technological and Environmental Dangers.* Berkeley: University of California Press.

Dunlap, R. E. (1998). Lay Perceptions of Global Risk: Public Views of Global Warming in Cross-National Context. *International Sociology, 13*, 473.

Europol (2007). High tech crimes within the EU: Old crimes new tools, new crimes new tools. *Threat Assessment 2007, High Tech Crime Centre.* Available at http://www.eurofinas.org/uploads/documents/policies/Europol_report.pdf [20.06.2014].

Gaßner, R. & Steinmüller, K. (2004). Scenarios that tell a story; Normative Narrative Scenarios – An efficient tool for participative innovation-oriented foresight. In *Proceedings of the EU-US Scientific Seminar: New Technology Foresight, Forecasting & Assessment Methods.* Seville, Spain, 3-14 May 2004.

Gaßner, R. & Steinmüller, K. (2006). Narrative normative Szenarien in der Praxis. In F. Wilms (Ed.). *Szenariotechnik. Vom Umgang mit der Zukunft* (133-144). Bern: Haupt Verlag.

Jacobs, L. & Worthley, R. (1999). A comparative study of risk appraisal: A new look at risk assessment in different countries. *Environmental Monitoring and Assessment, 59* (2), 225-247.

Johnston, B. R., & Nedelescu, O. M. (2006). The impact of terrorism on financial markets. *Journal of Financial Crime, 13* (1), 7-25.

Kahn, H. & Wiener, A. (1967). *Toward the Year 2000: A Framework for Speculation on the Next Thrity-Three Years.* New York: Macmillian.

Lupton, D. (1999). *Risk.* London: Routledge.

National Consortium for the Study of Terrorism and Responses to Terrorism (START). (2015). Global Terrorism Database [Data file]. Available at: http://www.start.umd.edu/gtd [08.08.2015]

Nisbett, R. (2004). *The Geography of Thought.* New York: Simon & Schuster.

Roxburgh, C. (2009). The use and abuse of scenarios. *McKinsey Quarterly, 11*, 1-10.

Schwartz, P. (1996). *The art of the long view: paths to strategic insight for yourself and your company.* New York: Broadway Business.

Silke, A. (Ed.) (2003). *Terrorists, victims and society: Psychological perspectives on terrorism and its consequences.* West Sussex, England: John Wiley & Sons.

Sjöberg, L., Moen, B. E. & Rundmo, T. (2004). Explaining risk perception. An evaluation of the psychometric paradigm in risk perception research. *Rotunde, 84,* Trondheim, Norway.

Slovic, P. (Ed.) (2000). *The perception of risk. Risk, society, and policy series.* London, England: Earthscan Publications.

Steinmüller, A. & Steinmüller, K. (2004). *Wild cards.* Hamburg, Germany: Murmann Verlag.

The FESTOS Scenarios

Karlheinz Steinmüller

The scenarios were improved and finalised with the help of feedback from external experts and the FESTOS team. They were expanded and rewritten in places where adjustments were useful. Since much of feedback was given, it was not possible to incorporate all of the details. However, with the help of all participants, the FESTOS scenarios are a methodological method for threat assessment, impact analysis and backgrounds for the identification of indicators. The four final scenarios are presented in the following sections.

How to read the scenarios?

Good scenarios are easy to read, but in doing so one should keep in mind several things.[1]

First of all, scenarios are not forecasts. They are aimed at providing insights about possible future developments; they do not and cannot depict “the future” as it will be. They convey consistent and plausible images of possible futures: “This is the way it *could* happen.” If you have alternative scenarios on one specific topic, it is uncertain which scenario – which option – will become the reality. But even taking this into account, the future will never look exactly like one of the scenarios. New elements will contribute to the future, developments, innovations and wild cards that no one foresees, and that obviously are unknown to the scenario writers.

These limitations, and this is the second point, do not devalue scenarios. Scenarios tell stories about the future, and one can learn from these stories. Their narratives and specific messages are aimed at inspiring thinking about the future and at encouraging mental experiments. Scenarios are intended to contribute to public or internal debates about possible pathways into the future, about lines of action, about strategies, policies, and instruments. They are tools that can lead to better decisions. Their main aim is to draw conclusions: “What do we wish to

[1] This advise to readers is based on joint work with my colleague Robert Gaßner.

R. Peperhove et al. (Eds.), *Envisioning Uncertain Futures*, Zukunft und Forschung 6, https://doi.org/10.1007/978-3-658-25074-4_13

achieve and how can we achieve it? And would it be robust in the long-term, would it be 'future proof'?"

Thirdly, scenarios can be regarded as coarse, "wood-cut" images that seemingly exaggerate present developments. They tend to carry present trends, developments, innovation or policies to extremes, sometimes to extremes that are barely inside the realms of the plausible. This is an advantage: Scenarios extend the "option space" we take into account. As mental experiments, scenarios draw conclusions from certain premises: "What if…?" At first glance, some of the implications may even seem counterfactual, since they contradict hidden convictions we all share. One of the most important advantages of scenario studies is that they make such convictions visible and open to debate and critique.

Ideally, scenarios display rather comprehensive pictures of a possible future. They describe actions from all actors relevant to the given topic; politicians, managers, stakeholders from society etc. They include strategies, measures, and policies that – seen from today – may seem either rather improbable or even outright undesirable. Therefore point four is that scenarios should not be misinterpreted as recommendations. One has to be cautious: It is never certain that the actions described in a scenario give rise exactly to the results indicated in the scenario, because circumstances may change. Our knowledge is at best limited. No scenario writer pretends that an action he describes has exactly the envisioned impact. Sure, the impacts envisioned are not nonsense, but as the saying goes: Forecasting is very difficult, especially about the future.

Fifth point: Even scenarios that describe a future that looks plainly horrific may lead to important insights. Interestingly, even scenarios that are dubbed "negative" combine desirable and undesirable aspects. There is always a bargain. Debating such bargains, the "pros and cons" of a scenario provides insights into options – and into the diverging preferences, values and future expectations of the debaters. To a large degree, the individual, professional and political perspectives of a participant determine whether he or she regards a scenario as highly realistic or rather improbable, as desirable or frightening, as barely conceivable or mainstream.

Final point: Scenarios are focused descriptions of possible futures. They are constructed around their main topic and emphasize the aspects related to this topic. Other aspects are treated, at best, in passing. A comprehensive description of "the whole future" is naturally out of reach. A scenario writer has to be rather selective, just because the human attention span is limited. He has to concentrate on the most pertinent aspects, the most influential actors, the most telling interactions, and the most relevant framing conditions. There are always intriguing side-ideas that could be added…

Depending on the situation or the project, scenarios may be used in different ways; to initiate a debate, or to provide additional food for thought, to help designing policies, or to test the robustness of strategies. In any way, they stimulate thinking about the future. For a first encounter with scenarios, the reader may ask:

- What is intriguing about the scenario?
- What makes the scenario plausible? Which elements of the scenario are implausible or rather far-fetched?
- Which present trends and developments are addressed in the scenario – and does the scenario extrapolate them or deviate from them?
- Who are the winners and the losers in the scenario?
- Are the lines of action taken by the actors in the scenario consistent with their present strategies, or do they implement new strategies?
- Which aspects of the scenario are desirable from my point of view? Which ones are not?
- What measures or actions could support the desirable aspects, and which ones could help avoid the undesirable aspects?

Interpreting scenarios is an important methodological step in itself. But for a first encounter one should simply immerse oneself into the future world of the scenario.

Scenario 1: Cyber-Insects attack!

Wild card: Swarms of cyber-insects attack people and animals.

"Mommy, Daddy, the synsects stung me!" Julie ran into the house in a fluster. Martin, who had just sat down to deal with the administrative stuff for his organic farm, looked over at his eleven-year-old daughter. On her face and all over her arms were red marks that looked like mosquito bites. "What happened?"

Artificial insects show strange malfunctions.

Julie had just been inspecting the rabbit hutches. Apparently, a swarm of these synsects had flown at her and attacked her. "There's one of them now!" One of the mini flying robots had gotten caught in the sleeve of her blouse. Martin picked it up carefully; synsects had some sharp points and edges. It looked completely normal.

"You know," he said, trying to calm his daughter down, "synsects are just artificial bees. They fly from field to field pollinating the plants. You were probably just in the way of one of the swarms that was flying into a new operation zone. You know that synsects don't do anything to people. They can't even sting!"

Background of the scenario: artificial bees replace extinct bee populations.

Synsects didn't fit in with Martin's ideal image of organic farming, which had successfully spread throughout the EU. Almost no one wanted synsects, but one had to be glad that there was a replacement for bees at all. Years ago, bee populations had collapsed. A strange, almost unaccountable disease had devastated them. Many of the populations had simply died out and others stopped producing queens. In some hives, bees simply never came back when they went out to collect nectar, as if they'd disappeared. People puzzled over the causes extensively: Was it some kind of mite? Too many pesticides? Too many chemicals in the environment? A bee disease carried over from the USA? Harvests rapidly declined and attempts with genetically-modified wasps and bumblebees didn't work out. For a farmer who, like the majority of the population, was suspicious of genetic engineering, they were a red flag anyway. At the time, everyone was happy when a robotics laboratory managed to produce "outdoor-proof" artificial pollinators. The synsects of the first generation were as big as hornets. They were powered by solar energy, navigated with a micro-GPS and, in good weather, could reach almost half as many flowers as a bee. The current, third-generation synsects were smaller, faster and more versatile, they even communicated with each other. They could get just as much done as a busy bee.

"But it hurts," Julie reminded him. Martin took her hand and went with her to Deb, his wife. A little skin cream wouldn't hurt.

"The cattle are so restless today." Deb gestured to the screen that showed the pasture. The cows were agitated and milling around frenetically. "I'll have a look," said Martin with concern.

A quarter of an hour later he came back to the house with red marks on his face. His hair was disheveled. He was on his mobile phone before the door had even closed behind him. "Hey Mike. Look, your artificial bees are going crazy! They've started going after my cows. They're worse than a swarm of gadflies used to be. What's up with these things?"

The artificial bees are out of control - and everywhere!

He put the mobile on speaker so that Deb could listen in. The beekeeper sounded distressed. "You're not the first, Martin. It's not just my bees, either. I've already called the Beekeeper's Association and the manufacturer. Nobody at SynBee, Inc. knows anything. I tried transmitting a return signal, but my bees aren't coming back. I don't know what to do."

While he was putting the cows into their stalls he had suffered countless "stings". Even if a synsect ran into you by accident, it hurt. Besides, you never knew if there might be some kind of germs on their legs or hairs.

Deb was already searching the Internet, trying to find any information she could. The "marauding" synsects were already being discussed on Twitter and in the local news. A spokesperson for SynBee, Inc. was saying that the occurrences, while isolated, were being taken very seriously. They were searching for the cause. If it was a matter of improper usage or manipulated control signals, however, it wouldn't be covered by the warranty.

Now and then, there were dull thumps on the door. A few synsects were bumping against the window, which evidently didn't damage them. To Julie it was clear: "They're knocking at the door! They want to get in!" It was difficult to calm her down. Martin pulled down the blinds on the southwestern side. The other windows didn't have any.

First reaction: panic!

By afternoon, the marauding synsects had taken over the number one spot in the national news. Apparently, the bees had nearly blanketed some regions. Martin turned on the TV while he searched the Internet. "Synsects inciting stampedes." "Do cyberbees carry diseases?" "Farmer loses control of his tractor." "Minister of Agriculture fears crop shortages." Also, a swarm had already been spotted in a city. There were various warnings being issued not to go outdoors unless it was absolutely necessary.

Instead of an explanation there were wild speculations and conspiracy theories.

Instead of an explanation there are wild speculations and conspiracy theories.

Deb was suspicious of the seed manufacturers. They always wanted to make those "single source solution for all of your needs" type of offers. Fourth-generation synsects had destroyed many businesses (e.g. selling seeds, herbicides, fertilizers), because they were equipped with high-quality flower-recognition systems and only pollinated useful plants. Weeds were left out to dry. Martin thought it was a manufacturing error. Maybe the mobile networks had started to confuse the synsects' sensitive electronics. On the Internet, however, it was speculated that radical environmentalists who renounced synsects as an unethical interference with the ecosystem and wanted to give them a bad name were carrying out political action. Or, as a government spokesperson suggested, it was an inhuman terrorist attack, meant to create panic. Perhaps the synsects had finally developed swarm intelligence, making them, effectively independent. Or, that a competing synsect manufacturer fighting for supremacy in the pollinator market had implanted a dormant worm into the synsect software which had just been activated. Or, a certain foreign power had prepared means of influencing the synsects, some backdoor into the synsects' control software, to be available for use in a time of armed conflict. Now, some accident – or some disgruntled individual – had activated this mechanism. Or, maybe the synsects had been real insects equipped with electronic coating from the very start, and SynBee had refrained from introducing them as cyborgs, fearing bad PR, and had profited from the natural swarm intelligence of the insects used. But nature is more flexible than engineers tend to assume and eventually the newly grown insect tissue/nerves had allowed the insects to overcome technical barriers and to regain their autonomy. Maybe they would even be able to reproduce soon. There were rumors that SynBee, Inc. had been blackmailed; someone had hacked into the synsects' remote controlling system. People come up with all kinds of speculations. "Nobody knows anything," as Deb summed it up. Perhaps, Martin mused, spreading all possible suspicions, creating havoc and panic was part of the perpetrator's game?

A few days later, Martin went out to inspect his land, protected by a kind of hand-made beekeeper's mask. The effects of the synsect plague were everywhere. Whoever could was staying indoors. In cities, entrances to the underground trains were being covered with fine-mesh metallic screens, street cafés were closed, open-air events and football games were cancelled. Air travel was suspended in large portions of Central Europe for safety reasons. Several sources reported that the Assassins, a fundamentalist bioterrorist group, were being arrested. There was a lot of false information going around, however. Emergency hotlines were ringing off the hook, mostly with false sightings. The synsects seemed to be everywhere at once. It seemed as if they had a penchant for attacking cars and bicyclists. Who was out there riding bikes at a time like this?

The pastures lay fallow. A few natural insects were buzzing around the fields. Every now and then, a threatening swarm of synsects would fly over, as if it was looking for a target.

"They all have to be destroyed," said Daniel, Martin's neighbor, who trudged with him along the old drainage ditches, "or caught somehow. What's going to happen next spring? We need to have pollinators one way or another. Otherwise, everything will collapse!"

Along with farming, the entire agro-food industry is affected.

"It's already collapsing," said Martin, "even if it doesn't seem that way just now." Even though only part of the EU was directly affected, panic spread everywhere. Where would the Assassins strike next? Along with the pollination of various grain crops, humanity's entire basis of existence was threatened. Grain and livestock prices were skyrocketing worldwide. All those involved in trade seemed only to want to stock up on reserves. Many countries had instituted export embargoes and the FAO had imposed a "Global Food Management Regime", intended to manage the predicted shortages. In Latin America and North Africa, the first riots due to dramatically increased food prices had begun.

One good thing at least, thought Martin, was that his stables were sealed. He closed up all the cracks and put a grate in front of the ventilation windows. His cows, however, used to the open country, were ill at ease, ate little and gave little milk. Even that was relatively harmless compared to what would happen if synsects broke in and incited the cows into a panic in those tight quarters.

Countermeasures are inadequate, insufficient and often purely symbolic.

Martin and Deb tried to leave the house as infrequently as possible. The animals needed to be fed and milked. It was impossible to do any farming without going out into the fresh air now and again! The media was full of "war reportage"; farmers and terrorists found dead, school children being attacked, sick people unable to go to the doctor, police and fire brigade deployments, who were trying to use water jets, flame throwers and anything else they could think of, so-called "synsect hunters" who charged horrendous prices to do their useless hocus-pocus with "magneto-adhesive" scarecrows or sugar water sprayers or smart phone apps that, allegedly, could control synsect swarms. Others endorsed simple household remedies, such as loud music, as deterrents. Governmental spokespersons assured the public that the situation was nearly under control, that scientists were working hard to remotely reprogram synsects, and that the "Rescue Plan for European Agriculture" would take effect soon.

All robotics fall under suspicion.

On the Internet and in almost every evening panel discussion on TV, public anger gushed out. People complained about the insufficiency of testing, of information about risks, of security measures and risk prevention. They were calling for the culprits to be punished. SynBee's stocks were in freefall, as were the stocks of every other mini- and micro-robotics manufacturer. Even for service robots, the sales were collapsing. Only one in ten people who were surveyed still trusted the government to competently deal with the crisis.

Martin and Daniel were standing at the gate where the pastures met the street. They had made an appointment with a "synsect hunter". He was an acquaintance of Daniel's who insisted that he was no charlatan. The synsect hunter let them wait, which Martin was sure was no accident. Only after an hour did his small van pull up. Carlson, a man in his mid-thirties, seemed overworked. "You're really lucky here," he said. "The synnis don't like damp areas. In other places, people have made huge plots, entire square kilometers, into no-go zones. A swarm attacks every couple of minutes in those places. The birds have all left already and the army is trying to set up wireless signal blocks all around the area."

As Carlson took out his makeshift equipment, metallic nets to be shot at the swarms with pneumatic guns, he talked about how there was still no real professional equipment for fighting the synsects. "Honey Pots", meant to attract the marauding synsects, were still in the experimental phase. There were also electro-magnetic pulse guns (EMPs) that short-circuited the synsects. "They are controversial. There's too much of a danger that the EMP guns will be misused after the Synsect campaign, for instance against mobile phone towers."

Mini-robots are meant to combat mini-robots.

-

Maybe not a good idea.

Allegedly, SynBee, Inc. was developing a new, better and more controllable generation of synsects, which provided weekly security updates. "They say that the new synsects should only be sold once the old synsects are at least 99.99% neutralized. It might just be a rumor, though."

Martin himself had also been hearing outlandish things. One company, word had it, was ready to release anti-synsect synsects and synsect spiders onto the market. The first were mini-robots that worked as flying synsect killers and the second were small robot spiders whose webs could hold synsects, unlike normal spider webs.

Daniel started to get steamed up: "All micro-robots should be banned! They're trying to get us out of the frying pan by throwing us right into the fire."

Maybe it's all just a front for the profiteers who are becoming rich from the whole mess? Competitors of SynBee, Inc. or SynBee itself? Indeed, they would make a killing if they managed to make what one commentator called a "necrosphere", a pseudo-biosphere made up of dead life.

On Daniel's paddock, they came across a swarm. Carlson loaded and shot, but he didn't account for the wind. The net landed in the bushes.Weeks later, the "war on synsects" was over. There were still a few of them around that had escaped the EMP weapons of the extermination teams, but the "surviving" micro-robots didn't pose a threat anymore. With time, they were overcome by nature and wear and tear.

Instead of compensation there is only more bureaucracy.

Whilst Martin was out cleaning up the robot carcasses, an official of the newly founded Federal Office of Agricultural Security contacted him. Deb was against even letting him in: "Does he have bees? Then he can stay outside!" Just then, the man appeared in the door, muttered a few words about how the plague was over, thank goodness, and pulled out his laptop. He couldn't promise any big compensation payments for the losses, but he wanted at least to assess the damages. "Oh, for the statistics?" Deb asked bitterly.

Preventative measures take place primarily on the regulatory level.

The vacationers who usually had brought in a fair amount of extra income had, of course, failed to appear that season, as was the case all over the region. The undersupply of milk had been partially compensated for by higher prices. The worst thing was the uncertainty about the future. On many nights, Martin had thought about selling the farm. It just wasn't worth it anymore.

Trust in the ability of political processes to solve real problems sinks even further.

In order to break the tension, the official rattled off the measures being taken by the government; strict licensing procedures for synsects, strict supervision of research, strict supervision of manufacturers, and strict supervision of synsect beekeepers, strict compliance of emergency shut-down rules for synsects. Everything was according to the new EU Directive on High-Tech-Supported Agriculture. And he even mentioned the initiative of the EU to establish a Global Micro-Robot Agency after the model of the IAEA. “We give aid and support where we can.”

“How? Now I’m supposed to register my pollination needs on the Internet four weeks in advance, including the acreage and each individual crop.” Martin understood that they wanted to know where every single synsect was each day. He didn’t understand why, once again, it was his responsibility. “They can’t even guarantee that all our planting won't result in nothing next spring!” In the end, it all came back to one thing; even more bureaucracy.

“I won’t vote for them anymore,” said Deb when the official had finally gone. “No one. Never again.” Martin, however, picked up the information pamphlet that the official had left for them. “We farmers,” he said bitterly, “have just lost another piece of our freedom.”

Scenario 2: The Genetic Blackmailers

Wild card: Individual DNA is misused for extortion.

Tony Raasonen could barely believe his eyes. Without a doubt the e-mail read: "If you don't vote against the Biobank Bill, we'll publish the results of an analysis of your DNA on the Internet. Freedom for our genes! - The Movement for Genetic Self-Determination."

Scenario background: a new bill addressing secure handling of individual bio-data and bio-samples.

He took a deep breath and went over to the window, where he had a good view of the snow-covered Hanse Square with its usual bustle of cars, trams and pedestrians. It was simply unbelievable: someone was trying to blackmail him. Him! An elected representative! And he had never heard of this movement before. True, bio-ethical issues had always been controversial. Now that the Biobank Bill was being put to vote, the conflict was flaring up again. Still, how could the supposed advocates of genetic self-determination use these kinds of criminal methods, thereby violating the very rights that they advocate?

Bio-ethical issues are controversial across party lines.

He probably wasn't the only one who had received a message like this one. He reached for the telephone. His party chairperson had promised to support and advise him, as he was a young Member of Parliament. But he hesitated. Should he, *could* he, confide in anyone? No matter how he voted, people would see his decision in the light of this blackmail. He hadn't even come to a decision yet. As with many bio-ethical issues, the party had lifted compulsory unanimity. There were good reasons for it and against it. Besides, what could the party chairperson even tell him? Undoubtedly, he would tell him to call the police. Then, in his mind, he heard the mumbling voice of his older colleague: "That's the most idiotic lobbying that I've ever seen."

Tony pulled himself together. He called Sari, his research assistant, into the room. Sari, a spirited woman in her mid-thirties, had done a lot of work on the Biobank issue. She always knew when it was best to keep quiet. With a casual gesture, he showed her the scurrilous message. Sari shook her head, more out of astonishment than outrage: "I don't understand it. You were thinking of voting against the bill, weren't you?"

"That's no longer an option. I won't allow myself to be extorted. Who's behind this?"

Sari had never heard of a "Movement for Genetic Self-Determination," either. It could just be a sick hoax perpetrated by web anarchists.

"You've researched who this new bill benefits and who it hurts. Cui bono, that applies as much to politics as much as it does to crime."

Sari nodded: "Just a moment. I'll get the records."

An individual genome analysis can reveal unpleasant facts.

Tony watched her go. How might this harm him? Two years ago, when the debates on what was then called the Genbank Bill were just starting to heat up, he had his DNA sequenced. Then, he had the data analyzed with MS-MyGene. One could draw a number of conclusions – true or false – from his genome; a predisposition for various allergies, a long list of intolerances to medicines, a reading and writing disability, a notable risk of Parkinson's, and a significantly increased risk of depression and alcoholism (potentially the most damaging thing for a politician). He had decided, at the time, to completely ignore the somewhat unflattering analysis. Maybe now people would say, that with this profile, he should have never gone into politics.

Individualized medicine requires individual data...

... but complex interests complicate the institution of biobanks.

Sari came back with her web tablet. The Biobank Bill was meant to update the out-dated legislation about what was formerly called "genetic data privacy". Particularly, it was meant to adapt the legislation to the needs of high-tech medicine, which was becoming more and more customized to the individual. According to the excessively narrow formulation of the former law, it was prohibited to even store or relay laboratory data from blood tests. The new bill was intended to provide unified regulation for handling this data, as well as individual bio-samples (e.g. tissue samples, DNA), and to make it possible to integrate the various biobanks, research laboratories, clinics, etc., into national infrastructure. There were still many questions, however, to be answered about the issue: Who has access rights? When? For what purposes? Researchers? Attending physicians? How should access rights be regulated? Which data would be made anonymous? When is the patient's explicit consent necessary? When do patients have only a right of objection? How can the data be protected against misuse, theft and fraud?

Does the identification of individual risks destroy solidarity?

The Medical Association viewed the law as an opportunity to obtain better and quicker diagnoses, as well as to offer targeted therapies designed for individuals (e.g. risks and intolerances, medicines that had reduced potency for particular individuals). Radical anti-genetic engineering activists and some patient associations, however, feared that it would make their lives too "transparent". If insurers had access to the data, floodgates would be opened for discrimination against people with health risks! They invoked the image of insurers who would trick their customers into handing over their samples by offering them reduced rates. Anyone who didn't play along would be penalized with higher rates! Behind it all was the threat of the worst-case scenario: the "removal of inferior life" and the "optimization" of human beings with the use of genetic technologies.

Regulation as a factor.

Most researchers endorsed the bill. Many experts had already left the country on account of overly restrictive regulations. Some of those interviewed implied that tissue samples had, at times, been smuggled across the border. With good biobanks and valid statistical data, the medical research industry could base future research on where need is greatest; social health care providers could plan far ahead; and people with genetic disease in their family could receive an early warning and early treatment or plan lifestyles to avoid risk. Others were not so optimistic and claimed that the bill would hurt the population, when data started to be leaked. Old "family secrets" about hereditary defects and bastard offspring would surface… And a famous economist even warned that the bill would foster the establishment of "health-monopolies". The bill would facilitate the creation of new forms of integrated businesses from insurance, to treatment at the optimum stage in life with customized drugs etc. This would restructure all of the healthcare, pharmaceutical and insurance industries; instead of three sectors there would be one sector with very powerful integrated companies along the supply chain.

Usage of DNA traces in criminology.

There were the paragraphs about "forensic usage". Under certain circumstances, such as violent crimes, law-enforcement agencies would be given access to the biobank in order to complete DNA profiling on suspects not found in the police department's DNA bank. It was this kind of "non-medical usage" that caused the most controversy, which was why Tony had been inclined to vote against the bill, until now. There was a veritable quagmire of data privacy problems. How could protection be provided against false or forged samples in the biobank? In extreme cases, it could be a matter of life and death.

He returned to the matter at hand. "I think we have to dig a little deeper." Sari nodded. She knew what he meant; a research assignment. "Also, notify the authorities".

Everyone leaves traces of DNA everywhere.

Tony settled back down to his desk reflectively. Who could have gotten hold of his DNA? When he thought about it, he realized that it was easy. One left genetic traces everywhere; flakes of skin, hair, all kinds of things. It would have been enough if someone had access to a hotel room where he had just stayed and had taken a few hairs from his comb. In any case, that would have been easier than breaking into a laboratory or hacking a biobank's security system. Or was it just an empty threat?

Someone knocked on the door. Two women came in and identified themselves as agents of the Department of National Security. They would have preferred to take Tony's laptop with them. They didn't reveal whether other officials had received blackmail messages. They couldn't, of course, promise that the culprits would be arrested before the vote.

A few days later, Tony returned from a visit to his constituency. His voters, down-to-earth people who mostly lived from the timber industry, had other problems than biobanks and genetic data privacy. If his predisposition to alcoholism became public, however, it might indeed interest them.

Individual DNA becomes a commodity.

Sari was immersed in the matter: "First the best part! Now, they're auctioning off our president's DNA on a foreign eBay site!" That seemed to really give her a kick. "Apparently, last August, someone found DNA samples of his at a total of 34 locations. The police spokesperson, of course, denies everything. But, that's not all."

"What's next, is someone going to find my DNA all over the place?"

Pater semper incertus est – even in the Bio-Tech Age.

She leafed through a stack of printouts on the table in front of him: "Not just that. Here, a paternity suit against a billionaire. At first, his lawyers argued that the child's DNA was forged and now they're talking about semen theft. They say his DNA was stolen from a medical biobank. According to the newspapers, digital semen theft, using synthetic DNA, will become a common crime. As will false accusations of rape based upon manipulated DNA. And there is a yellow press story about another billionaire who has engaged spies to find out whether a potential son in law is genetically suitable, even on the first date with his daughter."

She pulled out the next page: "The next trial; an insurance company is being charged with having procured the DNA of its customers, in order to be able to calculate its rates better and avoid undesirable risks. Here a service provider is announcing, 'bring us tissue samples from your employees and we'll tell you whether there will be problems with them!' But then the other way round, there is a foreign online shop where you can buy 'generically disease-free' DNA to outsmart your employer or your insurer. There are even reported cases of DNA phishing. We'll analyze your DNA for free. What it will be used for, however, is unclear."

"Has the Department of National Security sent any messages?"

Other processes replace forensic DNA tests.

Sari shook her head and continued with her report. Criminologists were saying that since there were so many forgeries, "DNA fingerprinting" had lost its value. As a replacement, they were proposing methods based on proteomes or other individual markers. It might be useful until organized crime found a way into that, too.

Crime is modern and has a high degree of division of labor.

Organized crime! They apparently had a very specific division of labor: specialists who procured DNA samples or general bio-samples, specialists who analyzed or reproduced it, specialists who distributed it on the Internet, specialists who managed the payment flows and probably also specialists for blackmail, money protection and other such things. Online pharmacies that need genetic data in order to sell individualized medicine were a favorite target. A national database would definitely be helpful for them.

Many rumors – little knowledge.

Tony started to grow impatient. "Could organized crime be behind this blackmail?" Sari hadn't found anything on that. She did, however, have reports on fierce debates in which the media speculated on whether stolen DNA could be used to clone human beings. Many people were in support of setting up "gen-free zones", which was obviously nonsense. It could have been a joke or an incitement. The broad public understood much too little about genetic technology and its limits, much too little about modern biotechnology, and nothing about individualized medicine. Old, almost archetypal fears were emerging, fears of things like doppelgangers and changelings. Bad science fiction had added to the confusion even more. It even included his colleagues in Parliament! More education and training was badly needed!

"What would you think, Sari, if I voted for the bill at this point? Would people accuse me of taking pay-offs from the biotech lobby?"

"As long as I've been your assistant, you've always said that your conscience would be your only guide."

"But what about when conscience alone isn't enough?"

A long time ago, Tony had agreed to appear on a talk show on the evening before the vote. For a young, still relatively unknown MP, it was a tremendous opportunity, as long as he didn't blow it. The topic was stated somewhat luridly: "Big Brother for your Genes". Tony felt as if he were sitting on hot coals. The Department of National Security hadn't sent any word, which was in the favor of the blackmailers.

Principles of data privacy from information technology are applied to bio-material.

During the small roundtable discussion, the participants soon agreed that the current danger wasn't from any "big brother" (i.e. the government), but rather from many "little brothers", whose business it was to diligently collect genetic and medical data (and often even tissue samples!). Then, they could create exhaustive profiles and sell them. One of the talk show guests suggested that all laboratories should be required to "splice" the identifiers in every DNA strand processed, preferably using steganographic principles, so that they would not be easily traceable by third parties.

Finally it was Tony's turn to speak. "I was skeptical at first, but an attempt to blackmail me helped me to see the national biobank infrastructure in a new light. I am supposed to vote against it or the blackmailers will publish an analysis of my genome. Everyone will learn that I have flat feet, but...all jokes aside. At first I suspected a radical anti-biotech activist, bio-ethics fundamentalists. They make a case against the infrastructure citing insufficient security and a fear of us becoming transparent people. We have been transparent for a long time now and we lost our genetic innocence a long time ago.

A national biobank infrastructure as a preventative measure.

The fact is that our old, inadequate laws have led to ever-larger amounts of individual genome data and bio-samples being offered on the gray market by a bio-mafia that doesn't care about data privacy or quality assurance. They make profits comparable to those in human trafficking from their deals with semi-criminal biotech companies and insurers. It is a matter of vitiation, misdirection and, of course, of counterfeiting. The national biobank infrastructure is intended to guarantee the integrity and the quality of the data and samples. Also, it secures the commercial usage that is allowed under certain circumstances, such as research and medical development. My argument is simple: the establishment of national infrastructure will incapacitate the gray market and the mafia who deal in bio-samples." He allowed himself to make a rakish conclusion and addressed his blackmailers directly: "You misjudged me, boys." The next morning, Sari slapped down a print-out of a Twitter message on the table. "Now it's your turn, boss! Your full DNA analysis is posted on a Chinese website, including your reading and writing disability and..."

Nobody is perfect – and that's a good thing.

"I know", said Tony, "the risk of alcoholism. The blackmailers got it wrong, however. I had some opinion pollsters check it out. My not-so-perfect genome will give me about three more percentage points in the next election."

Scenario 3: At the Flea Market

Wild card: Everyday intelligent nanotechnology-based products can be set to self-destruct with a wireless signal.

The dark side of nanotechnology: induced product destruction.

"Now it has gotten into the hairdryer!" Sandra cursed loudly. Yesterday, it was sitting on the shelf and today there was just an unsightly heap. The device had started to ooze like a block of Camembert. A couple of metallic parts protruded from the heap. A small sign that read "Made by NanoTrust, Inc. China" was visible.

Sandra cleaned up the mess with a hand broom and dustpan. Yesterday, she had been hoping that the hairdryer wouldn't be infected. The disintegration, however, crept into everything, especially the new ones. "Never again nano!" She swore that to herself weeks ago, when her television stopped working, closely followed by her espresso machine, her washing machine, her new living room lamp and her smartphone. At that time, the washing machine company had been accommodating, offering a life-long guarantee and providing a new machine. Then the plague started to afflict the entire city. One after the other, dealers started going bankrupt, manufacturers were no longer reachable and the military patrolled the streets to prevent looting.

As it stood, she needed a new – that is, an old – hairdryer. If she could get her hands on one at all, it would be at the flea market.

Sandra grabbed a wad of cash, took her bag from the hook and slipped into her street shoes. It proved to be quite helpful that she hadn't thrown out her good old shoes from the pre-nano times. All of the fancy new sneakers with their stylish colorful OLED lights had, like much else, disintegrated into dust and ash.

Local craftspeople profit from the collapse of high-tech devices.

On her way to the market, which was in the parking lot of a closed down shopping center, the streets buzzed with their normal hustle and bustle. Flower and vegetable sellers gave the boulevard a quaint feeling. Day laborers offered their services and repair shops in the side streets were full. It seemed as if the city was on its way to recovering from the crisis. Hand-made signs on the walls advertised ceramics and other products made by local craftspeople. All of this activity, however, was just a misleading front. The shock was simply too deep, and the crash was too abrupt.

Like many people, during the first tumultuous days when the horror stories started rolling in and commerce started collapsing, Sandra had feared that a sudden crash would send the country back to the Stone Age. It seemed that human beings didn't capitulate so easily to technology that refused to perform its services.

Near the entrance, Sandra ran into Mario, an old classmate who, like many others, had lost his job. Mario had worked in the EC card department of a major bank. Now, in the age of disintegration, no one used EC cards anymore. The cards themselves had proven strangely to be disintegration-resistant, but the card scanners had suffered the same fate as all other nano-based products. Besides, no one really trusted technology anymore. It was a different thing to have money jingling in your pocket.

Normal economic life comes to a standstill,

...

but the flea markets flourish.

"What have you been up to?" asked Sandra. Mario shrugged his shoulders and told her about a second cousin in the country who was desperately looking for people to work during the harvest. "But I'm not that hungry yet. First, I'll work my way through some temporary jobs. We'll see if I can find anything on the market."

She pushed her way through the crowd in the narrow entrance, which had been intended for cars. All around were stands with awnings or cheap fabrics to keep the sun off and in between were all kinds of things spread on blankets and tables. People jostled, rummaged and bargained. One could hear the noise, insults, shouts and cries of the marketplace. The stands that had, in the past, sold cheap textiles and electronics from the Far East were no longer there. Nobody knew when new clothing would be available again. Production and, more importantly, transport were at a standstill. There weren't even any more old books, comics or newspapers. No one cared about those things anymore. People wanted household items and electronic devices of all kinds, whole or broken. The main thing was that they came from the good, old, pre-nano times. They could be electronic, because technicians for energy suppliers had managed to get the energy networks running within three days. It was a good thing that so little had been invested in the ostensibly out-dated power lines during the last few decades!

Old
= good
= expensive

The next stand: it had old lamps, alarm clocks, mp3 players and even two power drills. Sandra stood in front of the stand, her gaze drifting across the table.

She talked to the older woman who was working there, who just shook her head.

"If you've got enough money, you should buy that drill," whispered Mario. "They'll always be useful and their price is bound to keep going up." He asked the old woman about it, then seemed indignant: "A thousand Euros for that piece of junk!"

"That junk is fully functional, young man!" rebuked the old woman. "It's not some indestructible garbage."

Thanks to their self-repair function, nano-products had virtually unlimited lifespans. For this reason, manufacturers preferred leasing models.

Indestructible. Sandra remembered all too well the advertisements for nano-based products. "Throw out your old odds and ends. Our products are indestructible, thanks to their nano-based self-repairing function. Cracks and impurities disappear on their own. Defects are automatically nano-fixed. You don't even need to buy it. Just pay for your actual use. During the license period, you even get free software updates. If you just spend a couple of Euros more, you even get premium service, which features hardware updates. You'll always have the latest model." Then she fell for that hairdryer ad: "Say goodbye to flecks of hair dye on your clothes. Say goodbye to overheating. Say goodbye to hairdryers that go on the blink. The best part: your intelligent hairdryer recognizes you and knows exactly what is good for your unique kind of hair. You just need to train it..."

In a way she was lucky that she had not invested too much into "smart" or "intelligent" things. Some weeks ago, a friend had bought self-dusting furniture, a very trendy table and a chest of drawers – which now had transformed into dust. It was even worse if you had installed an intelligent toilet or self-cleaning, self-shading windows.

"Are you daydreaming?" asked Mario.

Sandra shook her head and walked on. "I ask myself," said Mario, "what they did with all those things. I tried it myself, selling old razors, light bulbs and other things. There's just nobody dumb enough to hand over their good old things, not even the broken ones. The recycling plants were combed through by mobs of people long ago. There are probably families here selling things they have more than one of. They're all emptying out their cellars."

Self-destruction, through the auto-recycling function.

A man bumped into Sandra. She tightened her grip on her bag. Under a colorful awning, a young fellow was selling “safety technology”. His t-shirt read “safer nano”. That almost sounded like “safer sex”. A little bit raucously, he promoted software that was supposed to turn off the self-recycling mechanisms and prevent devices from self-destructing. He was at least three weeks too late. Were there even any intact nano-based devices to be found? Besides, none of the remedies from the first days of chaos had done any good; no quickly installed nano-firewalls, nothing! In hindsight, people were surprised at themselves for trying such crazy ideas. Sandra had put metal pots over her kitchen devices. Others had draped their houses in wire gauze in order to block infection-carrying radio waves.

Ineffectual counter-measures – on the part of the government, as well.

At the time, recommendations were circulating that devices should be held under the shower in order to wash out harmful nano-dust, and that smaller devices should be kept safely in the refrigerator. Supposedly, houses could be shielded with metal wallpaper spray. Inventiveness knew almost no limits. Reliable information was rare because radios, televisions, computers, and telephones were soon infected. Media companies had difficulties printing newspapers. At first, governmental programs intended to stop the catastrophe would be announced almost hourly. This included everything from countermeasures involving wireless signals to hastily constructed EU research programs, and even to “nano-stabilization” what ever this meant. After two or three days, a blame game started. The nano-manufacturer lobby was in the pillory, because it had undermined any strict regulation of self-recycling and self-destruction mechanisms. Perhaps, a “dual-key” system where the second “key” is held by a state agency could have prevented the disaster… Perhaps better product firewalls would have helped… As usual, the government had acted too late. When it finally obliged producers to provide detailed specifications of nano-products, it was too late for any hardware/software countermeasures. At some point, the media simply gave up on reporting about quality seals, imprisoned nano-hackers and discussions about measures never taken.

The young man, probably an ex-student, turned around. On the back of his t-shirt were the words “save nano”. He grabbed a stack of flyers and directed his attention to Mario and Sandra. “If you’ve lost a device, it might be possible to save it. The self-repair function is really quite powerful, if you use it correctly. I brought my smartphone back from the dead. It pulled itself together, so to speak.”

Mario didn't believe him. The best-case scenario would be to give the devices a zombie-like life. As proof, the presumptuous student held the smartphone up to Mario. The small display showed colorful, animated Internet sites. Mario wasn't impressed and pulled Sandra onwards. "That's a fake. The wireless networks collapsed a long time ago."

"Or it's a miracle cure", Sandra conjectured. "Some devices are supposed to be able to restore themselves." Only, she had never seen such a device.

"I'm telling you, it's the government's fault!" Snatches of a fight were spilling over from the next aisle. Out of curiosity, Sandra pushed her way between two handcarts. "They should have been there with security measures before it was too late and prohibited all of this crap. Instead of just saying, 'Nano creates jobs!' Maybe in China and Brazil it does."

"It's the Chinese, I say, they implanted something into their chips. They want to destroy us, and they don't even need a war. I'm a civilian employee, I have seen it; all the military equipment is infected, too."

Conspiracy theories – or truth?

"Everybody knows that this was a plan on the part of EuroNano AG to get at the Chinese nano-manufacturers. What was first to collapse? Come on! It was obviously a war between corporations; that's what I say."

Finally Sandra could see what was going on. Two men, all steamed up and with red faces, were yelling at one another. People were watching it like a commedia dell'arte!

"No, no," a third man was interjecting. "Luddites did it; I saw it on the Internet when it still worked. They described it on their website; 'we are not against technology. We are simply against intelligent technology that repairs itself and doesn't need people. Down with the world domination of nano-machines!' They say that they've saved us from the nanos."

"They didn't save us from anything!" The crowd called insults at him and might have beaten him up, if a feisty woman hadn't gotten in between them.

The original targeted and highly specialized malware transformed into a family of device viruses.

Mario had finally worked his way back up to Sandra. "Well, do you still have your bag?" he asked. "That was a staged fight". Of course he had his own hypothesis about what had caused the catastrophe. First, a company hired a hacker who could create self-destruct signals to shut down the Chinese or Brazilian, or whatever, competition. It was indeed not so difficult, since the products were intended to be "self-disassembling" in their recycling mode. Then came some copycats, non-professional hackers, who just wanted to see if they could make these indestructible things self-destruct. In the end, the signals started spreading into the networks uncontrollably and started changing so that new types of devices could be infected. Since many devices communicated with one another, for instance to exchange user profiles or situational analyses, the "killer signal" started to spread and could not be stopped. There were a few exceptions. Where the wireless networks were shut down in time, or at least certain frequencies blocked, like in Switzerland, the damage could be repaired to some degree.

"And how do you know all that?" asked Sandra. In school, Mario had never seemed to be such a nerd.

"I learned most of it while I was still working at the bank, at the emergency meetings, before my department was dissolved. Man, I had it good! I always had enough money in my pocket and always had a cool little spot in an air-conditioned office. Now, I walk around keeping my eye out for a few Euros. I should have become a maintenance technician, craftsman, or a baker ...anything down-to-earth!"

The sun was burning brightly in the sky. The smell of pizza wafted over the stands. Sandra started to grow impatient. Why didn't anyone have a hairdryer for sale?

"But that's nano!" someone suddenly yelled next to them. A small corpulent man who had wanted to buy a DVD player dropped the device like a hot potato. The seller tried to calm him down, but the man didn't want to be calmed down. "It looks like an old one, but it's nano."

Cheap nano-imitations have survived.

The seller stayed cool. Nobody was forcing the man to buy it. Mario looked at the DVD player with interest. Despite it's old-fashioned design, from the early 2000's, the springy, flexible buttons betrayed it as a nano-based product. Still, the thing worked. The screen, somewhat larger than the palm of a hand, showed a scene from the film “Aufstand der Dinge”. How was that possible?

“I just tried it,” explained the seller, “and it didn’t collapse into dust.”

“Yeah,” said Mario, “because it’s a fake. It’s a cheap imitation without a recycling mode.”

One of the causes of the catastrophe: The EU directive on nano-recycling.

It was not at all cheap, actually. Now, it was truly precious! Earlier, the governmental supervisors had checked up on counterfeits. After the third EU Electronic Waste Directive, new devices without a recycling mode were prohibited. Importing them was against the law. African dealers, in particular, had tried it anyway. Considering the current situation, no one, not even the authorities, cared about environmental regulations, trademark rights and other legal babble.

The market economy has survived – as a flea market economy.

After almost two hours, Sandra finally found the hairdryers. They were sitting on that very table; large hairdryers and small, travel-sized ones in a metallic retro style, as well as futuristic hotel hairdryers with wall holders. “Which one would you like, young lady?” asked the gaunt seller. As a monopolist, she determined the price.

“I’d rather dry my hair in the sun,” said Sandra later to Mario.

“It’s astounding,” he mused as they left the market, “how fast people are adapting to the new situation. After all, we've always been used to living in chaos.”

“And it is lucky”, continued Sandra, “that the catastrophe happened so early, before we constructed nano-houses, or else we would have been catapulted back into caves.”

Mario laughed: “I think I will move in with my second cousin in the country after all, just in case we do end up in the Middle Ages.”

Scenario 4: We'll change your mind...

Wild card: A terrorist group uses a virus to change the behavior of a portion of the population for a certain period of time.

An acoustic virus as a conspiracy theory that is intentionally spread.

"Have a look and see what strikes you." The chief editor set a stack of printouts on the desk in front of Viktor. He picked them up without interest. The somewhat gimmicky title on the top page read "Tonal Terror". "Separatists from the Southern Province unleash an inaudible acoustic virus. Are the elections in danger?" Sometimes, it was amusing to see the drivel that the competition would come up with. Viktor apathetically leafed through to the next page: "More blackouts, more depressions, more personality disorders. Alarming psychological statistics from the Southern Province."

"Do you see any connections?" he asked in bewilderment. Normally, he could depend on the chief editor's journalistic instincts. Those instincts had, after all, played a major role in the growth of the *Monitor* into one of the most important independent newspapers in the country. "At best, I think they both belong under one heading: Too much election campaigning drives people crazy."

The chief editor shook his head. "For a couple of days now, the number of people who intend to vote has been decreasing. The separatists see their chance. Do you remember the bomb attack five years ago? They won't make that same mistake again. They don't want to wait around until the province governor has lost the last remnants of the population's sympathies as a result of corruption and cronyism..."

"That's why they would use an acoustic virus, an inaudible one, whatever that may be? Why in the world would they do that? It's just absurd."

The acoustic virus is also a metaphor.

"To me, it is absurd." The chief editor seemed unmoved. "Still, there is real interest behind this report, regardless of whether it's actually a weather balloon or a smoke grenade. You are going to find out who is launching these things, and why. The best thing would be to get down there today on the southern express train."

Viktor groaned. On many editorial staffs, the whole team would decide together who would take on the research. Here, at one of the most liberal papers, it was authoritarianism that ruled. "Why don't we send Bruno? He's fit, likes to travel, and has to get a few more stories under his belt."

"He's too young. As online editor, Bruno is perfect, but in the South Province, it's the seniors who play the decisive role in the vote. For them, he won't cut it."

Implanted dosage systems, intelligent and networked, make life easier for the chronically ill.

The old hotel, made of pre-cast concrete, smelled like a labor union's holiday home. The *Monitor* couldn't afford to put him up in one of the new palatial five-star spots. Years ago, Viktor had some trouble finding a pharmacy, here in the capital of the Province, which even had the everyday medicine that he needed. It was a good thing that medical technology had advanced quickly since then. The implanted dosage system released exactly as much medicine from its small repository as his body needed. In case of a malfunction, "the robotic doctor" in his chest would transmit a wireless alarm. It was comforting to know that the wireless network here was just as stable as the one in the capital. It could regularly transmit his data to the MediNetwork. Some people, like Alzheimer's patients or those suffering from depression, even had had a neuro-chip implanted. Rumor had it that more and more drug release implants were being used for lifestyle medication with caffeine, sedativa, any kind of drugs, even nicotine during smoker dehabituation… Hopefully, he would never need anything like that.

A little later Viktor was sitting in a restaurant, a dive, as it could properly be called. He drank a thin regional beer, watched the sports station on TV, and tried to start up conversations with the people there. What did they think about the upcoming election and about the pension increases promised by the governing party? It was difficult to avoid creating the impression that he wanted to pick their brains.

"Let's just talk about the politics of love," said the corpulent older man sitting next to him at the bar. "Politics make us sick." Another man, who had clearly had enough to drink started suddenly to rant about Europe. "It all started with the EuroVision Song Contest, with that sick tearjerker." It took two beers until Viktor understood that by "sick tearjerker", he meant the national contribution to the contest, and that people believed that just listening to it made you crazy.

Memes as (acoustic) viruses.

"There's your acoustic virus", he thought later as he sank into bed. "Earlier, brain viruses were spread with propaganda, now it's pop music." Which was really worse?

Does voter abstinence stabilize or destabilize the political system?

"Surveys show a growing disenchantment with politics." The next day, the election researcher from the university, with whom Viktor had made an appointment, pulled up a statistic on her screen. "This is not abnormal in light of the economic situation. Also, since joining the EU, many thousands of people have left the country for Western Europe, especially in our Southern Province, which has always been somewhat poor. Our pensioners see themselves as the losers in the new epoch." She took a breath. "What none of my colleagues understand is the clear crash in the numbers which has been occurring for about three weeks now. At the moment, only about 40% of people are saying that they will even vote. We don't know of any event that could have caused such a surge in voter abstinence. Contrary to the typical effects of sinking voter participation, it's weakening the opposition more than anyone."

In the morning, Viktor had read in a local paper that the opposition party accused the province governor of trying to keep people away from the ballot boxes with "concealed threats" of attacks. It fit well with the general gloomy feeling in the Southern Province. The people here had always been known as somewhat backward and superstitious, at least in the eyes of people in the capital. That they would suddenly be suffering from mass psychological illnesses, however, was a new thing. Maybe there was some kind of connection to political disenchantment?

Target group for implants: seniors.

"There aren't any studies on that." The election researcher shook her head and thought for a moment. "That can't be determined in a survey." Suddenly it became personal. "I, myself, have seen how people are rushing to the doctor with all kinds of aches and pains. But why? They ought to be much healthier than they ever have been. Some of the most significant progress of our time has been for older people. Almost half the people here have some kind of implant, including my parents. Earlier they often forgot to take their medicine. Now, finally, that's all solved by 'the chip'. Even they have changed in the last few weeks. Earlier, when I would visit them at their cottage, they would always discuss politics with me. Now they don't even want to hear about what I'm researching. Not a word about the election, not a word about politics. They say they want to work it out on their own. I just don't understand what's happened to my parents."

Fear of "acoustic viruses" leads to strange preventative measures.

Half of the election posters had been torn down from the walls. The remaining posters showed men who were grinning as if assured of victory. Viktor had gone out amongst the people who were not so much surging as sauntering, in small groups, toward the province capital's central square. Apparently, the opposition leader had been able to mobilize his followers, after all. Here in the province, election events of all kinds were still the main way to reach the voters. The people here were suspicious of newspapers, ad spots on TV, and the Internet... everything that was "remote controlled from up above." The only thing that mattered to them was communication in person.

A young man rushed around from group to group, and then addressed Viktor: "Ear plugs, ear plugs against the virus. Only five Euros apiece; ten for both ears." Viktor was still considering if he should pursue this curiosity out of journalistic diligence, when the man moved on to his next victim.

Speculations flourish: a hypersonic virus?

People stood on the square in loose clusters. The notables from the opposition had gathered together on the improvised stage. Pithy words rang over the square, but Viktor couldn't quite focus. Somehow he wasn't feeling so well. It was a slight rush of faintness, like back when he was still having health problems. It was nothing serious, but he was glad that he had his "robot doctor" there in his chest. Maybe, he thought, it's something like this acoustic virus? The illness was said to be spread ultrasonically, but he saw only typical speakers. There was nothing on the surrounding roofs. Some people were leaving the event already.

And then the national anthem came on the speakers. It was sickening! The music was, after all, unimaginative. The text – proud Fatherland, you make our hearts sing; you waive the flag of our fathers who died for freedom – was pathetic rubbish from the 19th century. Viktor ground his teeth. He only peripherally noticed that crowds of people were hastily leaving the square. As he followed them, he felt as if his legs could barely carry him.

Only when he was back in his hotel room did he feel like himself again. He wiped the sweat from his brow and took a shower. Now, he understood that what the man had said at the bar was meant literally: politics makes you sick.

As Viktor entered the hotel lobby, some guests were leaving early. He asked the receptionist if the evening paper was out yet. Without saying anything, the man handed him the newspaper.

The local tabloid was completely in line with the province governor: "Opposition leaders send voters running". Obviously, the same had happened at a large formal reception yesterday. Opposition adherents had not even found the time to clear the banquet table.

On page 5, there was even a commentary about the increased cases of depression. Apparently, they were isolated cases and people had always had to struggle with mood swings in the spring season. In short, everything is under control.

With a lack of information, speculations and conspiracy theories arise.

It wasn't. You could almost reach out and grab the unrest. Although he was on-site and in direct contact with the population, Viktor got his news from the Internet. On news sites, blogs, and Twitter, all hell was breaking loose. "My parents are going crazy," one of the posts said. A blogger recommended setting up an "acoustic Maginot line" to keep the rest of the country from falling victim to the virus. Another post reported that the first cases began during the "infamous" broadcast of the EuroVision Song Contest. This could explain why people believed in an acoustic virus. One Tweet claimed that companies were carrying out tests to recognize "infected individuals." Apparently, to sack them due to reduced reliability. The short message didn't reveal how the tests were administered.

Danger of copycats.

Viktor sat in the lobby drinking a regional tea from the Southern Province and read all of the nonsense that people on the web came up with. There were conspiracy theories claiming that the government itself had released the virus in order to discredit the separatists. There were speculations about the degree to which people could be turned into remote-controlled zombies – slave workers and "slave voters". There was a story circulating about a man who had mortally wounded another man in a barroom brawl and was claiming to be innocent. He claimed that the virus made him do it. He hadn't been able to think clearly for days.

Implant viruses are almost impossible to detect medically.

The doctor's office was as full as Viktor had feared it would be. On the wall, there were signs warning against tick bites, recommending vaccinations against H1N3 and advertising neuro-pills. Without having to slip the nurse a single Euro over the counter, Viktor was called in as the next patient. The doctor, a wiry man in his mid-forties, seemed curious. "A journalist from the capital... what brings you to me?" He sounded as if he was expecting to be interviewed. Viktor started telling his story. For a couple of days, he'd been having problems with his implant. Apparently, the control gauge for the medicine wasn't working anymore.

"And remote maintenance is online?"

Victor nodded. On the small device that he used to test the functionality of the implanted "robotic doctor", the light on the display shone green.

The doctor nodded and looked concerned. "We'll check it out." He didn't sound like he was expecting any kind of results. He switched on a wireless interface for implants and clicked through diagnosis menus. "You know, for about three weeks now, patients have been filling up my office. Half of them are complaining about their implants. I can't, as with you, see anything wrong. The manufacturers have been informed. Some of them don't answer and others send letters saying that they don't detect any defects. The Association of Implant Manufacturers issued a very useful notice saying that we should check our water quality. Complaints are apparently only coming from our region."

"At the moment, I feel fine," explained Viktor.

"You're no exception as far as that goes." The doctor closed the wireless interface. "You should be glad that you don't have a pacemaker or need a neuro-stimulator for Parkinson's. With things like that, problems make themselves known in seconds. If I might give you a bit of advice: get back to the capital as quickly as you can. And then, you should consider resetting the implant and deleting all recent updates. I am not equipped for that, not even for shutting it down temporarily."

When he said goodbye, Viktor recalled a horror story from the time when drug release implants were introduced: Somebody had a car accident. The implant broke and the entire drug deposit was released at once.

Implant viruses can be spread and activated globally as well as locally.

"Bruno, I think I have a headline." Viktor sat in his hotel room conferencing with his colleagues. He could hardly recognize Bruno on the small screen, but that wasn't important. "It took me a long time to put two and two together. But now I'm sure: someone is interfering with the implants over a wireless network. It's a virus, but not an acoustic one. It's a completely normal network virus. It always strikes when there's a political event."

"You think that the virus is activated by a local signal, location-based or something like that? And the fact that the effect occurs primarily with bad music is just a staged diversion?"

"Don't ask me about the technical details, that's your area of expertise."

"We can't use a story about how you feel woozy every now and then for the online edition. Besides, as our boss always asks: Cui bono? Who's behind this? The separatists? A hostile foreign power? People from the domestic secret service? The governor? Are him and his clique the real beneficiaries?"

Behavioural conditioning using implants.

Viktor shut his eyes. He definitely didn't feel well. "If I knew the answer, I would probably be dead already. They're conditioning people like Pavlov's dogs! Politics, no thanks! Change, no thanks! The boss will take care of it. It all works without an official party, without an ideology, without an elaborate network of informants."

Protection with a Faraday cage?

Bruno thought about it. "Any dim-witted terrorist can make a bomb, but something like this? They would need network specialists, implant experts, virus makers. That is to say, they would need expertise and organization." He whistled through his teeth: "You know what, forget the Southern Province. It's just a test. They're checking out here how they can manipulate people en masse." Bruno took a breath and ruminated: "You're in danger. You'd better protect yourself by wrapping some aluminum foil around your torso. That should shield your implants."

Aluminum foil! Where did Bruno get that idea? Viktor ended the conversation and packed his bags hastily. He felt only one impulse - get out of here! What did these problems in the Southern Province matter to him! He carried his bag to the elevator and, as it started to descend, felt a little better.

As he checked out, there was quiet music resounding in the hotel lobby. At first it was classical music, then someone put on the national tearjerker from the Eurovision Song Contest. “They’ve got you”, thought Viktor, then he collapsed. The paramedic determined the cause of death to be an implant failure.

III. Synopsis

Reflections on how to Improve Future Scenarios

Roman Peperhove

Introduction

The given examples of scenarios in this volume vary according to their development, content, goals, and their utilization. The aim of this section is to reflect on scenarios as tools in different contexts. Against the background of the examples in this volume the challenges, potential weaknesses, and strengths of the method and its application are scrutinized. From a practical point of view, scenarios are intended to matter – for instance as a new perspective, a catalyst for discussions or a virtual test bed. However, whether they actually have an impact or not might not be measurable in all cases and sometimes their ways of influencing were not intended by the developers since the perceived impact is not controllable and depends on the recipient.

What is not in the hands of the recipient, but in the hands of the responsible researcher or a team of researchers, is the development process itself: The selection of methods and information, its processing and distribution in terms of a scenario.

In the following paragraphs, critical questions and problems will be analysed and advantages and disadvantages of scenarios will be presented in order to gain an overall impression of the chances, but also the limits of scenarios.

R. Peperhove et al. (Eds.), *Envisioning Uncertain Futures*, Zukunft und Forschung 6, https://doi.org/10.1007/978-3-658-25074-4_14

How to start?

First, it appears to be necessary to start with the term *scenario* itself. It seems that there exists several definitions of what a scenario actually is (e.g. Duinker & Greig, 2007). Some representatives of the method, like Pierre Wack, even refuse to specify concrete elements of a definition of a scenario (Schwartz 1996). Others describe it in a rather soft manner. Based on the fact, that scenarios can be a product of a number of foresight methods, that is to say a part of alternative futures so that "all descriptions of alternative futures are deemed to be scenarios" (Bishop 2007, p. 6). Michael Porter defined scenarios as "an internally consistent view of what the future might turn out to be - not a forecast, but one possible future outcome" (Porter 1985). For Jarke it is a "description of a possible set of events that might reasonably take place" (Jarke et al. 1998, p. 155). From van der Heijdens´ perspective, scenarios are therefore "a set of reasonably plausible, but structurally different futures" (Van der Heijden 1996, p. 29). Against this small selection of descriptions, the definition of Kahn and Wiener might be still the most appropriate one:

However, scenario construction is neither the only foresight method nor always the most suitable one. Scenarios seems to be popular for different reasons: First, even though there are a number of methodological descriptions on how to develop scenarios, all scenario approaches leave enough room for specifications, individual adjustments, and shortcuts. Popper listed 33 different methods, some qualitative, some quantitative, and some semi-quantitative (Popper 2008a). Furthermore, the members of the Millennium Project describe 35 varying methods and approaches in their catalogue (Glenn & Gordon, 2009).

Second, scenarios are the most known approach and therefore, the easiest path to choose. It seems that most people have a vague understanding of scenarios and accept scenarios more quickly than other results of foresight studies (Popper 2008b).

Third, the term scenario is regularly used to describe potential events in the present and potential developments in general both in everyday language and in scientific contexts. Not every study which claims to be a scenario is in fact a scenario in terms of a foresight study.

Challenges

Most scenarios are a hybrid between science and art, including formal methods and the creative and innovative application of knowledge production. “Scenario thinking is an art, not a science”, Schwartz wrote in *The Art of the Long View* (Schwartz 1996). However, on the other hand, other representatives, try to identify scientific criteria for the development and use of foresight methods and scenarios (Gerhold 2014; Kuusi et al. 2015; Gabriel 2014). As a whole, the whole procedure can be understood as *Operational Quality* (Operative Qualität). The whole process of scenario development consists of several consecutive steps and of various critical aspects. Each decision made at these critical steps influences the quality of the whole process. Quality in the development of scenarios enhances its reliability, intersubjective understanding, and trustworthiness (e.g. Peperhove 2014).

These opposing perspectives constitute a challenge for all foresight studies, - not only scenarios. One of the main crucial points is the understanding of chances and limits of a method. Scenarios do not predict the future. They are meant to describe potential futures which might even compete with one another. It is not rare that they raise more questions than hint at concrete answers. In this sense, scenarios display the ambiguity of life. The questions which emerge during the scenario development process and through the final scenarios are essential triggers to gain a better understanding of a topic. Such questions help to become aware of our own perspective, support a critical (re-)considering process, and help to structure complex constructions: What can we do to influence the described future? How can we reach or avoid it? What are the most influential factors in a scenario? Are we able to influence them? How should we react if the pictured situation or development really happens?

Since scenarios describe future events and situations, which might even be mutually exclusive, a “right” prediction should not be considered the value of a scenario. This aspect is not very problematic, because it does not decrease the value of the method or its results – still, users and clients have to be aware of this fact. Then it becomes clear that scenarios are a tool with two main goals: Enabling communication and structure the whole research process in a transparent was.

Research and practice can only learn through an open and transparent assessment which can help to improve future foresight studies and scenarios in particular because they process information from different sources and qualities.

Strengths

In order to highlight the most valuable strengths, two aspects seem to be crucial here.

First, scenarios are a communication instrument. Their development process promotes new perspectives, insights, and options for all participants and offers a space in which participants can share comments and questions that they might hesitate to formulate otherwise. Since all participants are required to agree on certain scenarios, they have to discuss different aspects and viewpoints. In the case of FESTOS, a number of participants became aware of a potential for misuse of emerging technologies for the first time[1]. This learning process, however, is only available for participants and enables them to gain a better understanding of the subject matter. At the same time, it is a communication instrument that brings the message to recipients. Narrative scenarios in particular have the ability to display vivid and comprehensive potential futures, and to be entertaining at the same time. In this way, readers internalize unconsciously a number of details and immerse themselves into the characters and the plot. Complex situations can be described without losing the interest of the recipient. Besides, this procedure activates emotions and values in readers and triggers an instant reaction, which can vary from rejection to acceptance. According to Schwartz, "Stories have a psychological impact that graphs and equations lack. Stories are about meaning. They explain *why* things could happen in a certain way. They give order and meaning to events – a crucial aspect of understanding future possibilities" (Schwartz 1996). This may be the reason, why scenarios are a widely used method (e.g. Popper 2008).

Secondly, scenarios are a transparent way to structure discussions, strategic management processes, and research projects and to keep them open to scrutiny. It is possible to go back and forth and re-think the reasons for all decisions. Scenarios are not mainly intended for data collection, but for processing and presentation. Influencing factors are defined, discussed and assessed (e.g. Kosow & Gaßner, 2008). "Driving forces often seem obvious to one person and hidden to another." (Schwartz 1996) At the same time, creative approaches are adapted for a better understanding of the research topic.

[1] For details see *The Development of FESTOS Scenarios* by Roman Peperhove in this volume

As illustrated by the examples in this volume, scenarios vary and it is neither useful nor possible to measure all scenarios with the same yardstick. They are developed with different goals and methodological steps as well as for different topics. All of them describe a potential future development of situations, but they differ in their style and details.

To develop and utilize scenarios in a successful way, however, the goal for the use of a scenario has to be addressed clearly right from the beginning. It is important to keep in mind who is being addressed and which goals are to be reached by the scenario. If there is ambiguity within the scenario (e.g. contradictions, unrealistic changes, different thematic foci), the scenario becomes unconvincing and useless. Scenarios have to be, inter alia, consistent, coherent, and plausible in order to reach recipients and trigger new thoughts (Gerhold 2014; Kuusi et al. 2015; Gabriel 2014). At the same time, clients should know exactly what kind of result they are going to receive. If it does not match their expectations, it is important to discuss solutions timely.

Furthermore, researchers might be limited regarding the performance of methods and projects due to limited resources, political guidelines or other influences. This can (not must) have a problematic impact on the quality of the results. A consideration of the abilities and the framework is essential and should be initiated in time.

Creative thinking is very valuable and essential for the development of scenarios - but should be well-structured to prevent losing sight of the main goal. External limits and boundaries like resources and timeframes may help to stay focused and work effectively. If these limits lead to an unprofessional performance, however, they can decrease the value of scenarios (e.g. presuppositions, cognitive biases). Therefore, it seems to be essential to calculate required resources very carefully. Foresights projects and scenario development should be feasible with the given resources, and include time and manpower for reconsidering methods of performance and goals and their adjustment.

New perspectives

People become increasingly prone to tunnel vision after a certain time in a special environment or context and are convinced that they know "what will come". Special knowledge and expertise might be useful for an assessment of developments in general. However, even experts on a single topic are not beyond neglecting new trends or events which might influence their own topic. It is important to be open to new perspectives and to develop diverging scenarios in order to discover new - and possibly surprising - perspectives. A number of possible scenarios challenge one's own perspective, which is important for the learning process. Through discussions during the scenario development process and especially about the scenarios themselves, new approaches for dealing with events which may materialize are triggered and enable a deeper understanding of the matter.

Among other aspects, the use of scenarios provides the opportunity to think about *unthinkable* developments and worst cases, which are neglected regularly – be it because of fear or simple denial (e.g. Kahn 1960; Kahn 1962). Both companies and individuals refuse to think about worst cases (e.g. breakdown of the market, war), reasoning that "it will not happen" or something is "too unlikely" to waste time thinking about it. Scenarios establish an environment in which people accept thinking about worst cases. If worst cases occur, such people and institutions might react quicker and more reasonably than others who are taken by surprise (the case of Shell during the oil crisis is perhaps the most known example). In this way, they might be able to note weak signals (e.g. Ansoff 1975; Ansoff 1980; Holopainen & Toivonen, 2012) and accordingly be prepared for the worst case so that they can prevent it or minimize its impact. Therefore, scenarios can be used to be compared with guidelines and strategies regarding their adequacy. Would the given regulations and strategies work in scenario A or scenario B?

Although scenarios are meant to describe different future events or developments, they rarely take the form of a short story. The use of characters, names and explicit descriptions allows recipients to immerse themselves into the story and become part of it. Perspective changes from an external observer to an involved actor, which leads to a more intense perception. This may be the reason why people react more emotionally to narrative scenarios than to neutral reports and studies. The reader is touched by the story and perceives it not only through analytical assessment, but also with emotional senses. Since emotions are influenced by culture, religion and public discourse, this layer of perception also comes into play (Lewis et al. 2010). A narrative scenario is usually not only an entertaining story, but a sophisticated way to activate the analytical and the emotional mind alike.

Regardless of the specific topic, narratives mostly possess two main advantages: (1.) They enable a more comprehensive understanding of a topic. Not only facts are given in a narrative, but also cultural aspects, emotions, as well as explicit and implicit implications, which are hardly ever mentioned in reports. Skilled writers will manage to combine all this information in an interesting story and thus offer a deeper understanding of threats and options. (2.) It is more fun to read narrative scenarios and they facilitate the dealing with complex or sensitive future developments. On first glance, this does not seem to be especially important, but it is indeed. Decision makers are usually overloaded with reports, statistics and complex information. Working under time pressure, the stories may not only be nice to read for a change, but help to get a comprehensive understanding of an issue rather quickly.

Complex issues – displayed in an intuitive way

It is necessary to reduce complexity to apprehend complicated topics – especially for non-experts. To reach such a reduction without omitting relevant information, an adequate means for the transport of a message is needed.

Narrative scenarios tell a story. All characters and circumstances mentioned transport a message - explicitly or implicitly. The story is easy to follow and demonstrates rather complex topics in a familiar framework. Usually, only a number of aspects are recognized as the message itself. Most aspects are implicitly mentioned and create the atmosphere whilst transporting a message without being recognized instantly. This technique requires a talented writer with a good sense for atmospheres transported in stories, which come to life only in the mind of the reader. Therefore, narrative scenarios are a method which may be rejected if no such writer is at hand. If a good writer is available, he or she can be a powerful instrument in distributing the message.

Both the FESTOS scenarios and Telangana scenarios mention only abbreviations or vague descriptions, but show vividly the message behind the story. Both cases target a rational and emotional understanding of the impact such a scenario would have. They allow an immersion into the story and a comprehensive understanding of the described situation – be it a technological threat or a political-administrative issue. Security 2025 uses scenarios rather analytically, similar to Peace operations 2025. By posing leading questions, both approaches utilize their scenarios in different ways.

Obstacles

Aside from the obvious advantages scenarios offer for a structured way to anticipate the future, there are several disadvantages of the use of scenarios.

One of the obstacles is the ambiguity of the term itself. There is no clear definition of what a scenario actually is. Researchers, practitioners and the client might define scenarios differently and expect diverging results. Wilson described them as "a exploration of an alternative future" (Wilson 1978). Kahn and Wiener stated that ''Scenarios are hypothetical sequences of events constructed for the purpose of focusing attention on causal processes and decision-points." (Kahn & Wiener, 1967).The definitions give room for interpretations and variations which is helpful to adjust a scenario to a specific task, but makes a common understanding difficult. Glenn therefore suggested that "Scenario is probably the most abused term in futures research." (Glenn 2009)

Another obstacle is the topic itself. Usually, all relevant drivers are identified and assessed as one of the first steps. In security-related topics, a number of drivers are a) not assessable, since information supply is weak (like the capabilities of a terrorist group), or b) not known. In such cases, scenarios have to focus on known factors and include other factors as much as possible in order to cope with a more-than-usual level of uncertainty. What differentiates security-related scenarios from scenarios in business contexts, is the intention behind it. In security research, scenarios are built to identify weaknesses in order to improve strategies, procedures or technologies – the described event is to be prevented or mitigated. In business (or social) contexts, scenarios are a tool to identify situations or developments which are desirable (e.g. increased profits, improvements of social conditions). This difference requires another perspective on the development and use of scenarios

What is the best method?

It is important to be very careful with the selection of the kind of scenario which should be applied in a future project. To identify the most suitable solution, the design of the study and most importantly, the envisioned results, should be reflected before the project team decides on a certain type or method. Ideally, this should happen before the research project or a study is designed – during the strategy development or the writing of the respective research proposal. If this procedure cannot be adopted, a kick-off meeting of a research project offers another chance to catch up. To gain a common understanding and agree on the best strategy, it is important to have profound discussions about the envisioned goals and the available resources.

However, foresight methods are often picked based on practical reasons instead of theory-based methodological ones. Popper summarizes the process of method selection in the following way: "So far this process has been dominated by the intuition, insight, impulsiveness and – sometimes – inexperience or irresponsibility of practitioners and organizers." (Popper 2008b)

That is why it is necessary to select the type of scenario based on several questions:

- Is it possible to develop reliable and plausible scenarios based on the given pool of information?
- Is the scenario type realizable with the given resources?
- Is it possible to include the relevant experts into the scenario process?
- Will the final scenario(s) serve the intended goal?

The scenario construction is mainly influenced by persons involved in the study (the client, the topic, the researcher, and the involved participants). The client (e.g. a governmental institution or a company) might have specific expectations about a foresight study. Even while conducting the study, their objectives may change, which can lead to costly rearrangements and diminish the quality of the results. Therefore, it seems necessary to be as clear as possible to inform the client about the chances, but also the limitations of a foresight method – especially scenarios, since these are not expressed through a statistical trend exploration nor through quantitative data. Through their inherent nature, scenarios might be equally valid regarding their picture of the future and do, at the same time, not guarantee a prioritization – a fact which is sometimes difficult to attribute.

The second factor is the topic itself. In the given examples in this volume, the topics vary considerably: technology forecast and threat assessment, future water distribution in tense Indian areas, the future development of security, etc. Although most of the topics are well-defined at the start of the research project, they are vulnerable to a number of shifts - even for research projects with an extensive horizon: A sudden and unexpected technological breakthrough might change the initial situation, a success secession in India may change a number of given factors, a political change or a serious attack (e.g. a dirty bomb) might shift the perception of security in Europe, or the perception and attitude towards privacy may vanish due to new technologies (e.g. brain scanners), which render the maintenance of privacy impossible. These simple examples show that in foresight research, sudden new information has potential to make changes necessary. Due to practical reasons, it might be necessary to adapt. A rule of thumb would be: Changes should be avoided if possible, but made if necessary.

One way to be able to prevent surprises to a certain degree is to include not only likely or desirable developments, but also unlikely or even worst cases to picture the whole spectrum of potential future developments right from the beginning. If surprising events or wild cards are included in the design and structure of scenario development, the process and the results may be less liable to change parameters.

The third influencing factor is the researchers themselves as well as the involved experts and participants. Especially in qualitative foresight methods like scenarios, the influence of the researcher on the interpretation of results is crucial – but often not discussed in studies. People are unique in different ways, i. e. they have different expertise, attitudes, mind-sets, cultural heritages and other characteristics. It is legitimate to have trust in the intuition and experience of single persons (e.g. Van der Steen 2012), but even "experts", who know their field, might act upon wrong self-perception (e.g. Barber et al. 2000; Tetlock 2005) – including a gender gap (e.g. Barber et al. 2001). They might be influenced by their individual mind-sets and cognitive biases and should be selected carefully and be exposed to other mind-sets (Heuer 2009). Besides, knowledge is always influenced by social and cultural means (Rooney 2003) and experts' knowledge can be influenced "by people's wants, motives, personalities, experiences, value systems, wishes, hopes, expectations, beliefs, feelings, attitudes, needs and concerns" (Amanatidou 2008). An appropriate selection of participants is an often neglected but crucial aspect. In the respective literature, the selection of experts is – similarly to the role of the involved researchers – mentioned only occasionally.

The importance of a single participant decreases when a great number of participants are involved. Big groups, however, hamper creativity and "out of the box"-thinking by strengthening the average. Scenarios, however, usually depend on creativity, new perspectives and uncommon ideas. That is why the significance of participants is enhanced in methods with a small amount of involved people.

Anonymity might conflict with a demand for transparency regarding involved experts and researchers. Anonymity supports honest statements of participants, but obstructs transparent assessment at the same time. The same applies to situations when details about participants are classified due to security reasons (e.g. if members of intelligence services are involved). However, it is necessary to give as much information as possible on involved participants to receive knowledge of their backgrounds and expertise. Besides, such information enable an estimate concerning potential misrepresentations or biases. To avoid overrepresentation of single groups of experts, it can be useful to apply tools such as an expert matrix to make sure that all desirable characteristics of experts are covered (e.g. field of expertise, gender, age, and country) or the desired expertise (e.g. Kuusi et al. 2006; Varho & Tapio, 2013).

Attitude matters

Based on the scenario projects described, it is obvious that the attitude of the participants and experts involved needs to be in favor of foresight studies and the methods used. It is necessary to be willing and able to leave common paths and break fresh ground. Without open-minded participants, it is not possible to develop scenarios, especially in a participatory way. Imagination and creativity are needed from all those involved, especially if scenarios for a longer time span are to be developed. Attitude is one of the most influential preconditions for a successful foresight approach and scenarios. It is necessary to emphasize that scenarios are meant to open up new chances for decision-making and strategic decisions. At the same time, the involved personnel should be willing and able to imagine new threats and dangers, which may threaten a future society – in the case of security scenarios as presented in this volume. The same applies to the opposite case: As Schwartz points out, he was surprised "how difficult it is to convince people of optimistic scenarios" (Schwartz 1996, p. 195). It seems that people tend to believe that developments are rather worsening a situation than brightening.

A culture of positive attitude toward scenarios paves the way for the successful and solid development and use of the method. Therefore, it is helpful to make sure participants are in the right mood and expand their mind-sets. This can be achieved with games ("Who wants to be a futurist?"), opening questions ("What kind of future would you like to have 10 years from now?") or introducing background stories ("Imagine you come from a distant planet with your space ship and experience the first contact with humans"). Such openings usually broaden perspective and bring about a creative and ludic drive.

How can scenarios be used and utilized?

It is surprising that only a few publications deal with the utilization of scenarios. Scenarios allow for new perspectives and fresh access to complex events or developments. However, it is problematic deciding upon howto "read" scenarios, how to "translate" them to recipients and decision makers. Against a security background, the pressure to deal with potential threats adequately is particularly high. The Irish Republican Army summarized correctly, in 1985 after an attack on the British Prime Minister Thatcher, "Today we were unlucky, but remember we only have to be lucky once. You will have to be lucky always" (Taylor 2014). The stakes are high.

There are competing potential threats and competing priorities and perspectives – especially when it comes to budgets. Besides, in scenarios experiences and statistics might be combined with innovative new threats. How should we assess scenarios and react accordingly?

Most articles deal with the use of scenarios from a business perspective (e.g. O'Brien & Meadows, 2013; Fink et al. 2010; Wilson 2000) and only few from a security perspective. The challenge is similar though. Scenarios deliver a message – be it implicit or explicit. The message will be uncovered by decoding the underlying assumptions, i. e. socio-cultural codes, by a hermeneutic analysis (e.g. Steinmüller 2012). Addressing the fact that details (e.g. names, associations, metaphors) might influence the perception and interpretation of scenarios, they can be used as a tool to uncover ideas, concepts and (social) perspectives that are taken for granted (e.g. Inayatullah 2009). It could be argued that an intensive engagement with scenarios does not happen to a satisfactory degree and scenarios are not deconstructed often enough (e.g. Steinmüller 2012). It seems that a lack of quality criteria, common understandings, and a missing willingness to analyse scenarios are reasons for the neglected analysis of scenarios.

On the other hand, scenarios struggle with an inherent challenge. They are designed to trigger fresh ideas, perspective and initiate discussions. For this reason, scenarios need to touch recipients intellectually and emotionally whilst being precise and reliable. This balancing act is difficult to realise. For security scenarios it is even more complex and difficult. What is the goal of using scenarios in security? It is of course the intention to anticipate a threat and prevent it or mitigate its impact; that is to say to be one step ahead of the opponent.

To sum it up, three critical aspects have to be kept in mind when using scenarios for and from a security-related context:

- We have to deal with a higher degree of uncertainty than usual, since information about the opponent might be wrong, incomplete, or not even exist. What makes it even more complex is the fact that in theory an indefinite number of threats and attacks are thinkable.

- The challenge of dealing with likelihoods and impacts is complicated. Most foresight experts refuse to work with probabilities in scenarios, but security experts usually demand a prioritization. Even with probability parameters, the expected impact is also important when it comes to the selection of scenarios. The same applies for reliability and creativity. If security experts do not believe in the reliability of a certain scenario, they do not pay attention to it. The problem is how to balance creativity and out-of-the-box thinking with reliability.

Summarizing, it is important to mention that: there are competing potential threats as well as competing priorities and perspectives – especially when it comes to the budget – and the challenge to work on the basis of statistics and known threats or to think about innovative and new threats. From a methodological point of view, scenarios about threats become more and more complex and it is difficult to say where to stop. We need to keep in mind that developments on the other side of the planet might trigger attacks over here. It is therefore a great challenge to identify the right drivers for a scenario. From a security perspective, scenarios can be utilized in three ways:

- First of all, to broaden perspective. While this sounds trivial, it is, in fact, not.

- Second, becoming aware of potential innovative action or perpetrators in order to prevent or mitigate a danger. To think about something in advance should accelerate your ability to react.

- Third, current security concepts and the whole administrative side as well as the interaction of involved players should be tested and evaluated.

On the other hand, there are various aspects which are not sufficiently addressed in scenarios. To mention just a few, the following questions come to mind: What is the effect of a good scenario? Which kind of impact does a good scenario have on decision makers and other participants? Most foresight studies are assessed by the evaluation of the impact alone (e.g. van der Steen & van der Duin, 2012; Amanatidou 2008; Li 2009). But the pure focus on the impact neglects the effects that scenarios might have on the perception of situations and developments.

For security research, this implies the following concern: In what ways do scenarios influence the comprehension and perception of threats? Could they lead to bad investments and create new vulnerabilities? How should we deal with good scenarios is this regard?

Such questions are hardly raised but have far-reaching consequences. People are influenced by good stories and the human mind can be influenced. We are influenced by heuristics and cognitive biases, like Kahneman showed in several experiments (e.g. Tversky & Kahneman, 1974). Our intuition misleads us when it comes to statistics, as the Monty-Hall-Problem shows (e.g. introduced by Selvin 1975). We overrate consistency compared to probability, which was illustrated by the Linda-Problem. And last, but not least, we are influenced by cultural and social factors in our ways of thinking (e.g. Nisbett 2010).

As shown by those influences mentioned, very convincing scenarios might affect the threat assessment and could lead to a kind of securitization (e.g. Wæver 1993). Transferred from International Relations to foresight and future studies, describing potential threats in a convincing way might lead to a security-driven regime of increased security measures. Especially unlikely scenarios might trigger this development. In the FESTOS project, recipients often stated, "I have never thought about that. It raises awareness, but introduces new threats at the same time."

If scenarios are convincing – and it is one of their fundamental goals to be convincing and influencing – could a very successful scenario possibly worsen a situation? Not only for experts, but also the public? The public might be scared by a scenario and demand preventive action, since the picture of a threat can be very powerful.

Finally, scenarios could even give advice to the enemy – as an example from al-Qaida illustrated. Only after mentioning a potential kind of weapon and attack did they started thinking about it:

> "Despite their extreme danger, we only became aware of them when the enemy drew our attention to them by repeatedly expressing concerns that they can be produced simply with easily available materials (…)" (Ayman al-Zawahiri about WMD in an email 1999; Cullison 2004).

Scenarios are the product of an intensive exchange of information, assessments, and expectations between a number of experts. They help to gain better and more comprehensive understanding of the problem by confronting people with different perspectives and perceptions.

Either way, scenarios are a method to apprehend a potential tomorrow and to derive insights from this vision. Anyhow, it is important to be aware of the features of scenarios in research projects. The research design should address the objectives clearly in order to enable the best possible utilization of scenarios and if it matches with the given resources; timeframe, manpower, and budget.

In this context, questions emerge as to if and how scenarios were utilized in their projects. If the scenarios were meant to serve a special goal in projects, it is necessary to evaluate whether the goal has been reached or – if not – why the goal could not be accomplished.

Are the scenarios utilized in the project and if so, could they provide additional input or new perspectives? In the FESTOS project, the envisioned goal could be reached. Most participants in the scenario development process became aware of the potential misuse of emerging technologies for the first time. All readers, that read the scenarios on different occasions, gave very positive feedback on the way the scenarios were used to shed light on the potential misuse of future technologies. In the logic of the project itself, the scenarios worked as a communication platform as intended. Through the scenarios, all project partners had a picture in mind when speaking of a potential misuse. They transformed the results from the survey and horizon scanning into a more accessible subject. Picturing technology misuse helped gaining a common understanding of the threat.

Whether the scenarios were noticed or used in other research projects or relevant institutions cannot be answered satisfactorily. It seems that research results of this type do not receive the attention intended. Even if there is occasional exchange between governmental institutions and research projects, the impact of scenarios on the security sector seems to be rather limited.

The scenarios in this book

The perception of scenarios is a very individual process. Accordingly, it is not surprising that recipients assess scenarios differently and draw their own conclusions – this is not a weakness, but a strength, as it leads to discussions, exchange of arguments and a better understanding of the topic eventually. A scenario which is perceived by one reader as convincing and useful may be assessed badly by another one. Scenarios are even more interesting if they do not convince the reader, since they challenge accustomed perspectives and usual ways of anticipating the future.

The bottom line is that scenarios can be helpful in different contexts for a better understanding of complex situations or developments. By describing possible futures, they support an engagement in thinking about challenges, options and threats, which may materialize in the future – to be aware of weak signals, which give the first notice or allow us to prevent threats through timely countermeasures. How do the given scenarios in this book fit in this context?

Most of them address security issues and are comparable in a way: Security 2050 displays potential threats in urban security and airport security, the FESTOS scenarios describe the potential impact of a technology misuse in a future society, the Telangana scenarios describe water distribution in an collapsing state and Peace Operations 2025 present varying developments and challenges for Peace Operations – they are all highly connected to political and social tensions; the scenarios in PRACTICE were used, however, as a vehicle to sketch privacy aspects of the next decades.

In this way, all scenarios, or aspects of them, point at futures that can be assessed as rather negative or threatening or to a certain extent challenging – at least from our perspective today. They picture indeed potential future tensions and dangers, and become a didactic instrument due to this. Through reading scenarios, recipients are forced to reconsider the current situation and strategies against the background of the described future situation or trend. The threat scenarios in FESTOS for example demand a trustful handling of evolving technologies and ask implicitly for methods and strategies to prevent misuse of these technologies. On a different level, the Telangana scenarios argue for a useful and fair distribution system for water supply in order to prevent social tensions, water shortages and high prices. Security 2025 exposes its topic already in the title and displays different shapings of potential future cities. Privacy is another important aspect of everyday life and occasionally considered as closely connected to security. The scenarios of Peace Operations 2025 describe the influence of different power constellations and their impact on local, regional, and global issues. The scenarios of the PRACTICE project address changes of privacy and the potential follow-up effects. Here, it becomes obvious that security aspects are touched upon by all scenario examples in this volume.

In the very sensitive field of security, scenarios have a special role: They depict potential threats and risks in order to improve our present and future societies. There are assets and drawbacks in the construction and use of scenarios. The biggest mistake would be, however, to neglect the enormous potential of scenarios because of drawbacks. They are not a panacea – but one of the best approaches to deal with an unknown future in an uncertain world.

References

Amanatidou, E. & Guy, K. (2008). Interpreting foresight process impacts: steps towards the development of a framework conceptualising the dynamics of 'foresight systems'. *Technological Forecasting and Social Change, 75* (4), 539-557.

Ansoff, H. I. (1975). Managing strategic surprise by response to weak signals. *Californian Management Review, 18* (2), 21–33.

Ansoff, H. I. (1980). Strategic issues management. *Strategic Management Journal, 1*, 131–148.

Barber, B. M., & Odean, T. (2000). Trading is hazardous to your wealth: The common stock investment performance of individual investors. *The Journal of Finance, 55* (2), 773-806.

Barber, B. M., & Odean, T. (2001). Boys will be boys: Gender, overconfidence, and common stock investment. *Quarterly journal of Economics, 116*, 261-292.

Bishop, P., Hines, A., & Collins, T. (2007). The current state of scenario development: an overview of techniques. *Foresight, 9* (1), 5-25.

Cuhls, K., & Georghiou, L. (2004). Evaluating a participative foresight process: 'Futur-the German research dialogue'. *Research Evaluation, 13* (3), 143-153.

Cullison, A. (2004). Inside Al-Qaeda's hard drive. *The Atlantic Monthly, 294*, 55-65.

Fink, A., Siebe, A., & Kuhle, J. P. (2010). How scenarios interconnect strategy, innovation, and early warning processes. *World Future Review, 2* (1), 5-30.

Glenn, J. C. (Ed.) (2009). *Futures research methodology. Version 3.0.* Washington, D.C.: The Millennium Project (CD-Rom).

Gabriel, J. (2014). A scientific enquiry into the future. *European Journal of Futures Research, 2* (1), 1-9.

Grunwald, A. (2013). Wissenschaftliche Validität als Qualitätsmerkmal der Zukunftsforschung. *Zeitschrift für Zukunftsforschung, 2*, 22-33.

Heuer, R. J. (1999). *Psychology of intelligence analysis.* Washington D.C.: Center for the Study of Intelligence, Central Intelligence Agency.

Holopainen, M., & Toivonen, M. (2012). Weak signals: Ansoff today. *Futures, 44* (3), 198-205.

Inayatullah, S. (2009). Causal layered analysis: an integrative and transformative theory and method. In J. C. Glenn (Ed.). *Futures research methodology. Version 3.0.* Washington, D.C.: The Millennium Project.

Jarke, M., Bui, X. T., & Carroll, J. M. (1998). Scenario management: An interdisciplinary approach. *Requirements Engineering, 3* (3-4), 155-173.

Johnson, R. B., Onwuegbuzie, A. J., & Turner, L. A. (2007). Toward a definition of mixed methods research. *Journal of mixed methods research, 1* (2), 112-133.

Kahn, H. (1960), *On Thermonuclear War*. New Yersey: Princeton University Press.

Kahn, H. (1962). *Thinking about the Unthinkable*. New York: Avalon.

Kahn, H. & Wiener, A. J. (1967). *The year 2000: A Framework for speculation on the Next Thirty-three Years*. New York: MacMillan

Kosow, H. & Gaßner, R. (2008). Methods of Future and Scenario Analysis. Overview, Assessment, and Selection Criteria. *DIE Studies, 39*. Bonn: Deutsches Institut für Entwicklungspolitik. Available at: https://www.die-gdi.de/uploads/media/Studies_39.2008.pdf [18.08.2015].

Kuusi, O., Cuhls, K & Steinmüller, K. (2015). Quality Criteria for Scientific Futures Research. *Futura, 1*, 60-77.

Kuusi, O. (2006). Suomen Terveydenhuollon tulevaisuudet. In: Terveydenhuollon tulevaisuus, Eduskunnan kanslian julkaisu, 3. [The futures of health care, in Finnish].

Lewis, M., Haviland-Jones, J. M., & Barrett, L. F. (Ed.) (2010). *Handbook of emotions*. New York: Guilford Press.

Li, S. S., Kang, M. H., & Lee, L. C. (2009). Developing the evaluation framework of technology foresight program: lesson learned from European countries. In *Atlanta Conference on Science and Innovation Policy* (1–12). Atlanta: Georgia Institute of Technology.

Nisbett, R. (2010). *The Geography of Thought: How Asians and Westerners Think Differently... and Why*. New York: Simon & Schuster.

O'Brien, F. A., & Meadows, M. (2013). Scenario orientation and use to support strategy development. *Technological Forecasting and Social Change, 80* (4), 643-656.

Peperhove, R. & Bernasconi, T. (2014). Operative Qualität. In L. Gerhold et al. (Ed.). *Standards und Gütekriterien der Zukunftsforschung. Ein Handbuch für Wissenschaft und Praxis* (121-130). Wiesbaden: Springer VS.

Peperhove, R. & Luoto, L. (2015). Scientific quality in foresight studies – Reflecting and discussing criteria for their assessment. Special Issue of *Foresight* (expected to be published in 2015).

Popper, R. (2008a). Foresight Methodology. In L. Georghiou, J. C. Harper & M. Miles (Ed.). *The handbook of technology foresight: concepts and practice* (44-90). Cheltenham: Edward Elgar Publishing.

Popper, R. (2008b). How are foresight methods selected? *Foresight, 10* (6), 62-89.

Rooney, D., Joseph, R., Mandeville, T., & Hearn, G. (2003). *Public Policy and the Knowledge Economy: Foundations and Frameworks* (New Horizons in Public Policy). Cheltenham: Edward Elgar Publishing.

Schwartz, P. (1996). *The art of the long view: paths to strategic insight for yourself and your company*. New York: Broadway Business.

Selvin, S. (1975). Problem in probability. *American Statistician, 29* (1), 67- 71.

Steinmüller, K. (2012). Szenarien – Ein Methodenkomplex zwischen wissenschaftlichem Anspruch und zeitgeistiger Bricolage. In: R. Popp (Ed.). *Zukunft und Wissenschaft. Wege und Irrwege der Zukunftsforschung* (101-137). Berlin/Heidelberg: Springer Verlag.

Taylor, P. (2014). *Brits: the War against the IRA*. London: Bloomsbury Publishing.

Tversky, A. & Kahneman, D. (1974). Judgment under uncertainty: Heuristics and biases. *Science, 185* (4157), 1124-1131.

Tversky, A. & Kahneman, D. (1983). Extensional versus intuitive reasoning: the conjunction fallacy in probability judgment. *Psychological Review, 90* (4), 293-315.

Van der Steen, M. & Van der Duin, P. (2012). Learning ahead of time: how evaluation of foresight may add to increased trust, organizational learning and future oriented policy and strategy. *Futures, 44* (5), 487-493.

Varho, V. & Tapio, P. (2013). Combining the qualitative and quantitative with the Q_2 scenario technique — The case of transport and climate. *Technological Forecasting and Social Change, 80* (4), 611-630.

Wæver, O. (1993). *Securitization and desecuritization.* Centre for Peace and Conflict Research.

Wilson, I. (2000). From scenario thinking to strategic action. *Technological forecasting and social change, 65* (1), 23-29.

Conclusion

Roman Peperhove

Scenarios enable a better understanding of complex contexts and are helpful to identify both threats and chances– be it for regional, national or international challenges and businesses, respectively. The scenarios presented in this book are intended to demonstrate the flexibility and usefulness of the method with regard to complex contexts and objectives within the fields of security, privacy and mobility research. Working as a catalyst, scenarios are not only products of a working process, but also facilitate internal and external communication. Participants involved in a scenario process acquire new knowledge and gain insights into different perspectives on a topic. This initiates the development of new strategies or an improved handling of sensitive issues.

The method of *narrative scenarios* gains increasing attention in foresight studies as narrative scenarios approach recipients in an innovative way. Narrative scenarios appear as short stories, but include a great variety of explicit and implicit information on the subject in question. That is why it is worth paying special attention to this particular kind of scenario and working on the method and potential application of the method further.

In this volume, one main focus lies on narrative scenarios as an innovative form to promote interest for a topic and display the whole range of aspects without losing the interest of the reader. Besides, socio-cultural aspects can be integrated, which enables a better understanding of the background. Narratives are generated to trigger discussions and work probably much better as a communication tool than other scenarios.

The examples of this volume give practical examples of how to develop scenarios – of different types – and use them for a various topics ranging from security to privacy and even whole sectors like the motor industry.

Scenarios can be a communication tool to become aware of internal and external challenges, to build a fundament for future strategies, and to deal with upcoming challenges. They have become popular, since the method is open to adjustment according to different topics and time frames. Using quality criteria for the development will increase the quality and therefore the impact and use of scenarios even more.

R. Peperhove et al. (Eds.), *Envisioning Uncertain Futures*, Zukunft und Forschung 6, https://doi.org/10.1007/978-3-658-25074-4_15

There is, however, a downside. First, developing scenarios – especially writing narrative scenarios – is not only an analytical work but also aform of art. It needs a novelist to work out a story line which is convincing and entertaining whilst including all necessary details; thus, a skilled writer is needed to transform individual information into an appealing story in an authentic way. This fact slightly hampers the implementation of this scenario type.

Another critical aspect is the utilization of narratives. Scenarios are powerful and they might change our perception and our assessment for the better or the worse. No matter, how often it may be repeated that scenarios display potential futures and that a single scenario should not be given too much weight, people cling to ideas and pictures. (Narrative) scenarios can produce neat and convincing illustrations, which may lead to an overestimation of single scenarios when it comes to decision making and strategy development. In a field like security for example, where a risk is by definition a future event and has to be balanced by other risks and threats, too convincing scenarios could interfere with other potential threats. The persuasiveness of a (threat) scenario might subtract attention from an important aspect only because it is not presented in such a way. The same applies to strategic decisions in business or politics.

Either way, scenarios are a (powerful) tool and have to be used analytically in a rational and distant manner in order to avoid securitization of a topic or an aspect of a scenario.

The articles presented prove the usefulness of (narrative) scenarios in business, political and security fields – be it in a disruptive Indian state or to display the future of military action. They work as metaphors, potential pictures of future situations and conditions. They warn of non-intended futures. By showing bright and dark futures, readers are enabled to discuss decisions and paths which avoid such futures. Taking decisions, developing strategies or paving ways for new options, is the job of decisions makers, managers or politicians.

The examples given in this book emphasize at least three ways in which scenarios can be used:

- As a communication tool: What are the priorities within a project (internally) and how can they raise awareness with scenarios (externally)?

- As a tool for strategy development: If the described future might materialize, how will we react? What is necessary to avoid envisioned negative events?
- As a political instrument: How can scenarios be utilized to develop innovative participation, new guidelines or instruments to be more resilient against the described or similar threats?

The experiences with the FESTOS scenarios powerfully show that style, specific foci and a selection of topics in scenarios raise a lot of questions - which is a positive by-product. Involved participants discussed whole scenarios as well as single details and balanced pros and cons of each approach against each other. Intensive discussions paved the way for a higher acceptance of scenarios and their utilization within the research project in different phases: In their preparation, the development, and the drafts as well as in the final version. The matter of discussion was a number of aspects in the scenario regarding their content as well as the storyline or the assumed likelihood of them happening. Without these critical discussions, a number of suggestions for improvement would have been missed and the result would not have been this good.

Such experiences with scenario development show that internal communication is needed among involved researchers, experts and clients, not only to identify the scope and approach of the scenario, but also to agree on foci and priorities. Especially in the context of political or technical challenges or threats, there is usually a broad range of potential developments and situations. Different perspectives are important in order to avoid a too narrow view right from the beginning. The proverbial tunnel vision exists in most minds and can be overcome by a broad discussion, at least to a certain degree.

In terms of external communication, the effect is similar. Depending on the style required by the client, scenarios transport a message to a single recipient or the broad public – in any case, they initiate a reaction, ranging from consent to rejection. In the case of dark scenarios, the warning is the critical part. Most People prefer to reject worst-case scenarios as they do not feel comfortable thinking about them. However, if scenarios describe negative trends, threatening situations or problems of which the recipient was not aware of before, they have fulfilled their purposes. Based on threats and descriptions of their impacts, recipients consider countermeasures almost instantly. And that is exactly the reaction which is intended: Showing a dark tomorrow initiates a discussion on strategies to avoid this dark future in favour of a brighter one. This applies to the examples given in this book.

After all, the crucial question remains: Do the relevant people receive notice of scenarios and are scenarios utilized optimally?

Both questions are difficult to answer. In publicly funded research projects, results are available for the client and usually for the public. However, such results are often difficult to access and understand. Inside the community, the existence of a project and its results might be known for interested researchers, but even here it is rather difficult to stay updated. Unfortunately, we are far from an intense mutual exchange between related projects regarding a synopsis of results and insights. It often happens that those who are in charge are not aware of a project or its results, even though it concerns their professional field. The usual places like conferences seem to lose substance since an increasing number of relevant events make it more difficult to address the relevant community – although the access to information was made very easy through the Internet. One thing is certain: There is room for improvements.

Whether scenarios actually have an impact on people's perception, is even more difficult to answer. It seems to be very difficult to "measure" the impact of ideas or "extrapolate" from an idea to a decision. Usually, scenarios are intended to open up perspectives, options, chances, and show potential developments, but it is actually not possible to build a cause and effect chain that determines whether the knowledge of specific scenarios actually influences a decision. This relation remains an interesting question. There are however increasing approaches to evaluate foresight studies for their impact.

Scenarios might be one puzzle piece which influence the assessment or decision process. In security research, this is much more delicate than in other fields. Scenarios in a security context are not focused on chances for improvement (e.g. new businesses), but more on a threat or a danger. Mostly, scenarios are designed to picture different perspectives in order to find a way to improve a situation. In security, scenarios picture situations or developments, which are a threat to the public and their likelihood of materialization should therefore be minimized. Thus, the problematic issue is to decide how and what should be addressed in a scenario. Should it be the most "likely" or the "worst"? This theoretical problem appears mainly in contexts of threats and less with positive examples. It is necessary to repeat continuously that scenarios are only generic. They depict potential futures by means of a selection of scenarios. Threats might have different shapes and intensities than addressed and described in the scenario. The client can use even a small number of scenarios for generic assessment; no matter if it is a security guideline of a company or the technical performance of a product. Even political decisions can be taken on the basis of plausible and consistent scenarios. However, it seems that scenarios are not as wide-spread as they could be. In the manageable field of security research, neither researchers nor security experts are aware of results – including scenarios about potential threats.

This lack of knowledge dissemination is caused by several factors. In a nutshell: First, the results are not often enough made public and “sold” to decision makers and relevant experts. Second, the form of the results (e.g. scientific reports, scenarios without background information) are not easily translatable. Third, results are not timed with political procedures and campaigns. Fourth, there is simply too much information available online and offline that make it difficult to keep track of relevant results. Broken down to the individual level, the question might be: If it were to happen as described, how would I react? On a systemic level, the very same question is raised for organizations, institutions and political bodies: Are we prepared for the depicted future? If not, are we able to prepare ourselves – and if so, how? Such questions are difficult to answer for individuals, but much more problematic in the broader context, for instance for local or nationwide governmental structures or (inter-)national companies. The more actors are involved in an issue, the more challenging a coordinated reaction becomes. For complex institutions, companies or even whole societies, a quick reaction is not usually possible unless structures are designed for flexibility. To be aware of challenges, thinking about them in advance may allow for a quicker reaction and can not only be a competitive advantage, but also help to improve the condition of societies and institutions in general – ranging from security to economic competitiveness. Here, the visualization of a (common) problem can be seen as a reminder of the challenge.

Scenarios provide the opportunity to be used as a test bed for new regulations or strategies. Although the described futures are generic, they can be used to develop strategies in order to alter a threat (dark scenario) into an improvement of the present (normative scenario). Matching scenarios with possible countermeasures can be helpful to “test” if described futures can be prevented or if their impact can at least be reduced. Would the development be influenced by timely countermeasures? Which actions would be necessary to be prepared appropriately? Is there anything to be done right now? Scenarios can be utilized in this way for a back casting procedure or for SWOT analysis.

The scenario processes described in this volume are based on different methodological approaches, which have proved to work sufficiently in their projects. Methods can be improved and an evaluation of processes and results may be helpful in this regard. It is neither intended to make scenario development a strictly regulated procedure nor to diminish its artistic aspect.

The influence of scenarios on political, economic or social decisions is not measurable in terms of a cause and effect chain. On a lower level –perhaps even a subconscious one – the perspective of people involved and recipients might be broadened by picturing potential threats and options. The impact, however, depends heavily on criteria like plausibility, consistency or transparency. Only if scenarios convince recipients of the idea that the pictured future is possible – and perhaps surprising – but generally possible, the recipient is willing to include it in a decision process.

More significant seems to be, however, that decision makers as well as everyone else are willing to reflect on future developments in order to prevent threats and make the world a better place. The future will remain unpredictable for complex issues in a remote future. Yet it is possible to think ahead and work on concepts and ideas to influence the future in a positive way. Foresight methods like scenarios can be an essential form of support for this task.

About the Authors

Sascha Dannenberg

Sascha Dannenberg holds a B.A. in Area Studies from the Humboldt University of Berlin and a M.A. in Futures Studies from the Free University of Berlin.

Since October 2012 he is a research fellow at the Department for Educational Futures Studies (Free University of Berlin). He is editor of the *European Journal of Futures Research (EJFR)* as well as of the *iF-Schriftenreihe Sozialwissenschaftliche Zukunftsforschung* and a contributing member of the *Millennium Projects German Node.*

Contact: dannenberg@institutfutur.de

Hans-Liudger Dienel

Prof. Dr. Hans-Liudger Dienel is full professor for Work, Technology and Participation at Technische Universität Berlin (www.technik.tu-berlin.de).

Before 2013, he was director of the Center for Technology and Society at the same university. He is scientific director of the nexus Institute for Cooperation Management, a private-non-profit-research institute for participation and future studies (www.nexusinstitut.de). Since the 1990s, Dienel is working on new methods for future research with special emphasis to the thematic fields of mobility, security and privacy. He studied history, philosophy, sociology (M.A. 1988) and mechanical engineering (Dipl.-Ing. 1990) in Hannover, Washington and Munich (Ph.D. in 1993). From 2006-2014, he served as President of the International Association for the History of Transport, Traffic and Mobility (www.t2m.org). He is member of the Board for Technology and Society of the German Association of Engineers (Verein Deutscher Ingenieure) and of the Competence Center for Critical Infrastructures.

Contact: hans-liudger.dienel@tu-berlin.de.de

Robert Gaßner

Dr. Robert Gaßner, psychologist, head of Preferable Future - Büro für Zukunftsforschung und Zielbildung.

Since 1985 he has been working in the field of interdisciplinary technology assessment and technology design and received a PhD on the "Psychological

R. Peperhove et al. (Eds.), *Envisioning Uncertain Futures*, Zukunft und Forschung 6, https://doi.org/10.1007/978-3-658-25074-4

consequences of computer use". In the beginning his research focus were the conditions and consequences of telematics and multimedia in work and leisure time, in industrial production, in transportation and in health care. In recent years Dr. Gaßner has been focusing increasingly on overarching topics, such as sustainable development as well as general and methodological questions of futures research, particularly using scenario planning and other participative approaches. As a well-trained facilitator Dr. Gaßner conducts futures workshops, future search conferences and scenario meetings.

Contact: gassner@preferable-futures.de

Lars Gerhold

Prof. Dr. Lars Gerhold is Professor for Interdisciplinary Security Research and head of the Research Forum on Public Safety and Security at Freie Universität Berlin.

After studying politics, psychology and sociology he received a PhD in psychology at the University of Kassel. He accomplished several research projects dealing with uncertainty there between 2002 and 2005. From 2005 to 2009 he participated in various research projects in the area of future oriented risk research and empirical methods at the Institut Futur at Freie Universität Berlin. In 2009 he joined the Research Forum on Public Safety and Security. His research focus lies on security foresight, risk research and futures research. Prof. Lars Gerhold is a member of the Board of the Netzwerk Zukunftsforschung (Network of Futures Research) and Editor of the Zeitschrift für Zukunftsforschung (Journal of Futures Studies).

Contact: lars.gerhold@fu-berlin.de

Aharon Hauptman

Aharon Hauptman (PhD) is a senior researcher in the unit for Technology and Society Foresight at Tel Aviv University (formerly the Interdisciplinary Center for Technology Analysis and Forecasting).

He studied Engineering at the Technion (the Israel Institute of Technology) and received M.Sc and Ph.D degrees from the faculty of Engineering at Tel-Aviv University. Dr. Hauptman specializes in Technology Foresight and in the evaluation of trends in emerging technologies and their various impacts on society. He has been involved in several foresight studies within projects carried out for the European Union, such as future developments in Nanobiotechnology (for the EU network of excellence “Nano-to-Life”), threat scenarios posed by the "dark side" of emerging technologies (project FESTOS), "wild cards" related to future research and innovation in Europe (project iKNOW), the impact of new technologies on privacy (project PRACTIS), and future scenarios and “wild cards” in transportation (project RACE2050).

Contact: haupt@post.tau.ac.il

Angela Jain

Angela Jain (PhD) has her academic background in spatial planning.

Since 2007 she is head of the division 'Infrastructure and Society' at the nexus Institute, Berlin (www.nexusinstitut.de). From 2009 until 2013 she worked in the Indo-German research project "Sustainable Hyderabad", funded by the German Federal Ministry of Education and Research (BMBF). She also supervised the project “Governance and Participation in the Telangana Region” with Focus on Scenarios for Water Governance (2011-2012), funded by the Foundation Friedrich-Ebert-Stiftung (FES), India. Her research focus lies on social-science oriented sustainability research, citizen participation in urban development and local governance in the South Asian context.

Contact: jain@nexusinstitut.de

Robin Kellermann

Robin Kellermann (M.A.) is a junior researcher at Technische Universität Berlin.

He graduated from cultural studies and historical urban studies and has investigated urban infrastructures in their iconic role as agents of political legitimation. His main research fields are the history and future of mobility and transportation in urban settings. He has worked as assisting project coordinator of RACE2050, an EU-FP7 project devoted to the past and future of European transport industries. Currently he is a PhD student focusing on the “history of waiting” in mobility context.

Contact: robin.kellermann@tu-berlin.de

Stefan Köppe

Stefan Köppe is project manager at the Berlin-based Center for International Peace Operations (ZIF) which is responsible in particular for Germany's UN, EU and OSCE contributions of civilian personnel.

He works in ZIF's Analysis Division where he coordinated and contributed to an interdisciplinary foresight project in 2011/12 which generated scenarios for "Peace Operations 2025." He studied Political Science in Potsdam, Berlin and Bordeaux.

Contact: S.Koeppe@zif-berlin.org

Annika Lonkila

Annika Lonkila, MSc, has a degree in Human Geography from the University of Helsinki, Finland, and currently holds the position of Junior Researcher in the University of Eastern Finland.

At the moment she is working on her PhD project examining transitions related to sustainabilities and genetic technologies in the field of animal agriculture and more specifically cattle breeding.

Contact: Annika.Lonkila@uef.fi

Liisa Hyttinen (née Luoto)

Liisa Hyttinen (M.Soc.Sc), is a senior adviser at Helsinki-Uusimaa Regional Council.

Her research focus lies with future studies (especially scenario planning, images of the future and SWOT analysis). Additionally, she has expertise in project management, security and privacy studies, youth research and rural studies. Previously, she has participated in two EU-funded 7th framework programme projects, namely FESTOS and PRACTIS at the Finland Futures Research Centre (FFRC). Additionally, she has participated in a national level project funded by the Finnish Ministry of agriculture and forestry. The project focuses on youth research and rural studies. Currently she is a project manager in a national level project, which focuses on youth research and future images.

Contact: liisa.hyttinen@uudenmaanliitto.fiis

Massimo Moraglio

Dr. Massimo Moraglio (PhD) is a senior researcher at the Technische Universität Berlin, working on technology and its wide effects on economic, social and cultural fields.

Currently he is focusing on the genealogy of the future in the mobility realm, with a special focus on 20th century prophecies about transport and technical systems. Massimo Moraglio has conducted research and taught in universities in Italy, France and Germany. Highlights of his career include an EU Marie Sklodowska Curie IEF fellowship conducted at the T.U. Berlin.

Contact: massimo.moraglio@tu-berlin.de

Roman Peperhove

Roman Peperhove studied History and Science of Islam with a focus on security issues like Islamist terror organisations and extremist movements.

He leads the Research Forum on Public Safety and Security of Freie University Berlin and works on national and international research projects dealing with issues of security, terrorism and foresight. Inter alia, he lead the German team of the EU founded project "Foresight of Evolving Security Threats Posed by Emerging Technologies" (FESTOS, FP7) and lectures on security-related issues. His professional interest lies with the interaction between society and security. He is member of several organizations and networks, such as, the European Expert Network on Terrorism Issues (EENeT) and German Middle East Studies Association for Contemporary Research and Documentation (DAVO). Additionally, he is member of the Board of the Netzwerk Zukunftsforschung (Network of Futures Research) and Editor of the Zeitschrift für Zukunftsforschung (Journal of Futures Studies).

Contact: roman.peperhove@fu-berlin.de

Yair Sharan

Dr. Yair Sharan is currently the director of TAM-C/FIRS2T (Foresight Insight Research Security Society and Technology) group active in the security and technology field.

He has been the director of the Interdisciplinary Center for Technological Analysis and Forecasting (ICTAF) at Tel Aviv University and a senior associate researcher in Begin-Sadat Center for strategic studies (BESA) in Bar Ilan University in Israel. He is a Col (res) in the IDF and served as the Israeli Science Attaché' in Germany and as senior consultant to the Israeli Ministry of Science. Yair Sharan is co-director of the Israeli node of the Millennium Project. Dr. Sharan earned his B.Sc. and M.Sc. in Mathematics and Physics in the University of Jerusalem. He earned his Ph.D. in Physics from the Weizmann institute of Science. His main fields of interest are research and science policy, the impact of technology on national strategy, technology foresight and security foresight, technology assessment. He participated in many EU projects including SIAM, Nano2Life, and Platform Foresight. He coordinated several EU projects including FESTOS in the security program and PRACTIS in Science in Society program. He is co-author of the book "Lone Wolf Terrorism Prospects and Potential Strategies to Address the Threat" as well as co-editor of several NATO books including "Terrorism on the Internet"(IOS press 2010) and recently "Lone Actors- an Emerging Threat" (IOS press November 2015).

Contact: sharany@gmail.com

Karlheinz Steinmüller

Dr. Karlheinz Steinmüller is scientific director of the consulting company “Z_punkt GmbH – The Foresight Company”.

He studied at TU Chemnitz and Humboldt-University Berlin. He graduated in theoretical physics and got his degree in philosophy of science. After his studies, he engaged in modelling and simulating of ecological systems at the East German Academy of Sciences. From 1982 to 1991 he worked as a free-lance writer. Together with his wife Angela he published ten science fiction books, three books about foresight and a biography of Charles Darwin. Since 1991 he works in the field of foresight, first at the Sekretariat für Zukunftsforschung in Gelsenkirchen and since 2001 as scientific director of the consulting company “Z_punkt GmbH – The Foresight Company” based in Cologne and Berlin. In addition to his work for Z_punkt he engages in research in the field of history and methodology of foresight and works as a university lecturer for future studies at Free University Berlin.

Contact: steinmueller@z-punkt.de

Björn Theis

Björn Theis, is a Foresight Manager at the Evonik AG Corporate Foresight Unit.

He studied cultural anthropology with a focus on network analysis, economic anthropology and ritual theory at the University of Cologne. He worked as a journalist as well as a research consultant for international companies. After his studies, he held the position of chief editor of the online magazine "Future Research" until 2009. Then he worked as Senior Consultant at Foresight Z_punkt The Foresight Company, an international consulting company. Here, as well as in his new position at Evonik, his work focuses on scenario development in the fields of society, politics, security, and consumer goods. Another of his priorities is to identify and analyze emerging issues and weak signals. Next to his work at Evonik he teaches future research at the Freie Universität Berlin.

Contact: bjoern.theis@evonik.com

MIX
Papier aus verantwortungsvollen Quellen
Paper from responsible sources
FSC® C105338

If you have any concerns about our products,
you can contact us on
ProductSafety@springernature.com

In case Publisher is established outside the EU,
the EU authorized representative is:
Springer Nature Customer Service Center GmbH
Europaplatz 3, 69115 Heidelberg, Germany

Printed by Libri Plureos GmbH
in Hamburg, Germany